I'LL BE GONE
IN THE DARK

I'LL BE GONE IN THE DARK

ONE WOMAN'S
OBSESSIVE SEARCH FOR THE
GOLDEN STATE KILLER

MICHELLE McNAMARA

An Imprint of HarperCollinsPublishers

I'LL BE GONE IN THE DARK. Copyright © 2018 by Tell Me Productions. All rights reserved. Printed in the United States of America. No part of this book may be used or reproduced in any manner whatsoever without written permission except in the case of brief quotations embodied in critical articles and reviews. For information, address HarperCollins Publishers, 195 Broadway, New York, NY 10007.

HarperCollins books may be purchased for educational, business, or sales promotional use. For information, please e-mail the Special Markets Department at SPsales@harpercollins.com.

FIRST EDITION

Designed by William Ruoto

Library of Congress Cataloging-in-Publication Data has been applied for.

ISBN 978-0-06-231978-4

18 19 20 21 22   LSC   20 19 18 17 16 15 14 13

No butler, no second maid, no blood upon the stair.
No eccentric aunt, no gardener, no family friend
Smiling among the bric-a-brac and murder.
Only a suburban house with the front door open
And a dog barking at a squirrel, and the cars
Passing. The corpse quite dead. The wife in Florida.

Consider the clues: the potato masher in a vase,
The torn photograph of a Wesleyan basketball team,
Scattered with check stubs in the hall;
The unsent fan letter to Shirley Temple,
The Hoover button on the lapel of the deceased,
The note: "To be killed this way is quite all right with me."

Small wonder that the case remains unsolved,
Or that the sleuth, Le Roux, is now incurably insane,
And sits alone in a white room in a white gown,
Screaming that all the world is mad, that clues
Lead nowhere, or to walls so high their tops cannot be seen;
Screaming all day of war, screaming that nothing can be solved.

—Weldon Kees, "Crime Club"

CONTENTS

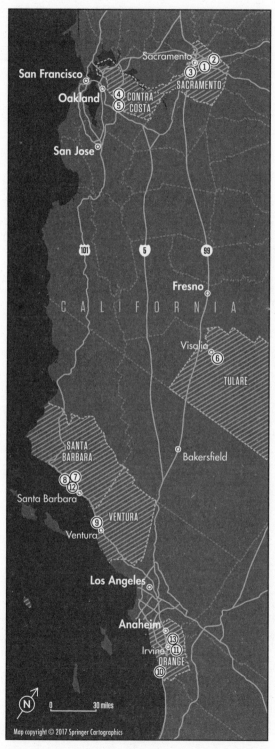

East Area Rapist Attacks
(June 1976 to July 1979) Northern California
Assaults 50 women across seven counties

① June 18, 1976 - Rancho Cordova
A 23-year-old woman (identified as "Sheila" in this book) is raped in her bed by a masked intruder. It would become the first attack of dozens by a man who'd come to be known in the press and to law enforcement as the "East Area Rapist."

② October 5, 1976 - Citrus Heights
The East Area Rapist strikes a fifth time, targeting 30-year-old housewife Julie Miller*. The rapist waits for the victim's husband to leave for work and enters minutes later. The victim's 3-year-old son remains in her bedroom throughout the ordeal.

③ May 28, 1977 - Parkway-South Sacramento
28-year-old Fiona Williams* and her husband Phillip are confronted by the EAR in his 22nd known attack—his seventh attack in which the man is present during the incident.

④ October 28, 1978 - San Ramon
The official case tally becomes 40 as the EAR targets another couple: 23-year-old Kathy*and her husband David*.

⑤ December 9, 1978 - Danville
32-year-old Esther McDonald* is awakened in the night, bound, and raped, becoming EAR victim #43.

The Visalia Ransacker Burglaries and Shooting
(April 1974 to December 1975)

⑥ Visalia
Possible link explored to several break-ins and the murder of Claude Snelling.

The Original Night Stalker Rampage
(October 1979 to May 1986)

⑦ October 1, 1979 - Goleta
The Original Night Stalker attacks a couple during an unsuccessful home invasion; the pair escape.

⑧ December 30, 1979 - Goleta
The ONS murders Dr. Robert Offerman and Debra Alexandria Manning.

⑨ March 13, 1980 - Ventura
The ONS murders Charlene and Lyman Smith.

⑩ August 19, 1980 - Dana Point
The ONS murders Keith and Patrice Harrington.

⑪ February 6, 1981 - Irvine
The ONS murders Manuela Witthuhn.

⑫ July 27, 1981 - Goleta
The ONS murders Cheri Domingo and Gregory Sanchez.

⑬ May 5, 1986 - Irvine
The ONS murders Janelle Cruz.

Denotes a pseudonym

CAST OF CHARACTERS

VICTIMS

RAPE VICTIMS
Sheila* (Sacramento, 1976)
Jane Carson (Sacramento, 1976)
Fiona Williams* (South Sacramento, 1977)
Kathy* (San Ramon, 1978)
Esther McDonald* (Danville, 1978)

MURDER VICTIMS
Claude Snelling (Visalia, 1978)†
Katie and Brian Maggiore (Sacramento, 1978)†
Debra Alexandria Manning and Robert Offerman (Goleta, 1979)
Charlene and Lyman Smith (Ventura, 1980)
Patrice and Keith Harrington (Dana Point, 1980)
Manuela Witthuhn (Irvine, 1981)
Cheri Domingo and Gregory Sanchez (Goleta, 1981)
Janelle Cruz (Irvine, 1986)

---

* Pseudonym
† Never conclusively linked to the Golden State Killer.

INVESTIGATORS

Jim Bevins—investigator, Sacramento County Sheriff's
Department

Ken Clark—detective, Sacramento Sheriff's Office

Carol Daly—detective, Sacramento County Sheriff's
Department

Richard Shelby—detective, Sacramento County Sheriff's
Department

Larry Crompton—detective, Contra Costa County Sheriff's
Office

Paul Holes—criminalist, Contra Costa County Sheriff's Office

John Murdock—chief, Contra Costa County Sheriff's Crime Lab

Bill McGowen—detective, Visalia Police Department

Mary Hong—criminalist, Orange County Crime Lab

Erika Hutchcraft—investigator, Orange County District
Attorney's Office

Larry Pool—investigator, Countywide Law Enforcement
Unsolved Element (CLUE), Orange County Sheriff's
Department

Jim White—criminalist, Orange County Sheriff's Department

Fred Ray—detective, Santa Barbara County Sheriff's Office

INTRODUCTION

BEFORE THE GOLDEN STATE KILLER, THERE WAS THE GIRL. MICHELLE will tell you about her: the girl, dragged into the alley off Pleasant Street, murdered and left like so much trash. The girl, a young twentysomething, was killed in Oak Park, Illinois, a few blocks from where Michelle grew up in a busy, Irish Catholic home.

Michelle, the youngest child of six kids, signed her diary entries "Michelle, the Writer." She said the murder ignited her interest in true crime.

We would have made a good (if perhaps strange) pair. At the same time, in my young teens, back in Kansas City, Missouri, I too was an aspiring writer, although I gave myself a slightly loftier moniker in *my* journal: Gillian the Great. Like Michelle, I grew up in a big Irish family, went to Catholic school, nurtured a fascination with the dark. I read Truman Capote's *In Cold Blood* at age twelve, a cheap second-hand purchase, and this would launch my lifelong obsession with true crime.

I love reading true crime, but I've always been aware of the fact that, as a reader, I am actively choosing to be a consumer of someone else's tragedy. So like any responsible consumer, I try to be careful in the choices I make. I read only the best: writers who are dogged, insightful, and humane.

It was inevitable that I would find Michelle.

I've always thought the least appreciated aspect of a great true-crime writer is humanity. Michelle McNamara had an uncanny ability to get into the minds of not just killers but the cops who hunted them, the victims they destroyed, and the trail of grieving relatives left behind. As an adult, I became a regular visitor of her remarkable blog, *True Crime Diary*. "You should drop her a line," my husband would urge. She was from Chicago; I live in Chicago; both of us were moms who spent unwholesome amounts of time looking under rocks at the dark sides of humanity.

I resisted my husband's urging—I think the closest I came to meeting Michelle was introducing myself to an aunt of hers at a book event—she loaned me her phone, and I texted Michelle something notably unauthorly, like, "You are the coolest!!!"

The truth was, I was unsure whether I wanted to meet this writer—I felt outmatched by her. I create characters; she had to deal with facts, go where the story took her. She had to earn the trust of wary, weary investigators, brave the mountains of paperwork that may contain that one crucial piece of information, and convince devastated family and friends to needle around in old wounds.

She did all this with a particular sort of grace, writing in the night as her family slept, from a room strewn with her daughter's construction paper, scribbling down California penal codes in crayon.

I am a nasty collector of killers, but I wasn't aware of the man Michelle would dub the Golden State Killer until she started writing about this nightmare, who was responsible for fifty sexual assaults and at least ten murders in California during the 1970s and '80s. This was a decades-old cold case; witnesses and victims had moved away or passed away or moved on; the case encompassed multiple jurisdictions—in both Southern and Northern California—and involved myriad crime files that lacked the benefits of DNA or lab analysis. There are a very few writers who would take this on, fewer still who would do it well.

Michelle's doggedness in pursuing this case was astounding.

In a typical instance, she tracked down a pair of cuff links that had been stolen from a Stockton crime scene in 1977 on the website of a vintage store in Oregon. But she didn't do just this; she could also tell you that "boys' names beginning in *N* were relatively rare, appearing only once in the top one hundred names of the 1930s and '40s, when the original owner of the cuff links was likely born." Mind you, this isn't even a clue leading to the killer; it's a clue leading to the cuff links the killer stole. This dedication to particulars was typical. Writes Michelle: "I once spent an afternoon tracking down every detail I could about a member of the 1972 Rio Americano High School water polo team because in the yearbook photo he appeared lean and to have big calves"—a *possible* physical trait of the Golden State Killer.

Many writers who have sweat and bled gathering this much research can get lost in the details—statistics and information tend to elbow out humanity. The traits that make one a painstaking researcher are often at odds with the nuance of life.

But *I'll Be Gone in the Dark*, while a beautiful work of reporting, is equally a snapshot of the time, place, and person. Michelle brings to life the California subdivisions that were edging out orange groves, the glassy new developments that made victims the stars of their own horrific thrillers, the towns that lived in the shadow of mountains that came alive once a year with thousands of scuttling tarantulas searching for mates. And the people, good God, the people—hopeful ex-hippies, striving newlyweds, a mother and her teen daughter arguing over freedom and responsibility and swimsuits for what they didn't realize would be the last time.

I was hooked from the beginning, and so was Michelle, it seems. Her multiyear hunt for the identity of the Golden State Killer took a harsh toll on her: "There's a scream permanently lodged in my throat now."

Michelle passed away in her sleep at age forty-six, before she could finish this remarkable book. You'll find case notes from her colleagues, but the identity of the Golden State Killer—who dunnit—remains unresolved. His identity matters not a whit to me. I want him captured; I don't care who he is. Looking at such a man's face is anticlimactic; attaching a name, even more so. We know what he did; any information beyond that will inevitably feel pedestrian, pale, somehow cliché: "My mother was cruel. I hate women. I never had a family. . . ." And so on. I want to know more about true, complete people, not dirty scraps of humans.

I want to know more about Michelle. As she detailed her search for this shadowy man, I found myself looking for clues to this writer I so admire. Who was the woman whom I trusted enough to follow into this nightmare? What was she like? What made her this way? What gave her this grace? One summer day, I found myself driving the twenty minutes from my Chicago home out to Oak Park, to the alley where "the girl" was found, where Michelle the Writer discovered her calling. I didn't realize until I was there *why* I was there. It was because I was in my own search, hunting this remarkable hunter of darkness.

—GILLIAN FLYNN

I'LL BE GONE
IN THE DARK

PROLOGUE

THAT SUMMER I HUNTED THE SERIAL KILLER AT NIGHT FROM MY daughter's playroom. For the most part I mimicked the bedtime routine of a normal person. Teeth brushed. Pajamas on. But after my husband and daughter fell asleep, I'd retreat to my makeshift workspace and boot up my laptop, that fifteen-inch-wide hatch of endless possibilities. Our neighborhood northwest of downtown Los Angeles is remarkably quiet at night. Sometimes the only sound was the *click* as I tapped ever closer down the driveways of men I didn't know using Google Street View. I rarely moved but I leaped decades with a few keystrokes. Yearbooks. Marriage certificates. Mug shots. I scoured thousands of pages of 1970s-era police files. I pored over autopsy reports. That I should do this surrounded by a half-dozen stuffed animals and a set of miniature pink bongos didn't strike me as unusual. I'd found my searching place, as private as a rat's maze. Every obsession needs a room of its own. Mine was strewn with coloring paper on which I'd scribbled down California penal codes in crayon.

It was around midnight on July 3, 2012, when I opened a document I'd compiled listing all the unique items he'd stolen over the years. I'd bolded a little over half the list: dead ends. The next item to search for was a pair of cuff links taken in Stockton in September 1977. At that time the Golden State Killer, as I'd come to call him, hadn't yet graduated to murder. He was a serial rapist, known as the East Area Rapist, who was attacking women and girls in their bedrooms, first in east Sacramento County, then snaking out to communities in the Central Valley and around San Francisco's East Bay. He was young—anywhere from eighteen to thirty—Caucasian and athletic, capable of eluding capture by vaulting tall fences. A single-story house second from the corner in a quiet, middle-class neighborhood was his preferred target. He always wore a mask.

Precision and self-preservation were his identifying features. When he zeroed in on a victim, he often entered the home beforehand when no one was there, studying family pictures, learning the layout. He disabled porch lights and unlocked sliding glass doors. He emptied bullets from guns. Unworried homeowners' closed gates were left open; pictures he moved were put back, chalked up to the disorder of daily life. The victims slept untroubled until the flashlight's blaze forced open their eyes. Blindness disoriented them. Sleepy minds lumbered, then raced. A figure they couldn't see wielded the light, but who, and why? Their fear found direction when they heard the voice, described as a guttural whisper through clenched teeth, abrupt and threatening, though some detected an occasional lapse into a higher pitch, a tremble, a stutter, as if the masked stranger in the dark was hiding not only his face but also a raw unsteadiness he couldn't always disguise.

The Stockton case in September 1977 in which he'd stolen the cuff links was his twenty-third attack and came after a perfectly bracketed summer break. Drapery hooks scraping against a curtain rod awakened a twenty-nine-year-old woman in her bedroom in northwest Stockton. She rose from her pillow. Outside patio lights framed a silhouette in the doorway. The image vaporized as a flashlight found her face and blinded her; a force of energy rushed toward the bed. His last attack had been Memorial Day weekend. It was 1:30 a.m. on the Tuesday after Labor Day. Summer was over. He was back.

He was after couples now. The female victim had tried to explain the foul odor of her attacker to the reporting officer. She struggled to identify the smell. Bad hygiene wouldn't account for it, she said. It didn't come from his underarms, or his breath. The best the victim could say, the officer noted in his report, was that it seemed like a nervous scent that emanated not from a particular area on his body, but from his every pore. The officer asked if she could be more specific. She couldn't. The thing was, it wasn't like anything she'd ever smelled before.

As in other cases in Stockton he ranted about needing money but ignored cash when it was right in front of him. What he wanted was items of personal value from those he violated: engraved wedding bands, driver's licenses, souvenir coins. The cuff links, a family heirloom, were an unusual 1950s style and mono-grammed with the initials *N.R.* The reporting officer had made a rough drawing of them in the margin of the police report. I was curious about how unique they were. From an Internet search I learned that boys' names beginning in *N* were relatively rare, ap-pearing only once in the top one hundred names of the 1930s and '40s, when the original owner of the cuff links was likely born. I Googled a description of the cuff links and hit the return key on my laptop.

It takes hubris to think you can crack a complex serial murder case that a task force representing five California jurisdictions, with input from the FBI, hasn't been able to solve, especially when your detective work is, like mine, DIY. My interest in crime has personal roots. The unsolved murder of a neighbor when I was fourteen sparked a fascination with cold cases. The advent of the Internet transformed my interest into an active pursuit. Once public records came online and sophisticated search engines were invented, I rec-ognized how a head full of crime details could intersect with an empty search bar, and in 2006 I launched a website called *True Crime Diary*. When my family goes to sleep, I time travel and re-frame stale evidence using twenty-first-century technology. I start clicking, scouring the Internet for digital clues authorities may have overlooked, combing digitized phone books, yearbooks, and Google Earth views of crime scenes: a bottomless pit of potential leads for the laptop investigator who now exists in the virtual world. I share my theories with the loyal regulars who read my blog.

I've written about hundreds of unsolved crimes, from chloroform murderers to killer priests. The Golden State Killer, though, has consumed me the most. In addition to fifty sexual assaults in Northern California, he was responsible for ten sadistic murders in Southern California. Here was a case that spanned a decade and ultimately changed DNA law in the state. Neither the Zodiac Killer, who terrorized San Francisco in the late 1960s and early '70s, nor the Night Stalker, who had Southern Californians locking their windows in the '80s, were as active. Yet the Golden State Killer has little recognition. He didn't have a catchy name until I coined one. He attacked in different jurisdictions across California that didn't always share information or communicate well with each other. By the time DNA testing revealed that crimes previously thought to be unrelated were the work of one man, more than a decade had passed since his last known murder, and his capture wasn't a priority. He flew under the radar, at large and unidentified.

But still terrorizing his victims. In 2001 a woman in Sacramento answered her phone in the same house where she'd been attacked twenty-four years earlier. "Remember when we played?" a man whispered. She recognized the voice immediately. His words echo something he said in Stockton, when the couple's six-year-old daughter got up to use the bathroom and encountered him in the hallway. He was about twenty feet away, a man in a brown ski mask and black knit mittens who was wearing no pants. He had a belt on with some kind of sword in it. "I'm playing tricks with your mom and dad," he said. "Come watch me."

The hook for me was that the case seemed solvable. His debris field was both too big and too small; he'd left behind so many victims and abundant clues, but in relatively contained communities, making data mining potential suspects easier. The case dragged me under quickly. Curiosity turned to clawing hunger. I was on the hunt, absorbed by a click-fever that connected my propulsive tapping with a dopamine rush. I wasn't alone. I found a group of hard-core seekers who congregated on an online message board and exchanged clues and theories on the case. I set aside any judgments I might have had and followed their chatter, all twenty thousand posts and counting. I filtered out creeps with iffy motives and concentrated on the true pursuers. Occasionally a clue, like the image of a decal from a suspicious vehicle seen near an attack, would appear on the message board, a bit of crowdsourcing by overworked detectives who were still trying to solve the case.

I didn't consider him a ghost. My faith was in human error. He made a mistake somewhere along the line, I reasoned.

On the summer night I searched for the cuff links, I'd been obsessed with the case for nearly a year. I favor yellow legal pads, especially the first ten or so pages when everything looks smooth and hopeful. My daughter's playroom was littered with partially used pads, a wasteful habit and one that reflected my state of mind. Each pad was a thread that started and stalled. For advice I turned to the retired detectives who'd worked on the case, many of whom I'd come to consider friends. The hubris had been drained from them, but that didn't stop them from encouraging mine. The hunt to find the Golden State Killer, spanning nearly four decades, felt less like a relay race than a group of fanatics tethered together climbing an impossible mountain. The old guys had to stop, but they insisted I go on. I lamented to one of them that I felt I was grasping at straws.

"My advice? Grasp a straw," he said. "Work it to dust."

The stolen items were my latest straw. I wasn't in an optimistic mood. My family and I were headed to Santa Monica for Fourth of July weekend. I hadn't packed. The weather forecast was lousy. Then I saw it, a single image out of hundreds loading on my laptop screen, the same style of cuff links as sketched out in the police file, with the same initials. I checked and rechecked the cop's crude drawing against the image on my computer. They were going for $8 at a vintage store in a small town in Oregon. I bought them immediately, paying $40 for overnight delivery. I walked down the hallway to my bedroom. My husband was on his side, sleeping. I sat on the edge of the bed and stared at him until he opened his eyes.

"I think I found him," I said. My husband didn't have to ask who "him" was.

PART ONE

IRVINE, 1981

AFTER PROCESSING THE HOUSE, THE POLICE SAID TO DREW WIT-thuhn, "It's yours." The yellow tape came down; the front door closed. The impassive precision of badges at work had helped divert attention from the stain. There was no avoiding it now. His brother and sister-in-law's bedroom was just inside the front door, directly across from the kitchen. Standing at the sink, Drew needed only to turn his head to the left to see the dark spray mottling the white wall above David and Manuela's bed.

Drew prided himself on not being squeamish. At the Police Academy they were being trained to handle stress and never blanch. Emotional steeliness was a graduation requirement. But until the evening of Friday, February 6, 1981, when his fiancée's sister appeared tableside at the Rathskeller Pub in Huntington Beach and said breathlessly, "Drew, call your mom," he didn't think he'd be required to use those skills—the ability to keep his mouth shut and eyes forward when everyone else went bug-eyed and screamed—so soon or so close to home.

David and Manuela lived at 35 Columbus, a single-story tract home in Northwood, a new development in Irvine. The neighborhood was one of the tendrils of suburbia creeping into what was left of the old Irvine ranch. Orange groves still dominated the outskirts, bordering the encroaching concrete and blacktop with immaculate rows of trees, a packinghouse, and a camp for pickers. The future of the changing landscape could be gauged in sound:

the blast from trucks pouring cement was drowning out the dwindling tractors.

An air of genteelness masked Northwood's conveyor-belt transformation. Stands of towering eucalyptus, planted by farmers in the 1940s as protection against the punishing Santa Ana winds, weren't torn down but repurposed. Developers used the trees to bisect main thoroughfares and shroud neighborhoods. David and Manuela's subdivision, Shady Hollow, was a tract of 137 houses with four available floor plans. They chose Plan 6014, "The Willow," three bedrooms, 1,523 square feet. In late 1979, when the house was finished, they moved in.

The house seemed impressively grown-up to Drew, even though David and Manuela were only five years older than him. For one thing, it was brand-new. Kitchen cabinets gleamed from lack of use. The inside of the refrigerator smelled like plastic. And it was spacious. Drew and David had grown up in a house roughly the same size, but seven people had squeezed in there, had impatiently waited their turn for the shower and knocked elbows at the dinner table. David and Manuela stored bicycles in one of their home's three bedrooms; in the other spare bedroom, David kept his guitar.

Drew tried to ignore the jealousy prickling him, but the truth was, he envied his older brother. David and Manuela, married for five years, both had steady jobs. She was a loan officer at California First Bank; he worked in sales at House of Imports, a Mercedes-Benz dealership. Middle-class aspiration welded them. They spent a great deal of time discussing whether or not to get brickwork done in the front yard and where the best place was to find quality Oriental rugs. The house at 35 Columbus was an outline waiting to be filled in. Its blankness conferred promise. Drew felt callow and lacking by comparison.

After the initial tour, Drew spent hardly any time at their house. The problem wasn't to the level of rancor exactly, but more like displeasure. Manuela, the only child of German immigrants, was brusque, sometimes puzzlingly so. At California First Bank, she was known for telling people when they needed a haircut or pointing out when they had done something wrong. She kept a private list of co-workers' mistakes that she wrote in German. She was slim and pretty, with prominent cheekbones and breast implants; she'd had the procedure done after her wedding because she was small and David, she told a co-worker with a kind of distasteful half shrug, seemed to prefer big chests. She didn't flaunt her new figure. To the contrary, she favored turtlenecks and kept her arms folded in against her body, as if anticipating a fight.

Drew could see that the relationship worked for his brother, who could be withdrawn and tentative and whose manner of speaking was more sideways than straight on. But too often Drew left their company feeling trodden, the power of Manuela's rotating grievances short-circuiting every room she entered.

In early February 1981, Drew heard through the family grapevine that David wasn't feeling well and was in the hospital, but he hadn't seen his brother in a while and didn't make plans to visit him. On Monday, February 2, Manuela had taken David to Santa Ana–Tustin Community Hospital where he was admitted for a severe gastrointestinal virus. For the next several nights, she kept the same routine: her parents' house for dinner, then to room 320 at the hospital to see David. They spoke every day and evening by phone. Late Friday morning, David called the bank looking for Manuela, but her co-workers told him she hadn't come in to work. He tried her at home, but the phone kept ringing, which puzzled him. Their answering machine always picked up after the third ring; Manuela didn't know how to operate the machine. Next he called her mother, Ruth, who agreed to drive over to the house and check on her daughter. After not getting an answer at the front door, she used her key to enter. A few minutes later, Ron

Sharpe,* a close family friend, was summoned in a hysterical call from Ruth.

"I just looked over on the left and saw her hands open like that and saw the blood all over the wall," Sharpe told detectives. "I couldn't figure out how it got on the wall from where she was lying."

He took one look in the room and never looked again.

MANUELA WAS IN BED LYING FACE DOWN. SHE WAS WEARING A brown velour robe and was partially wrapped in a sleeping bag, which she sometimes slept in when she was cold. Red marks circled her wrists and ankles, evidence of ligatures that had been removed. A large screwdriver was lying on the concrete patio two feet from the rear sliding glass door. The locking mechanism on the door had been pried open.

A nineteen-inch television from inside the house had been dragged to the southwest corner of the backyard, next to a high wooden fence. The corner of the fence was coming apart slightly, as if someone had fallen against it or jumped it too hard. Investigators observed shoe impressions of a small circle pattern in the front and back yards and on top of the gas meter on the east side of the house.

One of the first peculiarities investigators observed was that the only source of light in the bedroom came from the bathroom. They asked David about it. He was at Manuela's parents' house, where a group of family and friends had congregated after the news to grieve and console one another. Investigators noticed that David seemed shaken and dazed; grief was making his mind drift. His answers trailed off. He switched subjects abruptly. The question about the light confused him.

"Where's the lamp?" he asked.

---

* Pseudonym

A lamp with a square stand and a chrome metal cannonball-shaped light was missing from atop the stereo speaker on the left side of the bed. Its absence gave police a good idea of the heavy object that was used to bludgeon Manuela to death.

David was asked if he knew why the tape was missing from the answering machine. He was stunned. He shook his head. The only possible explanation, he told police, was that whoever killed Manuela had left his voice on the machine.

The scene was deeply weird. It was deeply weird for Irvine, which had little crime. It was deeply weird for the Irvine Police Department; it smelled like a setup to a few of them. Some jewelry was missing and the television had been dragged into the backyard. But what burglar leaves his screwdriver behind? They wondered if the killer was someone Manuela knew. Her husband is staying overnight at the hospital. She invites a male acquaintance over. It gets violent and he grabs the answering machine tape, knowing his voice is on it, and goes about prying the sliding door and then, in a final touch of staging, leaves the screwdriver behind.

But others doubted that Manuela knew her killer. Police interviewed David at the Irvine Police Department the day after the body was found. He was asked if they had had any problems with prowlers in the past. After thinking about it, he mentioned that three or four months earlier, in either October or November 1980, there had been footprints that he couldn't explain. They looked to David like tennis shoes and went from one side of the house all the way to the other side and into the backyard. Investigators slid a piece of paper across the table and asked David to draw the footprint as best he remembered it. He sketched it quickly, preoccupied and exhausted. He didn't know that police had a plaster-cast impression of Manuela's killer's footprint as he stalked the house the night of the murder. He pushed the paper back. He'd drawn a right tennis shoe sole with small circles.

David was thanked and allowed to go home. Police slapped his sketch next to the plaster-cast impression. It was a match.

Most violent criminals are impulsive, disorganized, and easily caught. The vast majority of homicides are committed by people known to the victim and, despite game attempts to throw off the police, these offenders are usually identified and arrested. It's a tiny minority of criminals, maybe 5 percent, who present the biggest challenge—the ones whose crimes reveal preplanning and unremorseful rage. Manuela's murder had all the hallmarks of this last type. There were the ligatures, and their removal. The ferocity of her head wounds. The several-month lapse between appearances of the sole with small circles suggested the slithering of someone rigidly watchful whose brutality and schedule only he knew.

Midday on Saturday, February 7, having sifted through clues for twenty-four hours, the police did one more run-through and then authorized release of the house back to David. This was before the existence of professional crime-scene cleanup companies. Sooty fingerprint powder stained the doorknobs. David and Manuela's queen mattress was gouged in places where criminalists had cut away sections to bag as evidence. The bed and wall above it were still splattered with blood. Drew knew that, as a cop-in-training, he was the natural choice for the cleanup job and volunteered to do it. He also felt he owed it to his brother.

Ten years earlier, their father, Max Witthuhn, had locked himself in a room at the family's home after a fight with his wife. Drew was in eighth grade and attending a school dance at the time. David was eighteen, the oldest in the family, and he was the one who beat down the door after the shotgun blast rocked the house. He shielded the family from the view and absorbed what he saw of his father's splintered brain alone. Their father committed suicide two weeks before Christmas. The experience seemed to rob David of certainty. He was suspended in hesitation after that. His mouth smiled occasionally, but his eyes never did.

Then he met Manuela. He was on solid ground again.

Her bridal veil hung on the back of their bedroom door. The police, thinking it might be a clue, asked David about it. He explained that she always kept it there, a rare sentimental expression. The veil provided a glimpse of Manuela's soft side, a side few had ever known—and now never would.

Drew's fiancée was studying to be a nurse practitioner. She offered to help him with the crime-scene cleanup. They would go on to have two sons and a twenty-eight-year marriage that ended in divorce. Even at the lowest points of their relationship, Drew could be stopped short by the memory of her helping him that day; it was an unflinching act of kindness that he never forgot.

They hauled out bottles of bleach and buckets of water. They put on yellow rubber gloves. The job was messy, but Drew remained dry-eyed and expressionless. He tried to view the experience as a learning opportunity. Police work called for being coolly diagnostic. You had to be tough, even if you were scrubbing your sister-in-law's blood from a brass bed frame. In a little under three hours, they rid the house of violence and tidied it up for David's return.

When they were finished, Drew placed the leftover cleaning supplies in his trunk and got behind the wheel of his car. He stuck the key in the ignition but then froze, seized up, as if on the brink of a sneeze. A strange, uncontainable sensation was winding its way through him. Maybe it was the exhaustion.

He wasn't going to cry. That wasn't it. He couldn't remember the last time he cried. Wasn't him.

He turned and stared at 35 Columbus. He flashed back to the first time he drove up to the house. He remembered what he'd thought as he sat in his car, preparing to go in.

My brother really has it made.

The tamped-down sob escaped, the fight to contain it over. Drew pressed his forehead against the steering wheel and wept.

Not a lump-in-the-throat cry but a tumult of brutal grief. Un-selfconscious. Purging. His car smelled like ammonia. The blood under his fingernails wouldn't come out for days.

Finally, he told himself he had to pull it together. He had in his possession a small object he had to give CSI. Something he'd found under the bed. Something they'd missed.

A piece of Manuela's skull.

ON SATURDAY NIGHT, IRVINE PD INVESTIGATORS RON VEACH AND Paul Jessup, in search of further information from Manuela's inner circle, rang the front door of her parents' house on Loma Street, in the Greentree neighborhood. Horst Rohrbeck, her father, met them at the door. The day before, shortly after the house was cor-doned off and declared a crime scene, Horst and his wife, Ruth, were taken to the station and interviewed separately by junior officers. This was the first time Jessup and Veach, who was the lead detective on the case, were meeting the Rohrbecks. Twenty years in the United States hadn't softened Horst's German com-portment. He co-owned a local auto repair shop and, it was said, could take apart a Mercedes-Benz with a single wrench.

Manuela was the Rohrbecks' only child. She had dinner with them every night. Her personal calendar had only two notations for the month of January, reminders about her parents' birthdays. *Mama. Papa.*

"Somebody killed her," Horst said in his first police interview. "I kill that guy."

Horst stood at the front door holding a snifter of brandy. Veach and Jessup stepped inside the house. A half-dozen stricken friends and family were gathered in the living room. When the investigators identified themselves, Horst's stony expression un-clenched and he erupted. He wasn't a big man, but fury doubled his size. He shouted in accented English about how disgusted he was with the police department, how they needed to be doing more. About four minutes into the tirade, Veach and Jessup realized that their presence wasn't necessary. Horst was heartbroken and conflict-starved. His rage was a projectile splintering in real time. There was nothing to do but put a business card on the foyer table and get out of his way.

Horst's anguish was also tinged with a specific regret. The Rohrbecks were the owners of an enormous, military-grade trained German shepherd named Possum. Horst had suggested that Manuela keep Possum at her house for protection while David was in the hospital, but she declined. It was impossible not to hit rewind and imagine Possum's gaping scissor bite, saliva dripping from his incisors, as he lunged at the intruder chipping at the lock, scaring him away.

Manuela's funeral was Wednesday, February 11, at Saddleback Chapel in Tustin. Drew spotted officers across the street taking photographs. Afterward he returned to 35 Columbus with David. The brothers sat talking in the living room late into the night. David was drinking heavily.

"They think I killed her," David said abruptly about the police. His expression was unreadable. Drew readied himself to hear a confession. He didn't believe David was physically capable of Manuela's murder; the question was whether he could have hired someone to do it. Drew felt his police training kicking in. The image of his brother sitting across from him narrowed to a pinhole. He figured he had one chance.

"Did you?" Drew asked.

David's personality, always a bit diffident, had acquired an understandable tremble. Survivor's guilt weighed on him. He'd been born with a hole in his heart; if anyone was going to die, it should have been him. Manuela's parents' grief roved in search of someone to blame. Their gaze had the increasing effect of a glancing blow. But now, in response to Drew's question, David bristled with certainty.

"No," he said. "I didn't kill my wife, Drew."

Drew exhaled for what felt like the first time since news of Manuela's murder. He'd needed to hear David say the words. Looking in his brother's eyes, wounded but flashing with assurance, Drew knew he was telling the truth.

He wasn't the only one who felt David was innocent. Criminalist Jim White of the Orange County Sheriff's Department helped process the crime scene. Good criminalists are human scanners; they enter messy, unfamiliar rooms, isolate important trace evidence, and block out everything else. They work under pressure. A crime scene is time-sensitive and always on the verge of collapse. Every person who enters represents the possibility for contamination. Criminalists come laden with tools for collection and preservation—paper evidence bags, seals, measuring tape, swabs, bindle paper, plaster of paris. At the Witthuhn scene, White worked in collaboration with Investigator Veach, who instructed him on what to seize. He collected flaky pieces of mud next to the bed. He swabbed a diluted bloodstain on the toilet. He stood with Veach as Manuela's body was rolled. They noted the massive head injury, ligature marks, and some bruising on her right hand. There was a mark on her left buttock that the coroner would later conclude was likely from a punch.

The second part of the criminalist's job comes in the lab, analyzing the evidence that's been collected. White tested the brown paint on the killer's screwdriver against popular brands, concluding that the best match was a store-mixed Oxford Brown made by Behr. The lab is usually where the job ends. Criminalists aren't investigators. They don't conduct interviews or run down leads. But White was in a unique position. The individual police departments of Orange County investigated crimes in their own jurisdictions, but most of them used the Sheriff's Department's crime lab. Thus the Witthuhn investigators knew only Irvine cases, but White had worked crime scenes all across the county, from Santa Ana to San Clemente.

To Irvine police, Manuela Witthuhn's murder was rare.

To Jim White, it was familiar.

DANA POINT, 1980

ROGER HARRINGTON READ THE HANDWRITTEN NOTE THAT WAS stuck under the doorbell. It was dated 8/20/80, the day before.

Patty and Keith,
We came by at 7:00 and no one was home.
Call us if plans have changed-?

It was signed "Merideth and Jay," names Roger recognized as friends of his daughter-in-law. He tried the front door and was surprised to find it locked. Keith and Patty rarely locked up when they were home, especially when they were expecting him for dinner. When Roger pulled into the driveway, he'd hit the garage door opener, and there were Keith's and Patty's cars, his MG and her VW. If they weren't inside, they must be out jogging, Roger figured. He reached for a key hidden above the patio trellis and entered the house, taking the mail, which at a dozen pieces seemed unusually bulky, inside with him.

The house at 33381 Cockleshell Drive is one of roughly 950 in Niguel Shores, a gated community in Dana Point, a beach town in southern Orange County. Roger owned the home, though his main residence was a condo in nearby Lakewood, closer to his office in Long Beach. His twenty-four-year-old son, Keith, a third-year medical student at the University of California–Irvine, and Keith's new wife, Patty, a registered nurse, were living in the house for the time being, a fact that made Roger happy. He liked to have his family close by.

The house was decorated in late-seventies style. Swordfish on the wall. Tiffany chandelier. Ropy plant hangers. Roger mixed himself a drink in the kitchen. Even though it wasn't yet dusk, the house was shadowed and still. The only thing moving was the ocean glinting blue through the south-facing windows and sliding glass doors. An Alpha Beta grocery bag with two cans of food sat in the kitchen sink. A loaf of sheepherder bread was out, three stale-looking pieces stacked beside it. Roger felt, by degrees, a creeping fear.

He walked down the ochre-colored carpeted hallway toward the bedrooms. The door to the guest bedroom, where Keith and Patty slept, was open. Closed shutters made it hard to see. The bed was made, the comforter pulled up to the dark wood head-board. An unusual bump under the bedspread caught Roger's attention as he was about to close the door. He went over and pressed down, feeling something hard. He pulled back the com-forter.

The contrast between the top of the undisturbed bedspread and what lay underneath was hard to compute. Keith and Patty were lying on their stomachs. Their arms were bent at strange angles, palms up. They seemed, in the strictest sense of the word, broken. Were it not for the ceiling, you might think they'd fallen from a great height, such was the spread of blood beneath them.

Keith was the youngest of Roger's four sons. Excellent student. All-conference shortstop in high school. He'd had one long-term girlfriend before Patty, a fellow undergraduate premed student whom everyone assumed he'd marry until, inexplicably to Roger, she chose another med school to attend and the couple broke up. Keith met Patty shortly after that at UCI Medical Center, and they were married within a year. In the back of his mind, Roger worried that Keith was rebounding and moving too fast, but

Patty was warm and clean-cut like Keith—she'd broken up with a previous live-in boyfriend because he used marijuana—and they seemed devoted to each other. Roger had recently been spending a lot of time with "the kids," as he referred to them. He'd helped install a new sprinkling system in the yard. The three of them had spent the previous Saturday clearing brush. Later that night they'd hosted a barbeque for Patty's father's birthday at the house.

In the movies, people who discover a dead body shake the corpse disbelievingly. Roger didn't do that. Didn't need to. Even in the dim light, he could see his fair-skinned son was purple.

There was no sign of a struggle, no evidence of forced entry, though one of the sliding doors had possibly been left unlocked. Patty bought groceries at 9:48 p.m. on Tuesday night, according to the Alpha Beta receipt. Her sister, Sue, called after that, at 11:00 p.m. Keith answered sleepily and handed the phone to Patty. She told Sue they were in bed; she was expecting an early morning call from the nurse registry. A metal fragment consistent with brass was found in Patty's head wound. That suggested that sometime after Patty hung up with her sister and before she didn't appear at work Wednesday morning, someone picked up one of the newly installed brass sprinkler heads from the yard and slipped inside the house. In a subdivision with a manned gate. And no one heard a thing.

REVIEWING THE EVIDENCE OF THE WITTHUHN CASE SIX MONTHS later, criminalist Jim White of the Orange County Sheriff's Department felt in his gut that it was connected to the Harrington murders. The cases shared similarities big and small. They involved middle-class victims bludgeoned to death in bed with objects the killer picked up at the home. In both cases, the killer took the murder weapon with him when he left. In both, the female victims were raped. The bodies of Keith and Patty Harrington showed evidence of ligature marks; pieces of macramé cord were found in and around their bed. In the Witthuhn case, six months later, ligature marks were also present on the body, but the binding material had been removed from the scene. The difference felt like evidence of learning.

The cases also shared an intriguing medical link. Keith Harrington was a med student at UC-Irvine, and Patty was a nurse who sometimes worked shifts at Mercy Hospital in Santa Ana. David Witthuhn, Manuela's husband, had been a patient at Santa Ana–Tustin Community Hospital when his wife was murdered.

A wooden match with a short burn was found on the Harrington's kitchen floor. None of the Harringtons were smokers; investigators believe it belonged to the killer.

Four wooden matches were collected from the flowerbed alongside the Witthuhn house.

Witthuhn was an Irvine PD case; Harrington was Orange County Sheriff's. Investigators on both teams debated the possible connection. Taking on two people, as the Harringtons' killer had, was considered unusual. It was high risk. It suggested the killer's pleasure was in part derived from raising the stakes. Would the same killer, six months later, target a single victim, as Witthuhn's had? The counterargument was that David's hospital stay had been a fluke. Was the killer surprised to find Manuela alone that night?

Theft (Manuela's jewelry) versus no theft. Forced entry versus no forced entry. They didn't have fingerprints to match; DNA was far in the future. The killer hadn't left an ace of spades at both scenes to identify himself. But small details lingered. When Keith Harrington was fatally struck, the wood headboard above him was dented. Investigators concluded from the location of a wood chip found between Patty's legs that Keith was killed first and then Patty was sexually assaulted. The chronology was planned for her maximum suffering. Manuela's killer spent enough time with her that she was stressed to the point of nausea: her vomit was found on the bed.

"Overkill" is a popular but sometimes misused term in criminal investigations and crime stories. Even seasoned homicide investigators occasionally misinterpret an offender's behavior when he uses a great deal of force. It's common to assume that a murder involving overkill means there was a relationship between offender and victim, an unleashing of pent-up rage borne of familiarity. "This was personal," goes the cliché.[†]

But that assumption fails to consider external causes of behavior. The level of force may depend on how much a victim resists. Tremendous injuries that look like a personal relationship gone horribly wrong might be the result of a protracted struggle between strangers.

Most violent criminals smash through life like human sledgehammers. They have fists for hands and can't plan beyond their sightlines. They're caught easily. They talk too much. They return to the scene of the crime, as conspicuous as tin cans on a bumper. But every so often a blue moon surfaces. A snow leopard slinks by.

Every so often investigators encounter a stranger murder involving the overkill of victims who didn't resist.

Considering that Manuela and Patty were bound and therefore by definition compliant, the amount of force used to bludgeon them revealed an extreme amount of rage directed at the female. It was unusual to see such frenzied anger combined with calculated planning. A forensic match between the cases didn't exist but a feeling did, a sense that a single mind was at work, someone who didn't leave many clues or talk or show his face,

---

[†] Michelle's understanding concerning the use of overkill in these cases had shifted somewhat after this was written. She had since reached the conclusion that only as much force as was necessary to kill was used in the GSK homicides. This information was gleaned from discussions with active investigators, including Paul Holes (who said he was "unimpressed" by the ferocity of the blows compared to other crime scenes he's analyzed). The messy/dramatic presentation of a bludgeoning death could initially register as overkill, which is likely what happened in some of the GSK cases.

someone who strolled undetected in the middle-class swarm, an ordinary man with a resting-pulse derangement.

The possible connection between Harrington and Witthuhn was never dismissed outright, just put aside as the cases went cold. In August 1981, several newspaper articles questioned whether or not the Harrington case was related to other recent double homicides in Southern California. "Is a psychopathic 'Night Stalker' murdering Southern California couples in their beds?" was the opening line of an article in the *Los Angeles Times*.

The Santa Barbara Sheriff's Department had been the first to raise the idea of a connection. They had two double homicides and a knife attack in which the couple escaped. But the other counties with proposed linked cases, Ventura and Orange, downplayed the idea. Ventura officials, still smarting from a highly publicized preliminary hearing where the case against their double homicide suspect fell apart, were quoted as saying they thought Santa Barbara had jumped the gun. Orange County was skeptical too. "We don't feel that," said investigator Darryl Coder.

And that was that. Five years passed. Ten years. The phone never rang with the right tip. The files, periodically reviewed, never divulged the necessary information. Roger Harrington obsessed over the details, trying to make sense of Keith and Patty's murders. He hired a private investigator. He offered a large reward. Friends and co-workers were reinterviewed. Nothing sparked. In desperation, Roger, a tough, self-made businessman, broke down and consulted a clairvoyant. The psychic couldn't lift the fog. Roger reexamined every moment he spent with Keith and Patty before their deaths. Their murders were a loop of fragmentary details that never cohered and never stopped rotating in his head.

HOLLYWOOD, 2009

PAPARAZZI FOUR-DEEP ELBOWED EACH OTHER ALONG THE RED CAR-
pet. My husband, Patton, mugged for the cameras in his smart
blue pinstriped suit. Flashbulbs deluged. A dozen hands thrust
microphones from behind the metal barricade. Adam Sandler appeared. Attention shifted. Clamor ratcheted. Then Judd Apatow.
Jonah Hill. Chris Rock. It was Monday, July 20, 2009, a little after
six p.m. We were at the ArcLight Cinemas in Hollywood for the
premiere of the movie *Funny People*. Somewhere there's probably
an unused photograph of a celebrity and in the background is a
woman in a black shift dress and comfortable shoes. I look dazed
and exhilarated and am staring at my iPhone, because at that moment, as some of the world's biggest stars brush against me, I've
just learned that a fugitive I'd been hunting for and obsessing over,
a double murderer on the run in the West and Northwest for the
past thirty-seven years, had been found.

I dodged behind a concrete column and called the one person
I knew would care about the news as much as I did, Pete King, a
longtime reporter for the *Los Angeles Times* who now worked in
media relations for the University of California. He picked up right
away.

"Pete, do you know?" I said. I could barely get the words out
fast enough.

"Know what?"

"I just got an e-mail with a link to a news story. There's been a shootout in some remote mountains in New Mexico. Two people are dead. A sheriff's deputy. And the guy they were after. A kind of mysterious mountain man stealing from cabins."

"No," Pete said.

"Yes," I said. "They fingerprinted the mountain man."

I admit I paused here for maximum dramatic effect.

"Joseph Henry Burgess," I said. "Pete, we were right. He was out there all this time."

Our stunned silence lasted only a moment. I knew Pete wanted to get to a computer. The premiere organizers were herding people inside. I could see Patton scanning for me.

"Find out more," I told Pete. "I can't. I'm at a thing."

This thing was not my thing. I realize confiding unease with movie premieres isn't the most relatable hang-up and falls under the exasperated "must be nice" category. I get it. Bear with me. I'm not being falsely humble when I say that I haven't yet attended a Hollywood event where someone hasn't tucked in a tag, adjusted a button, or told me I had lipstick on my teeth. I once had an events coordinator bat my fingers from my mouth when I was biting my nails. My red carpet pose can best be described as "ducked head, half crouch." But my husband's an actor. I love him and admire his work, and that of our friends, and occasionally attending these events is part of the deal. So you get fancily dressed and sometimes professionally made up. A driver in a town car picks you up, which makes you feel weird and apologetic. An upbeat public relations person you don't know leads you onto a red carpet where you're shouted at to "look here!" and "here" at a hundred strangers with flashbulbs for faces. And then, after those brief moments of manufactured glamour, you find yourself in a regular old creaky movie theater seat, sipping Diet Coke from a sweaty plastic cup and salting your fingers with warm popcorn. Lights dim. Mandated enthusiasm begins.

Walking into the afterparty, Patton was introduced to the directors of *Crank,* an action movie he loves starring Jason Statham. He began regaling them with his favorite bits from the movie. "I'm gay-tham for Statham," he confessed. After we parted ways with the directors, we paused and surveyed the crowd cramming into the ballroom at the Hollywood & Highland Center. Drinks, gourmet mini-cheeseburgers, and maybe even Garry Shandling, an idol of Patton's, awaited us. Patton read my mind.

"No problem," he said.

A friend intercepted us on our way out.

"Getting back to baby?" she said with a warm smile. Our daughter, Alice, was three months old.

"You know how it is," I said.

The truth, of course, was much weirder: I was foregoing a fancy Hollywood party to return not to my sleeping infant but my laptop, to excavate through the night in search of information about a man I'd never met, who'd murdered people I didn't know.

Violent men unknown to me have occupied my mind all my adult life—long before 2007, when I first learned of the offender I would eventually dub the Golden State Killer. The part of the brain reserved for sports statistics or dessert recipes or Shakespeare quotes is, for me, a gallery of harrowing aftermaths: a boy's BMX bike, its wheels still spinning, abandoned in a ditch along a country road; a tuft of microscopic green fibers collected from the small of a dead girl's back.

To say I'd like to stop dwelling is beside the point. Sure, I'd love to clear the rot. I'm envious, for example, of people obsessed with the Civil War, which brims with details but is contained. In my case, the monsters recede but never vanish. They are long dead and being born as I write.

The first one, faceless and never caught, marked me at fourteen, and I've been turning my back on good times in search of answers ever since.

OAK PARK

I HEAR TERRY KEATING BEFORE I SEE HIM. HE WORKS AS A DRUMMER and drum teacher, and his booming voice is probably a result of either hearing loss or a habit of yelling at his students to be heard. "It's Terry!" he shouts. I look up from my phone as I stand waiting for him and see a medium-size white guy with a flop of brown hair holding a Venti Starbucks cup. He's wearing Levi's and a green T-shirt that says SHAMROCK FOOTBALL. But he's not talking to me. He's crossing the street toward 143 South Wesley Avenue, the corner brick house in Oak Park, Illinois, where we have agreed to meet. He's calling out to a man in his fifties working on a car in the driveway. The man is tall, lanky, slightly stooped, his once dark hair gone gray. He's got what is sometimes unkindly referred to as a hatchet face. There is nothing warm about him.

But there's something familiar. He bears a strong resemblance to the family who lived in the house when I was growing up; some of the kids were close to my age, and I knew them from around town. He must be an older brother, I realize, and either bought or inherited the house from his parents.

The man looks at Terry with no recognition. I see Terry is undeterred, and unease washes over me. I have a mother's instinct to reach out, redirect, and quiet down. But I can see Terry wants to distinguish himself in the man's memory. They are old neighbors after all.

"I'm one of the boys that found the body!" Terry shouts.

The man stares at Terry from the side of his car. He says nothing.

The blankness is emphatically hostile. I look away, directing my gaze at a tiny Virgin Mary statue planted in the northeast corner of the front lawn.

It's Saturday afternoon, June 29, 2013—an unusually cold and windy day for midsummer Chicago. In the sky, a block to the west, I can see the steeple of St. Edmund Catholic Church, my family's old church, where I went to school from first through third grades.

The man returns to tinkering with his car. Terry peels off to the right. He spots me thirty yards down the sidewalk. I light up at eye contact and wave furiously at him, compensation for what just transpired. Terry was a year above me at St. Edmund's. The last time I remember seeing him was thirty-five years ago. I know little about him aside from the recent discovery that the same night in August 1984 changed both our lives.

"Michelle!" he shouts, walking toward me. "How's Hollywood?"

We hug awkwardly. His manner brings me back immediately to the Oak Park of my childhood. The flat vowels in his thick Chicago accent. The way he announces later that he has to "haul ass." He's got a cowlick, a raw, pink color to his cheeks, and an utter lack of artifice. No calculating mechanism filters his thought from speech. He starts in right away.

"So yeah, what happened was," he says, leading me back toward the house. I hesitate. Maybe it's fear of the already unhappy homeowner's reaction. Maybe it's my sense that walking might help transport us to that muggy summer night when we still rode bikes but had tasted our first sip of beer.

I look south down the alley.

"How about we retrace the path you guys took that night?"

Oak Park borders the West Side of Chicago. Ernest Hemingway, who grew up there, famously referred to it as a town of "wide lawns and narrow minds," but that wasn't my experience of the place. We lived in a drafty three-story Victorian on the 300 block of South Scoville, a cul-de-sac in the center of town. North of us was the Frank Lloyd Wright Home and Studio and an affluent neighborhood of prairie homes and liberal professionals intent on staying hip. My friend Cameron lived in one of the Wright homes. Her stepfather was a civil rights attorney, and her mother was, I think, a potter. They introduced me to vegetarian salt and the word "Kabuki." I remember the stepfather recommending that Cameron and I, who both tended toward black smocks and confessional verse, cheer ourselves up by going to see the Talking Heads' concert movie *Stop Making Sense*.

South of us was mostly blue-collar Irish Catholic families. The houses were always a few degrees too cold and the beds lacked headboards. Occasionally a father would disappear with a twenty-year-old, never to be seen again, but there would be no divorce. A college friend who spent sophomore year spring break with my family was convinced that my father was doing a comedy bit when he began updating me on the local gossip. The last names, she said, were so exclusively, defiantly Irish. The Connellys. The Flannerys. The O'Learys. And on and on. I overheard a weary Irish Catholic mother from Oak Park field a question about my family once. "How many McNamara kids are there?" she was asked.

"Only six," she said. She had eleven.

My family had a foot in both sides of Oak Park. My parents were natives, members of the tribe commonly referred to as West Side Irish. They met in high school. My father was gap-toothed and jolly. He liked to laugh. My mother was the teetotaling eldest daughter of two hard partiers. She loved Judy Garland and had a lifelong fascination with Hollywood. "People used to tell me I resemble Gene Tierney," she told me shyly once. I didn't know who that was. When I saw *Laura* years later, the mysterious central character who shared my mother's cascade of golden-flecked brown hair and delicately cut cheekbones mesmerized me.

The story is that my parents got together when my father knocked on my mother's door looking, allegedly, for a friend of his. I believe it. The indirect approach to emotional matters suited them. They both had enormous eyes, my father's blue, my mother's green, that expressed with great feeling what they frequently could not.

My father briefly considered the seminary while away at Notre Dame. They called him Brother Leo. My mother considered other suitors and doodled alternate possibilities of her future last name. But Brother Leo decided the seminarians didn't drink enough. Their friend, Rev. Malachy Dooley, officiated their wedding the day after Christmas, 1955. My eldest sister, Margo, was born the following September. Tease my mother with a raised eyebrow about the math and her cheeks burned. Her nickname in high school was Goody Two-Shoes.

After Northwestern Law School, my father went to work for the firm Jenner and Block downtown. He stayed thirty-eight years. Most days began for him in a chair on our screened-in front porch, one hand holding the *Chicago Tribune*, the other a cup of tea, and ended with a very dry Beefeater martini on the rocks with a twist. When he decided to get sober, in 1990, he announced the news in his usual quirky way. Each child received a typewritten form letter. "To my favorite child," it began, "I've decided to join the Pepsi Generation." He later claimed that only two children believed the salutation. I was one of them.

My siblings arrived in quick succession, four girls and a boy; I was the youngest, born after a six-year gap. My sister closest to me in age, Mary Rita, was too much older than me to be a real playmate. Looking back now, it feels as though I was born into a party that had started to wind down. By the time I came around, my parents had matching La-Z-Boy armchairs. Our front door was partly glass, and standing there you could see the back of my mother's beige armchair in the living room. When any of the kids' friends rang the doorbell, she'd stick her hand up and make a circling motion. "Go around," she'd shout, directing them to the unlocked back door.

The families on our block were close, but the kids were all the same ages as my older siblings. They ran in a pack and returned home at dusk. I have a keen memory of what it was like to be a teenager in the seventies because I spent a lot of time with them. My sister Kathleen, ten years older, was and is the most extroverted of our family, and she toted me around like a beloved toy. I remember teetering precariously on the back of her banana seat as she pedaled to the Jewel grocery store on Madison Street. Everyone seemed to know her. "Hey, Beanie!" they called, using her nickname.

In Beanie's freshmen year of high school, she developed an all-consuming crush on Anton, a quiet blond-haired boy who ran track. She took me with her to one of his meets. We hid high up in the bleachers to peek at him. I remember the love-wrecked expression on her face as we watched him explode forth from the starting line. I didn't realize it then, but I was losing her to the complexities of high school. Soon I was sitting alone on the top of the back stairs that connected our kitchen to the second floor, watching teenage boys in sideburns chug beers in our breakfast nook as the Steve Miller Band's "The Joker" played too loud.

Everyone in my family speaks mock reverently about the day in 1974 when the Van sisters—Lisa, my age; Kris, a year older—moved in across the street.

"Thank God," they tease. "What would we have done with you?"

MANY OF MY PARENTS' CLOSEST FRIENDS WERE FROM GRAMMAR school and high school. That they'd maintained such close bonds in an increasingly unmoored and transient world was a point of pride for them, as it should be, but it also had the effect, I think, of insulating them. Take them out of their comfort zone, and they became a little ill at ease. I think an undercurrent of shyness ran through them both. They gravitated toward bigger personalities. They used humor, sometimes sharply, to deflect tension. My mother especially seemed always in a state of suppressing— emotions, expectations. She had small, freckled hands and a habit of tugging her fingers when things got unpleasant.

I don't mean to give the wrong impression. They were bright, curious people who traveled the world once they could afford to. My father argued, and lost, a case in front of the Supreme Court in 1971 that's still studied in constitutional law classes. They subscribed to the *New Yorker*. They always had an interest in popular culture and what was considered good, or cool. My mother allowed herself to be taken to see *Boogie Nights*. ("I'm going to watch *The Sound of Music* twenty times in a row to forget that," she said.) They were Kennedy Democrats. "Politically progressive," my mother liked to say, "but socially conservative." My father took my older sisters when they were ten and eight downtown to see Martin Luther King speak. They voted for Mondale in '84. But when I was nineteen, my mother once woke me at dawn in a panic, shaking a handful of unfamiliar (to her) pills. She couldn't bring herself to say "pill."

"You're on the . . . ," she said.

"Fiber," I said, and turned back to sleep.

BUT THEN OUR RELATIONSHIP WAS ALWAYS FRAUGHT. MY SISTER Maureen remembers coming home when I was around two and finding my mother pacing the front porch. "I don't know if I'm crazy," she said, fighting tears, "or Michelle." My mother was forty then. She had endured alcoholic parents and the death of an infant son. She was raising six kids with no help. I'm sure I was the crazy one. Her lifelong nickname for me, only half-jokingly, was the Little Witch.

We button-pushed our whole lives. She stonewalled. I glow-ered. She scribbled notes on envelopes and slid them under my bedroom door. "You're vain, thoughtless, and rude," a notorious one went, concluding, "but you're my daughter and of course I love you very much." We had a summer cabin on Lake Michi-gan, and I remember one afternoon as a kid playing in the waves as she read a book in a chair on the beach. I realized that the waves were just high enough so that I could remain underwater and then rise for a quick breath when the wave was at its highest, shielding me from view. I let my mother straighten up and scan the water. I let her put down her book. I let her stand. I let her run toward the water preparing to scream. Only then did I pop up nonchalantly.

I wish now that I'd been kinder to her. I used to rib her about the fact that she couldn't bear to watch certain scenes in movies or on TV shows. She couldn't take scenes in which someone threw a party and no one came. She avoided movies about salesmen down on their luck. The specificity was what I found peculiar and amusing; I now see it as the mark of a deeply sensitive person. Her father was once a successful salesman whose career bot-tomed out. She witnessed her parents' problems with alcohol and the insistent mime of merrymaking that went on too long. I see her vulnerabilities now. Her parents valued social success and dis-missed signs of my mother's quick, eager mind. She felt thwarted. She could be undermining and cutting in her remarks, but the older me sees that as a reflection of her own undercut self-image.

We swim or sink against our deficits in life, and she made it a point to encourage me in ways that she had not been. I remember that she dissuaded me from trying out for cheerleading in high school. "Don't you want to be the one cheered?" she said. She thrilled at any of my academic or literary successes. When I was in high school, I came across a letter she'd started to write years before to Aunt Marilyn, my father's sister, who was a theology professor and accomplished archaeologist. My mother was looking for advice on how to best encourage me as a young writer. "How do I make sure she doesn't end up writing greeting cards?" she wrote. I thought of that question often in future years, during the many periods when I would have been ecstatic to be paid to write Hallmark greetings.

But I felt her expectations, the transference of hope, and I bristled. I both yearned for her approval and found her investment in me suffocating. She was both proud of the fact that she had raised a strong-minded daughter and resentful of my sharp opinions. It didn't help matters that my generation was deep into analysis and deconstruction, and hers was not. My mother didn't, or wouldn't, navel-gaze in that way. I remember talking with my sister Maureen once about the severe short haircuts we all had as children.

"Doesn't it seem like Mom was trying to desexualize us?" I asked. Maureen, the mother of three, suppressed a laugh mixed with irritation. "Wait until you have kids, Michelle," she said. "Short haircuts aren't desexualizing. They're easy."

THE NIGHT BEFORE MY WEDDING, MY MOTHER AND I HAD OUR biggest blowout. I was unemployed and adrift, not writing or doing much of anything, and I'd put a lot of time—too much, probably—into the wedding. At the rehearsal dinner, I seated small groups of people who didn't know each other together; the only thing I told them was that they all had one thing in common and had to figure out what it was. At one table everyone had lived at some point in Minnesota. Another table was avid cooks.

In the middle of dinner, my mother came up to me as I was making my way toward the bathroom. I'd been avoiding her because a friend had made the mistake of telling me that earlier in the evening she'd remarked to my mother that she thought I was the best writer she knew. "Oh, I know. I think so too," my mother said. "But don't you think it's too late for her?" Her words stung and batted around in my head all night.

I saw her out of the corner of my eye coming toward me. In retrospect, she was smiling. I could see she was pleased with everything; she was never good at giving compliments directly. I'm sure she thought she was being funny. She gestured at the tables.

"You have too much time on your hands," she said. I turned and faced her with what I'm sure was a mask of pure rage.

"Get away from me," I spit out. She was shocked and tried to explain, but I cut her off. "Walk away from me. Now."

I went to the ladies' room, locked myself in a stall and allowed myself to cry for five minutes, then went back out and pretended that everything was fine.

She was, by all accounts, devastated by my reaction. We never spoke of it, but shortly after the wedding, she wrote me a long letter detailing all the things about me that made her proud. We slowly rebuilt our relationship after that. In late January 2007, my parents decided to take a cruise to Costa Rica. The boat would leave from a port south of Los Angeles. The four of us—my husband, Patton, and I and my parents—had dinner the night before their trip. We laughed a lot, and I drove them to the dock in the morning. My mother and I hugged tightly good-bye.

A few days later, the phone in the kitchen rang at four a.m. I didn't get up. Then it rang again, but stopped before I could get to it. I listened to the voice mail. It was my father. His voice sounded strangled and almost unintelligible.

"Michelle," he said. "Call your siblings." *Click.*

I called my sister Maureen.

"You don't know?" she asked.

"What?"

"Oh, Michelle," she said. "Mom died."

My mother, a diabetic, had fallen ill on the ship due to complications from her disease. They helicoptered her to San José, but it was too late. She was seventy-four.

Two years later, my daughter, Alice, was born. I was inconsolable for the first two weeks. "Postpartum depression," my husband explained to friends. But it wasn't new-mom blues. It was old-mom blues. Holding my newborn daughter, I got it. I got the love that guts you, the sense of responsibility that narrows the world to a pair of needy eyes. At thirty-nine, I understood my mother's love for me for the first time. Sobbing hysterically, almost unable to speak, I ordered my husband to go down into our dank basement and find the letter my mother had written to me after the wedding. He spent hours down there. Every box was overturned. Papers littered the floor. He couldn't find it.

———————

SHORTLY AFTER MY MOTHER'S DEATH, MY FATHER, SISTERS, BROTHER, and I went to my parents' apartment in Deerfield Beach, Florida, to sort through her stuff. We sniffed her clothes that still smelled like Happy perfume by Clinique. We marveled at her bottomless collection of bags, a lifelong obsession. Each of us took something of hers. I took a pair of pink-and-white sandals. They sit in my closet still.

Afterward the seven of us went to an early dinner at the Sea Watch, a nearby restaurant overlooking the ocean. We're laughers, my family, and we told stories about my mother that made us laugh. Seven people laughing loudly create a scene.

An older woman with a bemused smile came up to our table as she was leaving. "What's the secret?" she asked.

"I'm sorry?" my brother, Bob, said.

"To such a happy family?"

We sat agape for a few moments. No one had the heart to say

what we were all thinking: *we've just been cleaning out our dead mother's belongings*. We dissolved into more shrieking laughter.

My mother was, and will always be, the most complicated relationship of my life.

Writing this now, I'm struck by two incompatible truths that pain me. No one would have taken more joy from this book than my mother. And I probably wouldn't have felt the freedom to write it until she was gone.

———

I WALKED THE SAME HALF MILE TO ST. EDMUND'S EVERY DAY, A LEFT on Randolph, a right on Euclid, a left on Pleasant. The girls wore gray plaid jumpers and white shirts; the boys, a mustard-colored collared shirt and slacks. Ms. Ray, my first-grade teacher, had an hourglass figure and a thick mane of caramel-colored hair, and she was always upbeat. It was Suzanne Somers herding a bunch of six-year-olds. Even so, she's not my most vivid memory of St. Edmund's. Nor, curiously enough, is any Catholic teaching or time spent in church, though I know there were a lot of both. No, St. Edmund's will always be welded in my mind with one image, that of a quiet, well-behaved boy with sandy brown hair and ears that stuck out a little: Danny Olis.

My schooltime crushes ranged wildly in physical and personality type, but I can say with confidence that they all shared one thing—they sat in front of me in class. Other people are able to develop feelings for people sitting next to them or behind them, but not me. That requires connecting with someone too directly, sometimes even craning your neck to make full eye contact. Too real. I loved nothing more than the back of a boy's head. I could project endlessly on the blank slate of a kid's slouched back. He could be sitting there with his mouth half-open or picking his nose, and I'd never know.

For a dreamy projectionist like me, Danny Olis was perfect. I don't recall thinking he was unhappy, but I also can't picture his smile. He was self-possessed for a little kid, and slightly solemn, as if he knew something the rest of us gap-toothed fairytale believers would eventually find out. He was the Sam Shepard of our first-grade class. I'd been gifted with a stuffed Curious George when I was born, and something about Danny's round, elfin face and big ears reminded me of my George doll. I fell asleep clutching him to my cheek every night. My love for Danny was big news in our house. Sifting through my old stuff during a move once, I came across a card Beanie had written me during her freshmen year at the University of Iowa. "Dear Mish, I miss you. How's Danny Olis?"

I switched to the local public school, William Beye Elementary, for fourth grade. My best friends, the Van sisters, who'd saved me from loneliness by moving in across the street, went there. I wanted to be with them. I wanted to wear whatever I liked. After a while, I mostly forgot about Danny Olis. My Curious George disappeared, along with my other childhood things.

One night in my junior year of high school, a friend was helping me prepare for a big party I was throwing while my parents were out of town. She'd been hanging out the last few months with some boys from Fenwick, the local all-boys Catholic high school, and asked if a few of them could come to the party. Sure, I said. Actually, she told me tentatively, she was sort of dating one of them.

"Just kind of," she said.

"That's great," I said. "What's his name?"

"Danny Olis."

My eyes widened and I half guffawed, half shrieked. I steadied myself and took a breath, the way you do when you're about to share a big secret.

"You're not going to believe this," I said, "but I had the biggest crush on Danny Olis in grade school."

My friend nodded.

"It started in music class because the teacher made you hold hands," she said. My confused expression prompted her to continue.

"He told me," she said.

I recalled nothing about holding hands and music class. And he *knew*? In my memory I was the quiet girl who sat in the back, faithfully but discreetly observing every swivel and dip of his head. Now it seemed my fixation had been about as subtle as a telenovela. I was mortified.

"Well, he's very mysterious," I told her, a little irritated.

She shrugged. "Not to me," she said.

That night teenagers with Solo cups spilled onto my lawn and into the street. I drank too much gin and ducked and weaved through the throngs of unfamiliar people in my house. Boys I'd dated were there, and boys I would date. Someone played "Suspicious Minds" by the Fine Young Cannibals on repeat.

All night I was acutely aware of a quiet, sandy-haired boy standing in the corner of the kitchen near the refrigerator. His hair now covered his ears. His face had lost its roundness and was more drawn, but through quick glimpses I could see the steady, cryptic expression remained. All night I avoided him. I never looked him in the eye. Despite the gin, I was still the girl in the back of the classroom, watchful, never watched.

———

TWENTY-SIX YEARS LATER, ONE AFTERNOON IN MAY, I WAS PREPARing to close my laptop when the familiar ring announced a new e-mail. I glanced at my inbox. I'm an inconsistent e-mail correspondent, and sometimes, I'm a little ashamed to admit, it takes me several days or longer to respond. The name in my inbox took a moment to register: Dan Olis. I clicked on the message hesitantly.

Dan, who was now an engineer living in Denver, explained that he had been forwarded a profile of me that ran in the Notre Dame alumni magazine. The article, "Sleuth," reported that I was the author of a website, *True Crime Diary*, that attempts to solve cold-case homicides. The writer asked the origin of my obsession with unsolved murders and quoted my reply: "This all started when I was 14. A neighbor of mine was brutally murdered. Very strange case. She was jogging, close to her house. [The police] never solved it. Everyone in the neighborhood was gripped with fear and then moved on. But I never could. I had to figure out how it happened."

That was the sound-bite version. Another version is as follows. On the evening of August 1, 1984, I'm basking in the hermetically sealed freedom of our house's renovated third-floor attic bedroom. Every kid in my family spent part of their teenage years up there. It's my turn. My father hated the attic because it was a firetrap, but for me, a fourteen-year-old tsunami of emotions who signed her journal entries "Michelle, the Writer," it's a glorious escape. The carpet is deep orange shag, the ceilings slanted. There's a bookcase built into the wall that swings open to a secret storage nook. Best of all is the enormous wooden desk that takes up half the room. I have a turntable, a typewriter, and a small window that overlooks my neighbor's tiled roof. I have a place to dream. In a few weeks I'll start high school.

At the same time, three-tenths of a mile away, Kathleen Lombardo, twenty-four, is jogging with her Walkman along Pleasant Street. It's a hot night. Neighbors out on their porch watch Kathleen go by about nine forty-five p.m. She has minutes to live.

I remember hearing someone walk upstairs to the second floor—my sister Maureen, I think—and a murmured conversation, an intake of breath, and then my mother's footsteps going quickly to the window. We knew the Lombardo family from St. Edmund's. Word trickled out quickly. Her killer had dragged her into the mouth of the alley between Euclid and Wesley. He cut her throat.

I had no particular interest in crime aside from reading the occasional Nancy Drew book growing up. Yet two days after the killing, without telling anyone, I walked to the spot near our house where Kathleen had been attacked. On the ground I saw pieces of her shattered Walkman. I picked them up. I felt no fear, just an electric curiosity, a current of such unexpected, searching force that I can recall every detail about the moment—the smell of newly cut grass, the chipped brown paint on the garage door. What gripped me was the specter of that question mark where the killer's face should be. The hollow gap of his identity seemed violently powerful to me.

Unsolved murders became an obsession. I was a hoarder of ominous and puzzling details. I developed a Pavlovian response to the word "mystery." My library record was a bibliography of the macabre and true. When I meet people and hear where they're from I orient them in my mind by the nearest unsolved crime. Tell me you went to Miami University of Ohio, and every time I see you I'll think of Ron Tammen, the wrestler and bassist in the school jazz band who walked out of his dorm room on April 19, 1953—his radio playing, the light on, his psychology book open—and vanished, never to be seen again. Mention you're from Yorktown, Virginia, and I'll forever connect you with the Colonial Parkway, the ribbon of road snaking along the York River where four couples either disappeared or were murdered between 1986 and 1989.

In my midthirties, I finally embraced my fascination and, thanks to the advent of Internet technology, my DIY detective website, *True Crime Diary*, was born.

"Why are you so interested in crime?" people ask me, and I always go back to that moment in the alley, the shards of a dead girl's Walkman in my hands.

I need to see his face.

He loses his power when we know his face.

Kathleen Lombardo's murder was never solved.

I would write about her case now and again, and mention it in interviews. I even called the Oak Park Police to fact-check some things. The only real lead was that witnesses reported seeing an African American man in a yellow tank top and headband watching Kathleen intently as she jogged. The police debunked a rumor I remember, that witnesses had seen the killer exit the El train and begin following Kathleen. The rumor's intent was obvious: the murderer had slipped in among us from somewhere else.

The Oak Park cops gave me the distinct impression that the case was a dead end. And that's where I thought it stood, until that day when Dan Olis's name appeared in my inbox. Dan had copied another person on his e-mail to me: Terry Keating. I vaguely recognized the name as a boy a year above us at St. Edmund's. Dan and Terry, it turns out, are first cousins. They were reaching out to me because they, too, were haunted by Kathleen Lombardo's murder, but for different, and far more personal, reasons. In his e-mail Dan said hello, how are you, then got right to the point.

"Did you know that some nice St. Edmund's boys found Kathleen?" he wrote.

The experience had been gruesome and rattling for the kids. They spoke of it often, Dan wrote, mostly because they were angry—the well-known, accepted theory of what happened to Kathleen that night was wrong, in their opinion. They felt they knew the identity of her killer.

In fact, they had encountered him that night.

———————

TERRY AND DAN ARE NOT ONLY COUSINS; THEY SHARED A HOUSE growing up. Dan's family lived on the first floor; Terry's, on the second; and their grandmother, on the third. Terry and I survey the back of the old place from the alley.

"How many people would that be?" I ask Terry. The house is about three thousand square feet at most.

"Eleven kids, five adults," he says.

Just a year apart, Dan and Terry were, and remain, close.

"That summer was a real transition time for us," Terry says. "Sometimes we stole beers and got drunk. Other times we messed around like when we were kids."

He gestures at the slab of concrete that abuts the garage in the backyard.

"I remember we were playing hockey, or maybe basketball, that night." The group comprised Terry, Danny, Danny's younger brother, Tom, and two grade-school friends, Mike and Darren. It was a little before ten p.m. Someone suggested they head down the alley to the White Hen, a small convenience store on Euclid, about a block and a half away. They went to the White Hen all the time, sometimes three or four times a day, for a Kit Kat or a Coke.

Terry and I head north from the house. He spent so much time in this alley as a kid, he can spot all the little ways it's changed.

"It was darker at night back then," he says. "Like a cave almost. The branches would stick out and hang down more."

An unfamiliar tree in a neighbor's backyard draws his attention. "Bamboo," he says. "Can you believe it?"

About fifty feet from where the alley intersects with Pleasant Street, Terry stops. A gaggle of preteen and teen boys shooting the shit, as Terry recalls them doing, can be raucous. They distracted themselves with goofball antics. This spot haunts him. Looking straight ahead you can see the mouth of the alley across the street.

"If we'd been paying attention, we might have seen her run by," he says. "We might have seen him grab her."

We cross the street to the alcove behind 143 South Wesley Avenue. The five boys were walking together in a straight line. Danny was on his right, Terry remembers. He puts a hand on the fence near the garage and rattles it.

"I think this is the same fence, but it was painted red then," Terry says.

He thought he glimpsed a rolled-up rug near the garbage cans. Kathleen's legs were very pale, and in the dark Terry mistook them for a light-colored carpet. Then Danny, who was closest to her, shouted.

"That's a body!"

Terry and I stare at the spot alongside the garage where Kathleen lay on her back. It was clear immediately that her throat had been slashed. Blood pooled around her feet. There was a terrible smell. Probably her stomach gases, Terry guesses now. Darren, a "delicate kid," as Terry describes him, walked slowly backward to the opposite garage with his hands on top of his head, bugging out. Tom took off toward the nearest back door, yelling for help.

The next moment is where the accepted narrative of Kathleen Lombardo's murder diverges from Terry and Dan's memory. They remember that Kathleen still had vital signs but died in the minutes between their discovery of her and the arrival of a swarm of police. They remember the detectives telling them they must have just walked up on the guy.

They remember a man emerging from the alley almost simultaneously as they discovered Kathleen's body. He was tall and appeared to be of Indian descent. He wore a linen shirt opened to his navel, shorts, and sandals.

"What's going on here?" he asked. Terry says the man never looked in the direction of the body.

"Someone's hurt. We need to call the police," Mike shouted at the man. The man shook his head.

"I don't have a phone," he said.

The chaos of the scene obscures the next sequence of events. Terry remembers the patrol car pulling up, driven by a skeptical uniformed cop with a mustache who asked sarcastically where the body was. He remembers the change in tone and urgent radio for help when the cop saw Kathleen. He remembers the cop's partner, a younger guy, maybe even a trainee, leaning against the side of the car, retching.

He remembers Darren against the garage, his hands still to his head, rocking back and forth. And then a siege of lights and sirens, the likes of which Terry had never seen before or since.

Seven years later, Terry happened to carpool to a concert with a guy named Tom McBride, who lived a few doors down from the murder scene. Terry and Tom had been enemies as kids, in the way you are when you don't know each other and go to different schools. Tom, Terry says, was a "public," as the Catholic kids called them. But Terry discovered that Tom was actually a really good guy. They gabbed all night.

"Weren't you one of the kids that found that body?" Tom asked.

Terry said he was. Tom's eyes narrowed.

"I always thought someone in the neighborhood did it."

An image came back to Terry, the man in the open linen shirt, the strange way he wouldn't look at Kathleen's body. The way he'd asked them what was going on here, when it was clear something horrible was.

Terry's stomach tightened.

"What did he look like?" Terry asked.

Tom described him. Tall. From India. A real creep.

"He was right there when we found her!" Terry said.

Tom's color drained. He couldn't believe it. He remembered

clearly that, in the clamor after the discovery of the body, the neighbor, who appeared freshly showered and was dressed in a robe, came out his back door to survey the police cars. He'd turned to Tom and his family, who were out on their back porch.

"Did he say anything?" Terry asked.

Tom nodded.

"What's going on here?" the neighbor said.

THEY NEVER CAUGHT HER KILLER. AND THOSE PIECES OF HER SHAT-tered Walkman that I picked up at her crime scene are jangling around in my head thirty years later as I steer my rental car onto Capitol Avenue in Sacramento. I take it east, out of town, until it turns into Folsom Boulevard. I stay on Folsom, past Sac State and the Sutter Center for Psychiatry, past the empty lots of scrub and scattered oak trees. Running parallel on my right is the Gold Line, a light-rail transit system that runs from downtown to Folsom, twenty-five miles east. The route is historic. The tracks were once used for the Sacramento Valley Railroad, built in 1856, the first steam railroad to connect the city with the mining camps in the Sierras. Crossing Bradshaw Road, I spot signs reading PAWN and 6 POCKET SPORTS BAR. Across the road are petroleum storage tanks behind a rusty chain-link fence. I'm at my destination. Where it all started: the city of Rancho Cordova.

SACRAMENTO, 1976–1977

IN THE SEVENTIES, KIDS WHO DIDN'T LIVE HERE CALLED IT RANCHO Cambodia. The American River bisects the east side of Sacramento County, and Rancho Cordova, on the south bank, is cut off from the leafier, more genteel suburbs on the other side of the river. The area began as a Mexican land grant of five thousand acres for farming. In 1848, after James W. Marshall, thirty-five miles upriver, glimpsed glittering metal flakes in a water-wheel drain and declared "I have found it," the gold dredges descended on Rancho Cordova, leaving huge piles of river rock behind. For a while, it was a vineyard. Mather Air Force Base opened in 1918. But it was the Cold War that really changed Rancho Cordova. In 1953 Aerojet, the rocket and missile-propulsion manufacturer, opened its head-quarters here, and with it came a boom in residential housing for its employees, the town's twisty roads (Zinfandel Drive, Riesling Way) suddenly paved and neatly divided into modest single-story tract houses. Everyone's family seemed associated with the military or Aerojet.

A rougher element lurked. A man who grew up on La Gloria Way in the midseventies remembers the day the ice cream man who worked around Cordova Meadows Elementary School dis-appeared. Turns out the guy with the long hair, big beard, and mirrored aviator glasses who had been selling the kids Popsicles was selling LSD and cocaine to a different set of clientele, and he was hauled away by the cops. Stories of growing up in Sacramento in the seventies are often bait-and-switches like this, a tangle of sweet and scary, small-town postcards with foreboding on the back.

On hot summer days, we waded in the American River, a woman recalls; then another memory, this one of running along the trails by the river and coming upon a homeless camp in the dense brush. Parts of the river were said to be haunted. A group of teenage girls hung out at Land Park and watched shirtless boys wax their cars; they went to Days on the Green in Oakland, that era's Lollapalooza, to see the Eagles or Peter Frampton or Jethro Tull. They drove up to the Sutterville Road levee and drank beer. They were on the levee drinking the night of April 14, 1978, when a convoy of squad cars, sirens blaring, flew past them on the road below. The convoy was endless. "Never saw anything like it before, or since," one of the teenagers, now a fifty-two-year-old woman, said. The East Area Rapist, or EAR—the man I would come to call the Golden State Killer—had struck again.

From Folsom I took a left onto Paseo Drive, into the heart of residential Rancho Cordova. This place meant something to him. He attacked here first and kept coming back. By November 1976, there were nine attacks in Sacramento County attributed to the East Area Rapist in six months; four of those took place in Rancho Cordova. In March 1979, when he hadn't attacked in a year and it seemed he'd left for good, he came back to Rancho Cordova one last time. Was it home? Some of the investigators, especially the ones who worked the case in the beginning, think so.

I pulled up to the site of his first attack, a simple L-shaped single-story house, about a thousand square feet, with a cleanly shorn tree stump in the center of the yard. It was here that the first call came in, at five a.m. on June 18, 1976, from a twenty-three-year-old woman who was speaking into the receiver as best she could from where she lay on the floor, her hands tied behind her back so tightly that she'd lost circulation. Sheila* had backed up to the phone on her father's nightstand, knocked it to the ground, and searched with her fingers for 0. She was calling to report a home-invasion rape.

She wanted them to understand that the mask was strange. It was white and made of a coarse, knitlike material, with eye-holes and a seam down the middle, but it fit very tight against his face. When Sheila opened her eyes and saw him in her bedroom doorway, she thought she was dreaming. Who wears a ski mask in Sacramento in June? She blinked and absorbed more of the image. He was about five nine, moderately muscular, wearing a navy blue, short-sleeved T-shirt and gray canvas gloves. Another detail, so unnatural it must have strayed in from her subconscious—a pair of pale legs with dark hair. The parts flew together and formed a whole. The man wasn't wearing pants. He was erect. His chest rose and fell, exhalations of the real.

He leaped onto Sheila's bed and pressed the blade of a four-inch knife against her right temple. She pulled the covers over her head to will him away. He yanked them off. "If you make one move or sound, I'll stick this knife in you," he whispered.

He tied her wrists behind her back with cord he brought with him, then tied them again with a red-and-white fabric belt he found in Sheila's closet. He stuffed one of her white nylon slips into her mouth as a gag. Already hints existed of the behavior that would become so recognizable. He put baby oil on his penis before he raped her. He rummaged and ransacked; she could hear the little knocker handles on the side tables in the living room clattering as he opened drawers. He spoke in a low guttural whisper, with a clenched jaw. A one-inch cut near her right eyebrow bled from where he'd pressed the knife, ordering her not to make a sound.

---

* Pseudonym

Common sense, and any cop, will tell you that the no-pants rapist is an unsophisticated teenage peeper who just graduated from misdemeanor to crudely conceived felony. The punk doing the no-pants dance suffers from poor impulse control and will be arrested swiftly. His lingering stare has no doubt afforded him creep status in the neighborhood. The cops will kick him awake at his agitated mother's house in no time. But this no-pants punk wasn't caught.

There exists something that I think of as the paradox of the smart rapist. Roy Hazelwood, a former FBI profiler who specializes in sexual predators, talks about it in the book *The Evil That Men Do*, co-written by Stephen G. Michaud: " 'Most people have no trouble connecting intelligence with a complex robbery. But rape-torture is a depraved act, which they cannot remotely relate to. They therefore resist crediting such offenders with intelligence. This is true even of police officers.' "

A closer look at Sheila's rapist's methods reveals a calculating mind at work. He was careful to never remove his gloves. Sheila received hang-up phone calls in the weeks leading up to the attack, as if someone were monitoring her schedule. In April she had the feeling she was being followed. She kept seeing a dark, medium-size American-made car. But it was curious—though she felt sure it was the same car, she could never quite make out the driver.

The night of the attack, a birdbath had been moved to a spot under the telephone line in the backyard, evidently to stand on. But the line was only partially cut, the clumsy hesitation mark of a trainee, like the bent nail of an apprentice carpenter.

Four months later, Richard Shelby was standing on a curb on Shadowbrook Way in Citrus Heights.

Based on the rules of the Sacramento Sheriff's Department, Shelby should not have been on this or any other case. He shouldn't have even been in uniform. Shelby knew the rules—to work for the Sacramento Sheriff's Department in 1966 you had to have all ten digits in their entirety—but he had passed the written exam and physical, and thought he'd try his luck. Luck had been good to him; even the fact that he was missing a good portion of his left ring finger was lucky. He should have been cut in half by the hunter's errant shotgun blast. The doctors told him he came very close to losing the whole hand.

When the screener spotted Shelby's finger, he halted the interview. Shelby was curtly dismissed. He wouldn't be joining the Sacramento Sheriff's Department after all. The rejection smarted. All his life, Shelby had heard his family speak reverently of an uncle who was a sheriff in Oklahoma. Maybe it was a sign. He wanted to work in a less populated county anyway. Yolo, or Placer. The Central Valley's open spaces were the landscape of his youth. Summers he'd worked outside on the ranches and farms of east Merced County. Skinny-dipped in the canals. Hunted rabbit and quail in the lower foothills of the Sierra Nevada. The SSD's "failure to pass" letter arrived a week later. Then, the next day, another letter arrived. This one told him where and when to report for work.

Shelby called for an explanation. Vietnam was becoming big news. In February 1965, the monthly draft was three thousand; the number had increased to thirty-three thousand by October. Protests began throughout the country, turning incrementally more raucous. Available young men were growing scarce. The SSD saw Shelby as a new and relatively rare phenomenon. He had joined the air force more than a decade before, thirteen days after his seventeenth birthday, and completed duty. He had a college degree in criminal justice. He was married. And despite what he was lacking fingerwise, he could outtype the sheriff's secretary. They changed the rules about finger length. Shelby reported for work August 1, 1966. He stayed twenty-seven years.

The SSD was far from a slick place back then. Everyone

competed for the one squad car that had a gooseneck lamp and clipboard affixed to the dash. The armory still had tommy guns from the 1920s. The sirens were located right on top of the cars; the cops who drove them wear hearing aids now. Specialized divisions like the one for sex crimes didn't exist. You were the expert with hands-on experience if you picked up the phone and were called to a rape scene once. That's why Shelby found himself on the morning of October 5, 1976, on the curb at Shadowbrook Way.

A bloodhound following a scent trail had brought him to the spot. The trail began at a child's bedroom window, continued over a fence and through a field of weeds, stopping at the curb. Shelby knocked on the nearest door and looked across the field toward the victim's house, a distance of about two hundred feet. He wished away his unease.

An hour and a half earlier, shortly after six thirty a.m., Jane Carson had been cuddling in bed with her three-year-old son when she heard a light switch go on and off, and then someone running down the hallway. Her husband had left for work moments before. "Jack, is that you? Did you forget something?"

A man in a greenish-brown ski mask came through the door.

"Shut up, I want your money, I won't hurt you," he said.

Shelby found the precision timing interesting. The man entered the house through the son's bedroom window just moments after Jane's husband left. They'd been the victims of an unusual burglary two weeks before, in which the thief took ten or so of their rings and left behind some neighbors' stolen jewelry. The thief had also entered and exited through the son's window. Same guy, Shelby thought. A methodical and patient one.

Jane's rape would end up being the fifth assault attributed to the East Area Rapist, but it was the first one worked by Shelby and Carol Daly, two detectives who would become inextricably linked to the series. A female detective with experience in sex crimes, Daly was a natural fit to conduct the victim interviews. Her people skills would eventually rocket her all the way to the job of undersheriff. Shelby, however, had a knack for pissing people off. He would call on colleagues to handle suspect interrogations, as his tended to devolve into chaos. He was always butting heads with "the fourth floor," the top brass. His problems stemmed less from arrogance than plainspokenness. He lacked finesse. A childhood spent roaming a flat landscape empty of people could keep one from developing certain communication skills. "The ability to be tactful has always eluded me," he says.

There were three more attacks in quick succession that October. At first many of his colleagues thought an unidentified serial offender known as the Early Bird Rapist was responsible, but Shelby knew they were up against a smarter and weirder man than the Early Bird. These were the days before criminal profiling, before terms like "signature" or "ritual behavior" became commonplace. Back then, investigators might say "the presence," "the personality," or "the smell of it." What they meant was the precise and peculiar arrangement of details, as distinct as an odor—the experience of crime-scene déjà vu. There was the consistent physical description, of course. He was white, in his late teens or twenties, about five nine, with a medium, athletic build. Always in some sort of mask. Forced, angry whisper. Clenched jaw. When he got upset, his voice rose to a higher pitch. Small penis. There was the odd deportment—his voice was often hurried but his manner was not. He would open a drawer and stand looking at it for several minutes in silence. Reports of prowlers seen in the neighborhood around the time of an attack often included the detail that the prowler, once alerted that he'd been seen, left the area in a leisurely manner. "Totally unhurried," one witness said.

His psychosexual needs were specific. He bound his victims' hands behind their backs, often tying and retying several times, sometimes with different material. He ordered them to masturbate him with their bound hands. He never fondled them. When he started attacking couples, he'd take the female into the living room and drape a towel over the TV; lighting seemed important. He got off on sexual questioning. "What am I doing?" he'd ask a blindfolded victim as he masturbated with hand lotion found in the house. "Is this like the captain's?" he asked Jane; her husband was a captain in the air force. He told her to "shut up" at least fifty times, Jane said, but when he was raping her, he had other demands, snapping at her like a director to his actress. "Put some emotion in that," he ordered her, "or I'll use my knife."

He was brazen. Twice he entered homes, pressing on undeterred when he knew victims had spotted him and were frantically dialing the police. Children didn't bother him. He never hurt them physically, but he would tie up the older ones and put them in another room. He put Jane's toddler son on the bedroom floor during her attack. The boy fell asleep. When he awoke, he peered over the bed. The EAR had left. His mother lay bound in strips of torn towels and was gagged with a washcloth. He mistook the ligatures for bandages.

"Is the doctor gone?" he whispered.

————

SHELBY WAS FAMILIAR WITH THE BRUTE WAYS OF SKI-MASKED PERverts, but he was unsettled by this one's commitment to reconnaissance. That was unusual. The hang-up phone calls. Pre-prowling. Burglaries. The EAR knew how to turn off outside lights even when they were on a timer. He knew where a hard-to-find garage opener was located. Interviews Shelby conducted suggested that the suspect hadn't cased out just Jane but her neighbors too, noting where he could park his vehicle, what time the neighbors took out their garbage and left for work.

Carol Daly, Shelby's colleague that day, would be quoted a year later in the *Sacramento Bee* saying about the case, "The typical rapist does not have such elaborate schemes." That was the thought going through Shelby's mind as he stood on the curb with the bloodhound, looking across the field toward Jane's house. Another detail troubled him. The offender had poked Jane's left shoulder with his paring knife. Jane felt he didn't intend to injure her, that the wound was an accident. Shelby wasn't so sure. He guessed the guy was suppressing an urge to inflict more pain; until he was caught, the urge would grow.

It did. The suspect began clicking scissors next to blindfolded victims' ears, threatening to cut off toes, one for each time they moved. He stabbed the bed next to where they lay. Psychological torment stoked him. "You don't know me, do you?" he whispered to one victim, using her name. "It was too long ago for you, isn't it? It's been a long time. But I know you." He would always let them believe he'd left their house, then, just as their bodies would slacken, their numb fingers inching for their ligatures, he'd shock them with a sudden noise or movement.

After Jane Carson's attack in October, rumors flew around the community about a serial rapist at large, but the Sheriff's Department asked the local press to not publicize the crimes, fearing that the spotlight might drive the suspect away from the east side, where they hoped to contain and catch him. Shelby, Daly, and their colleagues in the detective unit went about quietly chasing leads. They checked with parole and probation officers. They looked at deliverymen, milkmen, janitors, and carpet layers. They left their business cards on neighborhood doors and followed up on tips that came in, usually about young men who stared too hard or stayed out too late or were, as one tipster said about his younger brother, "fruity." They blindfolded Jane and played tape recordings of two suspects' voices for her. She lay on her bed; her arms shook. "Not him," she said. They canvassed pawnshops for the stolen items, and visited House of Eight, a porn shop on Del Paso Boulevard, inquiring about customers into bondage. They followed up on a tip about a man who was paying the DMV for women's registration information, then following them in his car. They questioned him outside his house, where they noted that he stood in the gutter, too distracted to notice the stream of water swirling around his nice leather dress shoes. He wasn't the EAR, but they got the DMV to stop allowing the practice of purchasing private information. They noted blushing, blinking, arm crossing, and repeating questions in a clear grab for time. None of it led to the EAR.

Meanwhile, gossip in the community mutated in the vacuum of official word. The police weren't telling the public about the rapes, the rumors went, because the details were too horrible to repeat. He was mutilating women's breasts. The rumors weren't true, but the press blackout meant that no one publicly refuted them. Tension peaked on October 18, when the EAR attacked twice in twenty-four hours. One of the victims, a thirty-two-year-old housewife and mother of two, lived on Kipling Drive in Carmichael, one of the more affluent neighborhoods on the east side. Some speculated that the EAR, fed up with his lack of press, was pushing into the nicer neighborhoods to ensure publicity. It worked. Five hundred people attended a town-hall meeting on crime prevention at Del Dayo Elementary School on November 3. Shelby and Daly took turns at the microphone awkwardly trying to answer heated and panicky questions about the EAR.

The next morning, the *Sacramento Bee* ran a story by police reporter Warren Holloway: MAN HUNTED AS SUSPECT IN 8 RAPES. The press blackout was over.

Maybe it was a coincidence, but on the evening of November 10, the same day the *Bee* ran a follow-up story (EAST AREA RAPIST . . . FEAR GRIPS SERENE NEIGHBORHOODS), a man in a leather hood entered the window of a house in Citrus Heights and sneaked up on a sixteen-year-old girl watching television alone in the den. He pointed a knife at her and issued a chilling warning: "Make one move and you'll be silent forever and I'll be gone in the dark."

This time the EAR took his victim outside the house, leading her down an embankment to a cement drainage ditch, about twenty feet wide and ten feet deep, where they walked about a half mile west to an old willow tree. The girl later retraced the path with Shelby and some other detectives; cut shoestrings, shredded Levi's and green panties lay in a heap in weeds near the tree. The girl said she hadn't been raped. Coaxing information from people in the aftermath of a violent attack is tricky, especially when, like Shelby, you're a blunt, six-three older male and the victim is a female teenager who's emotionally about to capsize. You look them in the eye and ask the hard question. You may or may not believe the answer. You ask later, less pointedly, maybe in the middle of talking about something else. They repeat their earlier answer. That's all you can do.

The EAR may have thought she was someone else. "Don't you go to American River College?" he asked her. When she answered no, he pressed his knife against her throat and asked again. Again she said no. The girl told the detectives she resembled a neighbor who had gone to American River College, a local community college. But there was the weird precision timing again. She was only going to be alone in the house for a short window of time. Her parents had gone to the hospital to visit her brother, and she had a date scheduled with her boyfriend later that night. Before he took her to the drainage ditch the EAR had carefully replaced the screen on the window he'd entered and turned off the television and the house lights, as if he knew people would be returning soon and didn't want to raise an alarm.

The girl added to the ever-growing catalog of fleeting details glimpsed in the dark through a loosened blindfold. Black, square-toed shoes. A small flashlight, small enough that it disappeared into his left hand. Military fatigue pants. While she was tied up, he kept scrambling up the west side of the embankment and looking out at something, the girl said. Back and forth. Fidgety like. Shelby climbed the embankment. They were, as always, minutes or hours behind him. You could plant your feet in the man's footprints, but without knowing what drew him to that spot, yours was the chump's view, dumbly scanning the horizon for a hint. Overgrowth of tangled brush. Fences. Backyards. Too much. Not enough. Square one.

The leather hood the girl described extended beneath the EAR's shirt and had slits for eyes and mouth; that sounded to Shelby like the kind of hoods arc welders wear underneath their helmets. He hit up welding equipment companies for customer names. Nothing panned out. Meanwhile, the phones rang at the Sheriff's Department with people spilling names. The detectives tried to eyeball everybody. Guys were eliminated if they had big feet, a sunken chest, a potbelly, a beard, a wandering left eye, a limp, custom arch supports, or a sister-in-law who confided that she skinny-dipped once with her husband's younger brother and he had a big penis.

The EAR attacked another teenage girl, this one in Fair Oaks, on December 18. There were two more victims in January. RAPIST STRIKES AGAIN, 14TH TIME IN 15 MONTHS read the headline in the January 24 edition of the *Sacramento Bee*. A quote by an anonymous sheriff's detective conveyed the brittle weariness setting in: " 'It was exactly the same as all the rest.' "

ON THE MORNING OF FEBRUARY 2, 1977, A THIRTY-YEAR-OLD woman in Carmichael lay bound, blindfolded, and gagged on her bed. After listening for a long time and hearing nothing, she worked the gag out of her mouth and called out for her seven-year-old daughter, whom she sensed was in the room. "Are you okay?" she asked. Her daughter shushed her. "Momma, be quiet." Somebody pushed down on the woman's bed abruptly and let go, as if to tell her he was still there. For several minutes she lay with her eyes wide open against her orange-and-white terry-cloth blindfold, listening to him breathing somewhere close by.

Hypnotists elicited details about suspicious sightings. Detectives looked for a black-and-white motorcycle with fiberglass saddlebags. A black, possibly ex–California Highway Patrol car with a loud exhaust. A white van with no side windows. A biker named Don with muttonchops and a large mustache. A woman called about an employee at a local grocery store. The man's penis, she said knowingly, "is very rough like it's been used to death."

Desperate for fingerprint evidence, the detectives tried a method called iodine–silver plate transfer for lifting latent prints from human skin; Carol Daly was tasked with blowing a fine powder through a tube over the victims' naked bodies. Nothing. There were small victories. In February, a woman in Carmichael struggled with the EAR for his gun. He beat her over the head. When Shelby and Daly examined the victim's head wound they noticed a spot of blood on her hair about two inches from the injury. Daly snipped the bloodied hair and had it sent to the crime lab for typing. The victim's blood was type B. This spot, determined to be the EAR's, was A positive.

[EDITOR'S NOTE: The section that follows was pieced together from Michelle's notes.]

IT WAS AROUND TEN THIRTY ON THE NIGHT OF FEBRUARY 16, 1977. The Moore* family was settled into their home on Ripon Court

---

* All Moore family names are pseudonyms.

in the Sacramento neighborhood of College-Glen. Eighteen-year-old Douglas cut himself some cake in the kitchen while his fifteen-year-old sister Priscilla watched TV in the living room. Suddenly, an unexpected noise capsized the ordinariness of their weekday evening—a crash that came from the backyard. It was the family's electric smoker. Someone had just hopped the fence and knocked into it.

Mavis Moore turned on the patio light and peered through the drapes just in time to glimpse a figure running through the backyard. Douglas impulsively began pursuit, and his father, Dale, grabbed a flashlight and followed him through the side door.

Dale found himself trailing behind as he watched his son chase the blond-haired man who had been prowling their backyard—across Ripon Court and into the space between two neighboring residences, where the prowler disappeared over the fence. Douglas followed, and as he reached the crest of the fence, a loud pop sounded. Dale watched as his son fell backward onto the grass.

"I've been shot," Douglas cried out as his father attended to him. Another shot followed, without consequence. Dale moved Douglas out of the line of fire.

An ambulance arrived and rushed Douglas to the hospital. The bullet had entered his stomach and left multiple holes in his intestines, bladder, and rectum.

AS THE POLICE WENT DOOR TO DOOR CONDUCTING A NEIGH-borhood canvass, their notebooks began to fill up with details eerily similar to the descriptions detectives would hear when canvassing after an EAR attack: neighbors heard sounds in their yards as though their fences had just been scaled; one neighbor heard someone walking on her roof; fence slats were discovered kicked out and side gates were found open. A rolling tide of barking dogs seemed to indicate the direction of a phantom prowler.

Residents in the general area reported prowler incidents and burglaries in the weeks leading up to the Moore shooting.

And all witness reports, including Doug Moore's, yielded a familiar set of descriptors: a white male between twenty-five and thirty years old, five nine to five ten, with heavy legs and sandy blond neck-length hair, wearing a watch cap, a windbreaker, Levi's cords, and tennis shoes.

Among the clues collected was the usual outlier, an intriguing potential lead that may have had no relationship at all with the incident culminating in Doug Moore's shooting—and even if it did, it seemed to offer little in the way of concrete information: A custodian leaving his shift at the nearby Thomas Jefferson School crossed paths with a pair of loiterers in front of a building on campus. One of them asked him the time as he passed, while the other appeared to be concealing something—possibly a transistor radio—beneath his coat.

Both subjects appeared to be eighteen or nineteen years old and around five nine. One was apparently a Mexican male with dark shoulder-length hair, wearing a blue windbreaker and Levi's, while the other was a white male in an identical outfit.

The custodian had worked at the school for seven years and was well acquainted with the regulars who'd hang around campus after hours. He had never seen either subject before.

————

THE EAR HIT AGAIN IN THE EARLY MORNING HOURS OF MARCH 8, in Arden-Arcade. The *Sacramento Bee* ran an article ("Rape May Be Linked to Series") about the attack. The reporter noted that "the victim was separated from her husband and had a small child, who was staying elsewhere Monday night. The east area rapist has never attacked while there was a man in the house, although occasionally there have been children." If there was ever a question about whether the EAR was reading his press, it was put to rest after the article was published. His next victim was a teenage girl, but after that he targeted heterosexual couples, eleven in a row, and from then on, couples remained the main focus of his attacks.

On March 18, the Sheriff's Department received three phone calls between four fifteen and five p.m. "I'm the EAR," a male said, laughed, and hung up. The second call was a repeat of the first. Then the third: "I'm the East Area Rapist. I have my next victim stalked and you guys can't catch me."

That night in Rancho Cordova a sixteen-year-old girl returning home from her part-time job at Kentucky Fried Chicken dropped her take-out bag on her kitchen counter and picked up the phone to dial a friend. Her parents were out of town and she intended to stay at the friend's house. The call had rung one and a half times when a man in a green ski mask emerged from her parents' bedroom, a hatchet raised above his head.

This time the victim had a somewhat better look at the EAR's face, as he wore a ski mask with the center cut out. Acting on a hunch that the EAR was a young Rancho Cordova local, Shelby and Daly brought over a stack of neighborhood yearbooks and watched as the victim flipped through them. She stopped on a page in the 1974 Folsom High School yearbook. She handed the book to Shelby, pointing at a boy's picture. "That looks most like him." They ran down the kid's history. Instability, check. Weirdness, yes. He was working at a gas station on Auburn Boulevard. They hid the victim in the back of an unmarked car and had her peer at him from three feet away as he filled the gas tank. She couldn't make a positive identification.

THE HOUSES HAD DIFFERENT LAYOUTS. SOME OF THE VICTIMS were young teenagers who clutched couch pillows to their stomachs and, pain-faced and confused, shook their heads when they were asked if they knew what a "climax" was. Others were in their midthirties, had recently divorced their second husbands, and were enrolled in beauty school classes and active in singles clubs. But for the detectives called out of bed in the early morning hours, the scenes record-skipped with a numbing sameness. Cut shoe-laces on a shag carpet. Deep red indentations around wrists. Pry marks on window frames. Kitchen cabinets left open. Beer cans and cracker boxes scattered on backyard patios. There was the sound of some sort of bag, paper rustling or a zipper opening, as he stole engraved jewelry, driver's licenses, photos, coins, occa-sionally money, though theft was clearly not his driving motive, as he bypassed other valuables, and often what he stole, like a cherished wedding ring ripped violently from a swollen finger, was found dumped somewhere close by.

On April 2, he added a twist to his method, one he would continue to use. The first couple he targeted awoke to a bright, square-lensed flashlight shining in their eyes. He gruffly whis-pered that he had a gun ("a .45 with fourteen shots") and threw a length of twine at the woman, ordering her to tie up her boy-friend. When the male was bound, the EAR placed a cup and saucer on his back. "I hear the cup rattle or bedsprings make any noise, I'll shoot everybody in the house," he whispered. To the woman he remarked at one point, "I was in the army and I fucked a lot while I was there."

That the EAR may have a military connection was frequently discussed. There were five military installations within an hour's drive of Sacramento; Mather Air Force Base, adjacent to Ran-cho Cordova, had roughly eight thousand personnel alone. There was his penchant for army green and the occasional report of black lace-up military-style boots. Several who encountered him, including those with military backgrounds, felt his authoritative posture and unyielding demeanor were reminiscent of someone with a background in the armed forces. "The dishes trick," as his unusual alarm system came to be known, struck some as a technique right out of jungle warfare.

There was also the galling fact that he was outmaneuvering them. He remained free. The Sheriff's Department borrowed treetop cameras from the State Department of Forestry normally used to catch arsonists. They depleted their overtime budget sending undercover patrols to roam the neighborhoods the EAR frequented. They borrowed military nightscopes and movement detectors used in Vietnam. Yet he was still out there blending in, a man whose ordinariness was his mask.

The Sheriff's Department brought in an army colonel trained in Special Forces techniques to help them understand the EAR's tactics. "The major point in training is that of patience," the colonel told them. "The specially trained person can and will sit in one position for hours if necessary and will not move." The EAR's sensitivity to noise—he often turned off air-conditioning and heating units to hear better—was a skill honed in Special Forces personnel. Ditto knives, knots, and planning multiple escape routes. "He can and will make use of any point of concealment," the colonel said. Look for him "in the place most unlikely for a human being to be, i.e., the bottom portion of an outhouse, the middle of blackberry bushes." The colonel reiterated: remember the patience. He believes he's got more stamina than anyone else, and that searchers will give up when he will not.

Shelby wondered if they hadn't caught him for another reason. He noticed that they would station undercover patrols in a neighborhood he was known to frequent, but that night the EAR would attack somewhere else. He seemed more aware of police procedure than the average citizen. He always wore gloves and parked outside the standard police perimeter. "Freeze!" he shouted once at a woman as she tried to scramble away from him. Shelby wasn't the only one to bring it up. The thought crossed other minds in the Sheriff's Department too. Was he one of them?

One night Shelby followed up on a prowler tip. The woman who called in the tip seemed surprised when Shelby knocked on the front door and announced himself. For the last several minutes she thought an officer was already there, she told him; she could swear she heard the sound of a police radio just outside her house.

"He will let the searchers walk within an inch of him and will not move," the colonel had warned.

By the end of April, the victim count was seventeen. The EAR was averaging two victims a month. If you were paying attention, and most people were, it was bad.

Then came May.

———

THE SHERIFF'S DEPARTMENT ACCEPTED AN OFFER FROM A PSYCHIC who said she could identify the EAR. She chanted and ate raw hamburger. They looked into having the EAR's "biorhythm chart" done but were told it wouldn't work without his birth date. Around midnight on May 2, a little over two weeks since the last attack, a thirty-year-old woman on La Riviera Drive heard a thump outside, the same sound her young sons made when they jumped the fence from the levee into the yard. She went to the window, but didn't see anything. The abrupt glare of a flashlight, the first hint of danger, startled her and her husband, a major in the air force, around three a.m.

Two days later, a man in a beige ski mask and dark blue jacket, resembling a US Navy jacket, lunged out of the darkness at a young woman and her male co-worker as they walked to her car parked in his driveway in Orangevale. Both cases had the familiar smell. The hang-up phone calls beforehand. The dishes trick.

The unsettling pairing, in one instance, of brutal rape followed by a break to eat Ritz crackers in the kitchen. Both couples told the detectives the EAR seemed like someone straining to appear tough, a bad actor who took gulping breaths in an attempt to seem angry and unhinged. The woman in Orangevale said he entered the bathroom for several minutes; it sounded to her that he was hyperventilating in there.

EAST AREA RAPIST ATTACKS 20TH VICTIM IN ORANGEVALE read the headline in the next day's *Bee*.

Pressure was building at the Sheriff's Department. Normally hands-off bosses became agitatedly hands-on. It was only May and their overtime budget was nearly depleted for the year. They were elbow-deep in dead-end calls about ex-boyfriends and Public Works employees checking street lighting. Slouching and leisurely sipping from Styrofoam cups of coffee disappeared from daily briefings, replaced by pacing and restless legs. Detectives stared at maps and tried to predict his next attack. They had a feeling he would hit next in the area around Sunrise Mall, in Citrus Heights; reports of prowling and break-ins were emanating from there.

Around twelve forty-five a.m. on May 13, a family on Merlindale Drive, not far from Sunrise Mall, heard someone on their roof. Dogs in adjacent yards began barking. A neighbor called the family around one a.m. to say they heard someone crawling on their roof too. Squad cars arrived within minutes; the roof creeper was gone.

The next night, a block over, a young waitress and her husband, a restaurant manager, were the next victims.

Disbelief set in. A roughly ten-mile corridor following the American River east into unincorporated Sacramento County was under siege. No one required context anymore. There was no "Have you heard?" You had heard. "There's this guy" was replaced by "He." Teachers at Sacramento State gave up teaching and entire class sessions were devoted to discussions about the EAR, any student with new information pumped for details.

People's relationship with nature changed. Winter's drizzle and dense tule fog, the weather of dread, had given way to a lovely warmth, to vistas of freshly scrubbed green studded with red and pink camellia petals. But Sacramento's prized abundance of trees, all those Oregon ash and blue oaks flanking the river, were recast in their eyes, a once verdant canopy now a hunting blind. An urge to prune took over. East siders hacked off tree limbs and uprooted shrubs around their houses. Reinforcing sliding glass windows with dowel rods wasn't enough. That might keep him out, but they wanted more; they wanted to strip him completely of the ability to hide.

By May 16, a surge of newly installed floodlights lit up the east side like a Christmas tree. In one house tambourines were tied to every door and window. Hammers went under pillows. Nearly three thousand guns were sold in Sacramento County between January and May. Many people refused to sleep between one and four a.m. Some couples slept in shifts, one of them always stationed on the living room couch, a rifle pointed at the window.

Only a madman would strike again.

MAY 17 WAS THE DAY EVERYONE HELD THEIR BREATH AND WAITED to see who would die. They'd awakened that morning to news that the EAR had struck for the fourth time that month, the twenty-first attack attributed to him in less than a year; the latest victims, a couple in the Del Dayo neighborhood, told police he threatened to kill two people that night. In a single twenty-four-hour period, between May 17 and May 18, the Sacramento Sheriff's Department received 6,169 calls, almost all of them about the East Area Rapist.

The officers responded to the call at 3:55 a.m. on May 17. The thirty-one-year-old male victim was outside his house in light blue pajamas, a length of white shoelace dangling from his left wrist. He spoke angrily in a mix of English and Italian. "What's the hurry," he said to the officers. "He's gone. Just come on in!" When Shelby pulled up to the scene, he recognized the man immediately. Back in November, when he and Daly had led a packed town-hall discussion on the EAR, the man had stood up and criticized the investigation. He and Shelby had exchanged heated words. The incident had taken place six months ago, and maybe it was a coincidence, but the connection contributed to the impression that the EAR was brazen enough to attend events dedicated to his own capture, that he blended in, observed, remembered, and excelled at a certain kind of malevolent patience.

The attack, right off American River Drive in Del Dayo, near a water treatment plant, echoed the previous ones, though this time the EAR's mood, like the community's, was especially jittery. He stuttered; it didn't seem like a put-on. And he had a message to convey, one he practically spit out at his female victim with excited anger. "Those fuckers, those pigs—do you hear me? I've never killed before but I'm going to kill now. I want you to tell those fuckers, those pigs, I'm going to go home to my apartment. I have bunches of televisions. I'm going to listen to the radio and watch television and if I hear about this, I'm going to go out tomorrow night and kill two people. People are going to die."

But he gave the husband, who was tied up in another room, a slightly different message. "You tell those fucking pigs that I could have killed two people tonight. If I don't see that all over the papers and television, I'll kill two people tomorrow night."

He devoured Cheez-It crackers and half a cantaloupe before he left.

The city awoke to a jarring headline in the *Sacramento Bee*: EAST AREA RAPIST ATTACKS NO. 23, NEXT VICTIMS DIE TONIGHT? The article reported that the Sheriff's Department had consulted with a panel of local psychiatrists and concluded that the EAR was "a probable paranoid schizophrenic" and that he was likely in "a homosexual panic because of inadequate (physical) endowment." The inadequate-endowment detail was repeated several times in the article. Whether or not this was the kind of press the EAR sought, or whether he sought press at all, was anyone's guess, as was the question of whether he'd make good on his threat to kill.

May 1977 was the month the wrought-iron bars went up and the all-night vigils began, when a group of three hundred neighborhood men patrolled east Sacramento County in pickup trucks outfitted with CB radios. Hard acrylic panels were bolted behind windows and doors. Deadbolts were on back order. Meter readers held their identification cards in front of them and announced themselves repeatedly, loudly, when they entered people's yards. Orders for backyard floodlights went from ten a month to six hundred. A letter to the *Sacramento Union*, typical of the time: "We used to open our windows at night for fresh air. Not anymore. We took the dog for a walk in the evenings. Not anymore. My sons used to feel safe and secure in their own home. Not anymore. We all used to sleep without waking to every normal evening's noise. Not anymore."

Around this time, Shelby found himself in south Sacramento in an unmarked car with another detective on daytime surveillance detail. They were facing east, and to their left was a short street where, midway down the block, a game of tag football was being played. A car headed eastbound, going very slowly, passed by. The car's speed was unusual, but what really caught Shelby's attention was the extreme focus with which the driver watched the game. Shelby looked closer at the players; they were all boys except the quarterback, a young woman with long hair, about twenty years old. A few minutes later, the same car returned, inching by, the driver again staring intently at the players. Shelby noted the make and model of the car. When the car circled a third time, he jotted down the plate and radioed it in. "If he comes by again, let's pull him over," Shelby told his partner. But that was the last time the driver, a pencil-necked blond guy in his early twenties, came by. His ardent concentration is what lingers in Shelby's memory. That, and the fact that days later the EAR would attack in south Sacramento for the first time, about a mile away; that crime scene would be the last Shelby worked on before being pulled off the case and reassigned.

The license plate came back unregistered.

———

THERE'S A KIND OF PROUDLY SELF-RELIANT, NO-FUSS QUALITY that I've come to recognize in longtime Sacramentans. I once scheduled a breakfast interview at the boutique hotel I was staying at downtown. The interviewee's husband, a cabinetmaker, accompanied her to the meeting. I had already ordered my breakfast, a deconstructed yogurt parfait that came in a tiny mason jar with an antique silver spoon. I encouraged my guests to get something, but when the waitress turned to the husband he shook his head politely and smiled. "Made my own breakfast myself this morning." I literally had a silver spoon in my mouth when he said it.

I bring this up only to help make sense of certain things. For example, two days after the May 17 attack, a local dentist publicly announced that he was contributing $10,000 to the reward (raising it to $25,000) and, with another businessman, forming the grassroots EARS (East Area Rapist Surveillance) Patrol. Hundreds of local men attended a rally and, with CB radios, began patrolling the east side all night in their cars. The undersheriff conveyed his dismay over this development in a *Bee* article on May 20; essentially his message was: please don't. The citizen manhunt pushed on undeterred, accompanied by the noise and light of a surveillance helicopter on loan from the California Highway Patrol that circled relentlessly overhead.

Another example: an article in the *Sacramento Union* on May 22, "Two Victims Recall East Area Rapist," quoted Jane using a pseudonym; there were enough identifying details that the EAR, reading it, would have known who it was, which makes what she said all the more remarkable.

"I'd feel cheated if someone blew his head off. I'd ask them to please aim low," she said.

THAT FRIDAY MORNING, MAY 27, THE START OF MEMORIAL DAY weekend, Fiona Williams* did some chores around the house, then took her three-year-old son, Justin, with her to Jumbo Market on Florin Road to shop for groceries. She dropped him at the babysitter's and went to an optometrist appointment. She picked up her paycheck at the library, where she worked part-time, deposited it at the bank, and did some more shopping at Penney's. After that, she picked up Justin at the sitter's, and they went to Mel's Coffee Shop for dinner. When they got home, they swam for a while in the pool. Around dusk she watered the front lawn, still in her swimsuit, as Justin toddled around.

Fiona was aware of what was happening, of course; the local TV news blared with fresh hysteria every night. But she wasn't necessarily on high alert. He was the East Area Rapist, after all. He'd never hit in south Sacramento, the neighborhood where Fiona lived in a new house with her husband, Phillip, and Justin. But the EAR lingered in their minds. Phillip worked as a supervisor at a water treatment plant in Del Dayo. The most recent victims, the couple attacked on May 17, lived just yards from the plant. Phillip worked the swing shift, so when he came in, his colleagues had filled him in on the swarming police presence across the way. The EAR had put a gun to the husband's head. "Shut up, if you say one more thing I'll kill, do you understand?"

---

* All Williams family names are pseudonyms.

Phillip didn't know the couple; they were strangers cloistered behind police cars, the subject of murmured workplace gossip. But he would come to know them soon.

When Phillip returned home from work around twelve thirty a.m. Fiona and Justin were asleep. He drank a beer and watched some television, then climbed into bed and dozed off. About twenty minutes later he and Fiona woke at the same time, and reached for each other. They began fooling around. Several minutes later a scratching sound in the bedroom startled them. The sliding glass door to the patio opened and a man in a red ski mask entered. That they knew instantly who it was didn't lessen the shock. The feeling was surreal, as if a larger-than-life movie character, someone you'd just been watching on television, emerged from behind the drapes and began talking to you. He carried a two-cell flashlight in his left hand. He held what looked like a .45 pistol in his right hand, extending it into the flashlight's beam to show them.

"Lay perfectly still, or I will kill all of you," he said. "I will kill you. I will kill her. I will kill your little boy."

He threw a length of cord at Fiona and ordered her to tie up Phillip. The EAR tied her next. He rummaged and threatened, slashing his flashlight across the bedroom in jarring motions. He stacked plates on Phillip's back, then led Fiona into the living room.

"Why are you doing this?" she asked him.

"Shut up!" he hissed at her.

"I'm sorry," she said impulsively, in response to being yelled at.

"Shut up!"

He pushed her onto the living room floor, where he'd already laid down towels. After raping her several times he said, "I have something for you to tell the fucking pigs. They got it mixed up the last time. I said I would kill two people. I'm not going to kill you. If this is on the TV or in the papers tomorrow, I'll kill two people. Are you listening? Do you hear me? I have TVs in my apartment and I'll be watching them. If this is on the news, I'll kill two people."

When he mentioned the TVs in his apartment, an image flashed in Fiona's mind of LBJ in the Oval Office watching a trio of televisions he had next to his desk, a clip often played on the news back in the sixties. The EAR noticeably stuttered on *l* words, particularly "listening." His breathing was rapid—loud, sucking inhalations. She almost hoped he was faking, because if he wasn't, he sounded seriously unhinged.

"It scares my mommy when it's on the news," he said between gulping breaths.

It was a little after four a.m. when the first officer entered the opened rear patio door, hesitantly making his way toward the woman calling out to him. She lay face down on her living room floor, naked, her wrists and ankles tied behind her with shoelaces. A ski-masked stranger had just spent an hour and a half terrorizing Fiona and her husband. He brutally raped her. Fiona was five two, 110 pounds—a wisp of a woman. She was also a native Sacramentan, in possession of a dry, matter-of-fact manner, a clear-eyed resilience that belied her petite size.

"Well, I guess the East Area Rapist is the South Area Rapist now," she said.[†]

Shelby arrived at the yellow house with brown trim at five a.m. A crime-scene technician had laid plastic bags over the area on the floor where the rape occurred to preserve evidence. A green wine bottle and two packages of sausages were scattered on the back patio, about fifteen feet from the door. Shelby accompanied the bloodhound and his tracker as the dog nosed its way through the

---

† This was the only known EAR attack in the South Area. The dentist who co-founded the EARS Patrol and offered the $10,000 reward—which had been well-publicized in the week leading up to the attack—had a practice less than half a mile away, which may or may not have been purely coincidental.

backyard toward a flowerbed in the northeast corner, where they found shoe impressions.

Highway 99 ran adjacent to the house, and where the dog lost the scent, at a spot on the shoulder of the northbound lanes, were tire tracks from what looked to be a small foreign car, a VW bug maybe. A technician pulled out a measuring tape. The tire tracks measured four feet three inches center to center.

Right after the attack, when the investigators with their notepads asked Fiona to search her mind, the only thing she could point to that was slightly odd that evening was the garage door. She'd been going back and forth from the house to the garage doing laundry, and she was certain the side door leading to the carport had been closed. When she came back in one time, the door stood open. The wind, she thought. She closed and locked the door. They'd only lived in the house for three weeks and were adjusting to its contours and quirks. It was a corner house, boasting four bedrooms and an in-ground pool in the backyard. One image that would continue to nag at Fiona was that of a man at the Realtor's open house, standing next to her as they looked out at the pool at the same time. She didn't know why the impression stayed with her. Had he stood too close? Stayed a beat too long? She tried in vain to build a face, but he was blank. A man, that was all.

Highway 99 ran adjacent to the house, separated by a hundred yards of dirt and a row of large conifers; directly behind them, on the other side of a dinky chain-link fence, was an empty lot. Fiona would come to view the open space around them differently than she first had; what was once a pleasant expanse became a vulnerable point of entry. It wasn't part of their original plan, but after what happened to them that Memorial Day weekend, she and Phillip spent $3,000 they couldn't afford to build a brick wall around their new house.

Shelby noted the Realtor's Sold sign on the front porch. One of the significant avenues in the investigation was trying to find a common thread among the victims. The detectives gave the victims detailed questionnaires and carefully examined their checks. Areas of interest, or backgrounds that seemed overrepresented, included students and education, medical workers, and the military. Several were noted to have frequented the same pizza restaurant. But by far the most recurrent pattern was real estate. At Jane's, the first attack Shelby investigated, back in October '76, he observed a Century 21 sign on a lawn directly across the street. Several victims had just moved in, were moving out, or were next door to new units being sold. As one decade turned to the next and the case grew more complex, the real estate factor would consistently crop up, its significance—if any—remaining murky, right up to the moment a Realtor casually extracted a key from a lockbox and stumbled upon the EAR's last known victim, a beautiful girl, unrecognizable in death.

After Fiona and Phillip's attack on Memorial Day weekend, the EAR disappeared from Sacramento for the summer. He wouldn't return until October. By then Shelby was off the case, reassigned back to patrol. His skirmishes with the higher-ups had begun to flare more openly. High-profile cases are magnets for hierarchical politics, and Shelby could never quite play the game. When he first made detective, in 1972, his boss, Lieutenant Ray Root, had a loose, proactive philosophy. Go out and develop informants, Root instructed, and uncover felonies that might never be reported; develop your own cases rather than wait to be assigned. That philosophy suited Shelby's temperament. Showing courteous interest in his bosses' ideas did not. The transfer didn't upset him, he insists. He was stressed from the manhunt. Exhausted by the infighting. Working a high-profile case like the EAR meant constant scrutiny, and Shelby bristled at the surveillance; inside him lived the memory of that proud young man standing hopefully in front of the Sheriff's Department panel, dismissed because it was decided he was lacking the right parts.

IN THE DAYS AFTER HER ATTACK, FIONA FOUND HERSELF STUTTER-ing as the EAR had. Carol Daly organized a meeting among the female victims at one of their homes. Fiona recalls a lot of mur-mured exchanges—"You're doing so well" and "I didn't leave my home for five days." Daly played for them a couple of recordings of male voices, but Fiona doesn't remember any of the victims rec-ognizing them. For some time afterward, she became irrational about personal safety. At night she refused to go into the back of the house where the bedroom was until Phillip came home. She sometimes kept a loaded gun under the driver's seat of her car. She found she had a lot of nervous energy, and one night when she was using it to furiously vacuum, she blew a fuse, and the whole house and backyard went dark. She became hysterical. Her neighbors, a kind elderly couple who knew what had happened, rushed over and fixed the fuse.

During a break from work not long after the attack, Phillip walked over to the other victims' home and introduced himself. He didn't tell Fiona until years later, but he and the other hus-band would meet sometimes in the early morning hours to ride around in a car together, scanning yards and empty lots. Speed-ing up. Slowing down. Looking for the outline of a figure slink-ing along hedges. The two men's bond was unspoken. Few men would experience what they had, would understand the shatter-ing rage of lying face down on a bed, bound and gagged, as your wife whimpers from another room. They hunted a man whose face they didn't know. Didn't matter. The action of moving for-ward, their hands unrestrained, of physically doing something, was all that did.

AN EXCERPT FROM AN ARTICLE PUBLISHED ON FEBRUARY 28, 1979, in the now defunct chain of suburban weekly newspapers known locally as the Green Sheet might help convey what Sacramento was like in the 1970s. THREE RAPE TRIALS LOOM is the headline, with the subhead, "Questions of Publicity." The first paragraph: "The public defender's office will attempt to prove publicity about the East Area Rapist makes it impossible for three men charged with multiple rapes to get a fair trial in Sacramento County."

In February 1979, the East Area Rapist hadn't attacked in Sacramento County in ten months. Signs indicated he'd moved on and was prowling the East Bay. Yet the article describes how the Public Defender's Office was conducting phone surveys of Sacramento residents, trying to gauge "to what extent an aura of fear exists in this community because of the East Area Rapist." The Public Defender's Office worried that the East Area Rapist's top-dog infamy would poison the jury pool, that jurors would convict their clients—the Woolly, Midday, and City College Rapists—in a misguided attempt to punish the unidentified offender whose moniker still caused such terror that many potential survey responders, upon hearing the caller's question, didn't get past the four words "the East Area Rapist" before hanging up.

It might help convey what Sacramento was like in the seventies to know that in an article about three serial rapists overshadowed by a fourth, a fifth at-large serial rapist isn't even mentioned. The Early Bird Rapist was active in Sacramento from 1972 to early '76, when he seemed to go underground. Four years of break-ins and sexual assaults and approximately forty victims, and yet a Google search shows references to him only in relation to the EAR.

A woman wrote me an e-mail about a close encounter she believes she had with the East Area Rapist when she was a teenager. She and a friend were taking a shortcut to their high school in Arden-Arcade, a neighborhood on Sacramento County's east side. She remembers the morning was cold, and believes it was either fall or winter of 1976 or '77. They decided to walk down a cement path that ran along a creek and ended up hitting a dead end, a fenced-in backyard. When they turned around a man was standing twenty feet from them. He wore a black ski mask that covered his face except for his eyes. He started toward them, keeping one hand in his jacket. The woman, thinking quickly, reached her hand up and felt around for a lock on the fence. The gate pushed open, and the two friends ran screaming into the backyard. The homeowners, alerted by the racket, came out and herded them into the house. She remembers being interviewed by investigators at the time. She was writing to tell me that the masked man was built differently than I'd described in my magazine article about the EAR. The man she encountered was extremely muscular, the woman wrote. "Overkill so."

I forwarded the e-mail to Shelby, now retired from the Sacramento Sheriff's Department. "Probably did see the EAR," he wrote back. "However muscle description sounds like Richard Kisling perfectly."

Richard Kisling? I looked Kisling up—yet another serial rapist once active in the Sacramento area who, like the EAR, wore a ski mask and tied up the husbands while he raped their wives.

Sacramento's was not an isolated problem. US crime rates show a steady rise in violent crime throughout the 1960s and '70s, peaking in 1980. *Taxi Driver* came out in February 1976; the bleak and violent film was hailed as an encapsulation of its time, to no one's surprise. Many retired cops I talk to, from Sacramento but other places too, uniformly recall 1968 to 1980 as a particularly grim period. And unlike some other places, Sacramento, a city built by pioneers who forded rivers and passed over snowy mountain ranges to get there, is known for its flinty survival instincts.

My point is not to declare a plague but to underscore prominence: in a city inhabited by tough locals and lousy with violent offenders, one predator stood out.

It might help convey what Sacramento was like in the 1970s, and something about the EAR, to know that whenever I tell an inquiring native that I'm writing about a serial rapist from Sacramento, no one has ever asked which one.

VISALIA

[EDITOR'S NOTE: The following chapter was pieced together from Michelle's notes and early drafts of "In the Footsteps of a Killer," a piece Michelle wrote for Los Angeles *magazine, originally published in February 2013 and later supplemented online.]*

ONE FRIDAY MORNING IN LATE FEBRUARY OF 1977, RICHARD SHELBY was at his desk at the Sacramento County Sheriff's Department when his phone rang. On the other end was a Sergeant Vaughan of the Visalia PD. Vaughan thought he had potentially useful information for their EAR investigation.

From April 1974 until December of the following year, Visalia had been plagued by a rash of bizarre burglaries committed by a young offender they dubbed the Ransacker. The Ransacker struck as many as 130 times over a period of less than two years, but there had been no activity since December of 1975, and the EAR series began in Sacramento just six months later. Moreover, there seemed to be a host of similarities between the two offenders. Perhaps it was an angle worth exploring.

THE RANSACKER WAS AS PROLIFIC AS HE WAS WEIRD. HE OFTEN HIT multiple homes in one night—sometimes four, sometimes five, once as many as a dozen. The Ransacker targeted the same four residential neighborhoods repeatedly. He preferred personal items like photographs and wedding rings, leaving behind things of greater value. Investigators noted that he seemed to have a thing for hand lotion.

But he was a perv with a mean streak, and with an apparent bone to pick with the domestic unit. If there were family photos around, he'd tear them up or hide them, sometimes breaking the picture frames, sometimes stealing the photos entirely. He'd pour orange juice from the refrigerator onto clothing from the closet, like a bratty child with a bad temper. He'd thoroughly trash the place. This seemed to be his paramount objective over theft, hence his moniker. For good measure, he'd remove cash from its hiding places and leave it on the bed. He'd stick to stealing trinkets and personalized jewelry, piggy banks and redeemable Blue Chip stamps. He unplugged appliances and clock radios. He liked to take single earrings from pairs. The Ransacker was big on spite.

The sexual element of the Ransacker's burglaries was evident in his penchant for rifling through female undergarments, often leaving them strewn about or posed. In one instance, he piled them in a baby's crib. On another occasion, he neatly laid out the man's underwear in a line down the hallway, extending from the bedroom to the bathroom. He had a knack for knowing where to find anything in the house that could be used as lubricant—with a particular affinity for Vaseline Intensive Care hand lotion. He was also shrewd; he'd almost always leave more than one point of escape open so that if the homeowners returned before he was finished, he'd have multiple exit options. He'd implement his own makeshift alarm system by placing items like perfume bottles or spray cans on the doorknobs.

In the early morning hours of September 11, 1975, the Ransacker's criminal path made a frightening pivot.

It was around two a.m. The sixteen-year-old daughter of Claude Snelling, a journalism professor at College of the Sequoias, awoke to find a man straddling her, his gloved hand cupped tightly over her mouth. A knife was pressed against her neck. "You're coming with me, don't scream or I'll stab you," the ski-masked intruder whispered in a raspy voice. As she began to resist, he produced a gun: "Don't scream, or I'll shoot you." He led her out the back door.

Snelling, alerted by the noise, ran out onto the patio.

"Hey what are you doing, where are you taking my daughter?" he shouted.

The intruder took aim and fired one round. It hit Snelling in the right side of his chest and spun him around. Another shot was fired, and this bullet struck Snelling in his left side, traveling through his arm before piercing his heart and both lungs. He staggered into the house and was dead within minutes. The assailant kicked his victim three times in the face before running away. He was a white male, about five ten, with "angry eyes," the intended victim reported to police.

Ballistics tests revealed that the handgun used in the crime was a Miroku .38 that had been stolen in a Ransacker burglary ten days earlier. Investigators also learned that in February of that year, Claude Snelling had returned home to find a peeper crouched beneath his daughter's window. He chased the subject, but lost him in the darkness.

EVIDENCE STRONGLY POINTED TO THE RANSACKER. NIGHTTIME police presence was ramped up, with surveillance units assigned for nocturnal stakeouts. One residence of particular interest was a house that had been targeted three times before on West Kaweah Avenue, in an area of heavy Ransacker activity. On December 10, Detective Bill McGowen startled the Ransacker outside of the house; the suspect vaulted a fence and a chase ensued. When McGowen fired a warning shot the suspect gestured in surrender.

"Oh my God, don't hurt me," he squeaked in an oddly mannered, high-pitched voice. "See? My hands are up!"

The baby-faced man turned slightly, sneakily, and drew a gun from his coat pocket, promptly firing it at McGowen. McGowen fell backward and things suddenly went dark. The bullet had struck the officer's flashlight.

ON JANUARY 9, 1976, VISALIA POLICE DETECTIVES BILL MCGOWEN and John Vaughan rose early and drove three hours south to Parker Center, the LAPD's headquarters in downtown Los Angeles. McGowen had recently come face-to-face with a criminal whose ability to elude authorities defied the laws of logic and whose capture, it's fair to say, consumed the entire Visalia Police Department. His encounter with the Ransacker was considered an important break in the case, and so arrangements were made with a special investigative unit of the LAPD for McGowen to undergo hypnosis, with the hope that new details might be elicited.

At Parker Center, the two Visalia detectives met with Captain Richard Sandstrom, director of the LAPD's hypnosis unit. They briefed Sandstrom on the details. McGowen drew a diagram of the residential neighborhood where his confrontation with the Ransacker took place. A police artist created a composite sketch based on McGowen's input. The group then convened to room 309. Diagram and composite were laid on the table in front of McGowen. At 11:10 a.m., the hypnosis session began.

Sandstrom quietly encouraged McGowen to relax. Legs were uncrossed, fists unclenched, breathing deepened. He directed the detective's memory back a month, to the evening of December 10, 1975. That night a half-dozen police officers had been deployed in the neighborhood around Mt. Whitney High School, some in fixed, hidden locations, others on foot, and one in an unmarked vehicle. The goal of the coordinated stakeout was to "detect and apprehend" their greatest adversary, the Visalia Ransacker.

The night before, McGowen had taken a call of particular interest. The caller identified herself as Mrs. Hanley* from West Kaweah Avenue. She was calling about shoe tracks. Did he remember what he'd told her about checking around for shoe tracks? He did.

In July the Hanleys' nineteen-year-old daughter, Donna,* had encountered a ski-masked intruder in their backyard. Upon reporting the incident, she was advised by McGowen to check her backyard periodically for shoe tracks and alert him if any turned up. Well, they had.

On the basis of this information, McGowen was assigned to stake out the residence the following evening.

In his chair at the Parker Center, under the hypnotherapist's guidance, McGowen's mind eased back into that night.

He chose to position himself in a front-facing garage at 1505 West Kaweah Avenue. He had a feeling the Ransacker might return to the Hanley house, where his tennis-shoe impressions had been observed under Donna's bedroom window.

At seven p.m. McGowen set up his simple surveillance operation. He kept the garage door open. All the lights were shut off. He sat in the dark, watching the neighbor's house through a side window but also keeping an eye out for anyone passing the garage. An hour went by. Nothing moved. Another half hour passed.

Then, around eight thirty p.m., a crouching figure crept by the window. McGowen waited. The figure appeared in the garage doorway and looked around. Possibilities cycled through McGowen's head. The homeowner? A fellow officer? But his eyes had adjusted to the dark and he could see that the figure was dressed in black and crowned with a watch cap.

---

* Pseudonym

McGowen observed as the figure moved along the side of the garage, toward the rear of the structure. The subject had a large, ungainly frame, oddly proportioned. McGowen walked outside and followed, shining his flashlight on the figure as he fiddled with a side gate.

Vaughan, his colleague, took notes as McGowen, under hypnosis, recounted what happened next. The surprise confrontation. The chase into the backyard. The scream like a woman's scream.

"Oh my God! Don't hurt me!"

"Was it a woman?" Sandstrom, the hypnotist, asked McGowen. "No," he said.

McGowen kept his Kel-Lite flashlight fixed on the figure running from him and shouted repeatedly for him to halt. The Ransacker appeared to be hysterical, screaming "Oh my God, don't hurt me, don't hurt me!" over and over, darting this way and that, finally diving over a short slate fence into an adjacent yard. McGowen grabbed his service revolver from his holster and fired a warning shot into the ground. The Ransacker froze and wheeled around. He raised his right hand in surrender.

"I give up," he quavered. "See? See, I've got my hands up."

Remembering the moment during hypnosis pulled McGowen into a deeper trance. He fixated on the face illuminated in the beam of his flashlight.

"Baby. Round. Soft-looking baby."

"Doesn't even shave."

"Very light skin. Soft. Round. Baby face."

"Baby."

Standing at the fence, McGowen must have been exhilarated. The grueling eighteen-month manhunt was over. He was seconds from collaring a criminal who'd remained so cunningly invisible that more than one officer had wondered if they were chasing a ghost. But the Visalia Ransacker was real. And a bad man.

Yet their evil adversary was hardly intimidating in the flesh. A doughboy, McGowen thought, haplessly plodding around begging in a high-pitched whimper for McGowen not to hurt him. McGowen didn't intend to hurt him. He was a religious man, an old-fashioned, by-the-book cop. The thrill was in knowing the nightmare was over. The creep was toast. McGowen started over the fence to arrest him.

But the Ransacker had raised only his right hand in surrender. With his left hand he withdrew a blue steel revolver from his coat pocket and fired with unambiguous aim straight at McGowen's chest. Fortunately McGowen had his flashlight at arm's length in front of him—muscle memory from police training more than anything else. The bullet struck the lens. The force of the shot knocked McGowen back. His partner, alerted by the gunfire, sprinted into the yard and saw McGowen motionless on the ground. Thinking he had been shot, he ran to where he thought the Ransacker had fled, radioing for help at the same time. Suddenly he heard movement behind him. He whipped around. It was McGowen. Powder burns streaked his face. His right eye was red. Otherwise, he was fine.

"There he goes," McGowen said.

Seventy officers from three different agencies sealed off a six-square-block area. But nothing. The awkwardly built man-child ran away and disappeared into the night—a moth swallowed by the dark—leaving behind a sock full of collectible coins and jewelry, and two books of Blue Chip stamps.

MCGOWEN'S ACCOUNT OF THE RANSACKER'S DISTINCTIVE APpearance and his bizarre manner was consistent with reports of previous close encounters Visalians had with the near-ubiquitous Peeping Tom.

They decided he never went outside during daylight hours. He was that pale. The few people who'd glimpsed him remarked on his complexion. It's hard to maintain the skin tone of a fish's underbelly in Visalia, a farm town in central California where temperatures top 100 degrees in the summer. To understand why his pallor marked him as unusual, it helps to know that Visalia is heavily populated with descendants of Dust Bowl refugees. Native Visalians follow an internal clock set by nature. They remember the epic floods. Anticipate the droughts. Lean against pickups and watch ash fall from wildfires torching chaparral and timber forty miles away. The outdoors isn't a concept but hard fact. Sun damage is shorthand for knowledge and trust. It says, I understand what it means to hedge a citrus tree; I know that to "chop cotton" means to hack weeds from cotton plants with a hoe; I've drifted down the St. John's River on an inner tube, alkali dust from my feet dissolving into water the color of weak coffee.

His paleness conveyed no such local familiarity. It was uncommon and therefore suspicious. It suggested a cloistered life spent plotting. His pursuers in the Visalia Police Department didn't know who he was or where he shut himself away. They knew he moved around at night. They had a good idea of what drew him out.

To the teenage girls closing their bedroom curtains, he registered as a glint in the shadows. A flicker of stray light that made them pause. But it was hard to see clearly at night. It was sometime in the winter of 1974 when Glenda,* a sixteen-year-old who lived on West Feemster, was pulling her curtains shut and happened to glance down, noticing a marbly, moon-shaped object in the bushes. Curious, she raised her bedroom window for a closer inspection. The moon-faced object returned her stare, a screwdriver clenched in its left hand.

Like that, he was gone. Where hard, small eyes had been, there was darkness. Skittering sounds could be heard, like some crea-

---

* Pseudonym

ture with a muscly tail running from light. Bushes rustled. Fences thudded. The clambering grew fainter, but it didn't matter. A distress call drowned out everything else. At the time, in 1974, Visalia businesses closed at 9:00 p.m., and trouble was mostly confined to men huddled around irrigation ditches fighting over water rights. But there was no mistaking the sound when you heard it. Movies don't capture the effect of the real thing. It's impossible to reproduce in a studio. Conversations stop. Heads jerk. Eardrums pound with dread, for nothing signals terror like a teenage girl's wild, unrestrained scream in the night.

The paleness of the stranger's face wasn't its only unsettling feature. A week after the prowling incident, Glenda's boyfriend, Carl,* was waiting for her outside her house. It was an early autumn evening, warm still, already dark. Glenda's house was similar to others in the middle-class neighborhood near Mt. Whitney High School in southwest Visalia: single-story, solidly built in the 1950s; at roughly 1,500 square feet, not especially large. Carl sat on the lawn, his presence shadowed in contrast to the glow cast from the brightly lit picture window fronting the house. From his cloaked position in the yard, Carl observed a man emerge from a path that bordered the canal across the street. The man was ambling along but stopped short when his eyes locked on something. Carl followed his absorbed gaze to the window, where Glenda, dressed in a halter top and shorts, was talking with her mother in the living room. The man dropped to his hands and knees.

Carl had been at Glenda's when she spotted the prowler outside her bedroom; he'd chased him into a neighbor's yard before losing him in the dark. He knew he was looking at the same man. Even knowing that couldn't prepare him for what happened next. On his hands and knees, as if magnetized by what he saw in the

---

* Pseudonym

window, the man began a military-style crawl toward Glenda's house.

Carl remained still and obscured in the dark. He let the man snake his way to the front hedges. He clearly had no idea Carl was there. Achieving maximum shock effect meant choosing the precise moment to speak. Carl waited until the man had risen slightly and was peeking over the hedges into the window.

"What are you doing here?" Carl shouted.

The man recoiled in shock. He screamed something unintelligible and took off in a panicked, almost vaudevillian run. Glenda had described her prowler as chubby. He was on the heavy side, Carl confirmed, with sloping shoulders and big legs. He ran awkwardly and not particularly fast. The chase ended abruptly when the man cut to the left and ducked into a neighbor's alcove that was screened on one side. Carl planted himself in front of the alcove, blocking the way. The man was trapped. Street lighting gave Carl a chance to observe his girlfriend's prowler up close. He was about five ten, 180 to 190 pounds, with short, fat legs and stubby arms. His hair was blond, combed over and stringy. He had a button nose. The ears were short and fleshy, his eyes squinty. His lower lip pushed out a little bit. His face was round and expressionless.

"What were you doing looking in my girlfriend's window?" Carl asked.

The man looked away.

"Well, Ben, it looks like the guy's got us here!" he said loudly, excitedly, as if calling to an accomplice off to the side.

There was no one there.

"Who are you? What are you doing here?" Carl asked.

Getting no answer, Carl moved closer.

"Leave me alone," the man said. "Go away."

His speech was slow and dull now, with a hint of an Okie accent.

Carl took another step forward. The man responded by sticking his hand in his pocket. He was wearing a brown cotton jacket with woven cuffs; it was a style that had been popular years earlier but had since gone out of fashion.

"Leave me alone," he repeated flatly. "Go away."

Carl noticed a bulge in the pocket where the man's hand was. The detail took a split second to compute; when it did, Carl's instincts ordered him to stand back. It was the strangest, most unsettling sense, glimpsing for a moment the dark circuitry at work behind the dull-eyed mask. The round-faced simpleton in unfashionable clothes with the flat voice of an Okie bumpkin was, as evidenced by the move for what was most certainly a concealed gun, someone else altogether. Carl stepped aside. He noticed when the man passed him that his face was pale and unusually smooth; Carl felt certain that he was at least twenty-five years old, but oddly for someone who had, as they might say in Visalia, "reached his majority," it didn't appear he could even shave.

Carl watched the man walk north up Sowell Street. He kept swiveling around every few seconds to make certain Carl wasn't following him. Even then, with jittery body language of suspicion and fear, the man's pale round face remained inert, smooth, and blank as an egg.

Even further back, in September of 1973, Fran Cleary* had a strange encounter in front of her West Kaweah Avenue home. As she was getting into her car, she heard a noise and looked up, spotting a man with light blond hair and a smooth round face emerging from her backyard. As he jogged into the street, he noticed Cleary and did an about-face, yelling out, "Catch you later, Sandy!" before jogging northbound onto a perpendicular road and disappearing from view. Fran told her fifteen-year-old daughter, Shari,* about the incident, and Shari revealed that she'd seen someone matching the same description peeping into her

---

* Pseudonym

bedroom window a week earlier. The prowler would pester them for two months, visiting the residence one last time in October.

From 1973 through early 1976, numerous other teenaged and young adult women in the neighborhood had run-ins with a window peeper who fit the same description.

But once the composite sketch based on Bill McGowen's run-in with the Ransacker was released to the local press in mid-December 1976, he never struck Visalia again.

––––––

AND YET THE RANSACKER INVESTIGATION BARRELED ON FULL TILT. For an unsolved serial case to advance, it needs to go back. Early reports are pored over, hindsight wielded like a magnifying glass. Victims and eyewitnesses are recontacted. Dulled memories sometimes sharpen. Occasionally an overlooked clue shakes loose. Someone will remember an incident that wasn't necessarily officially reported. They'll have a name but not a number. Calls are made.

Visalia detectives in contact with Sacramento authorities in 1977 noted at least a dozen similarities between the two offenders. Among them: Both offenders ransacked. Both stole trinkets and personalized jewelry while leaving items of greater value behind. Both employed a similar manner of approach, climbing astride their sleeping victims and placing a hand over their mouths. Both used household items to create a makeshift alarm system. Both used a similar breaking and entering method, using a pry tool to chip around a doorjamb and bypass the striker plate. Both hopped fences; both were about five nine; both removed purses from inside the residence and dumped the contents outside. It was a compelling list. Visalia investigators thought they were onto something.

Sacramento County Sheriff's personnel compared the two

series and saw insurmountable differences. For starters, six of nine m.o. factors didn't match. The shoe impressions differed. The shoe sizes even differed. The EAR didn't steal Blue Chip stamps. And the physical descriptions were fundamentally different. After all, descriptions of the Ransacker pointed to a highly distinctive appearance: an outsize baby with stubby limbs and fingers and a smooth, pale complexion. The EAR was described as anywhere from medium to slight in build, with one victim going so far as to call him "puny." In the summer months, he appeared tanned. Even if the Ransacker had lost weight, it seemed unlikely he was a shape-shifter.

Visalia disagreed and went to the press. In July 1978, the *Sacramento Union* published an article in which the possibility of a link was promoted and the Sacramento County Sheriff's Department was criticized for its closed-mindedness. The following day, the Sacramento County Sheriff's Department struck back in the press, denouncing the *Union* for irresponsible journalism and accusing the Visalia Police Department of publicity seeking and desperation.

The Sacramento city police department, however, remained open to the possibility of a connection. Richard Shelby occasionally mined the avenue too. The Sacramento Sheriff's Department asked local utility companies for lists of employees who had transferred from the Visalia area between December 1975 and April 1976. They found two. Both were subsequently eliminated.

Forty years later, official opinion is still divided, though more amiably so. Ken Clark, Sacramento's current lead investigator, believes the two series are the work of the same offender. The FBI agrees. Contra Costa's lead investigator, Paul Holes, does not. An endomorph does not magically become an ectomorph, Holes is quick to observe.

ORANGE COUNTY, 1996

ROGER HARRINGTON DEVELOPED ONE BELIEF THAT HE MAINTAINED steadfastly, despite the uncomfortable implications. He was quoted in an October 1988 *Orange Coast* magazine story, eight years after the murder of his son and daughter-in-law, as saying he was sure the motive lay somewhere in Patty's background, not Keith's. They'd been married only a few months. Patty seemed unassailable, but how much did they really know about her past? One detail made him certain the couple must have known the killer: the bedspread. The killer had taken the time to pull the cover over their heads.

"Whoever did it knew them and was sorry they'd done it," Roger told the magazine.

In the old days, unsolved cases were solved by the unexpected phone call—the shrill ring of a rotary phone that signaled a death-bed confession or a tipster with verifiable facts. But the phone never rang for Keith and Patty Harrington or Manuela Witthuhn. In-stead, the break came in the form of three glass tubes stored in manila envelopes that hadn't moved in fifteen years.

Few people could be expected to greet the news of a break with more enthusiasm than Roger Harrington. The blank face of his son's killer dominated huge empty tracts of his mental map. The *Orange Coast* magazine profile about his search for Keith and Patty's killer ends with a grim, plainspoken quote.

"That's why I keep living: I don't want to go till I find out."

The three tubes that advanced the mystery closer to an answer were opened and tested in October and November 1996. By December, results in hand, Orange County Sheriff's investigators were ready to make phone calls to the families. But Roger Harrington never learned the news. He'd died a year and a half earlier, on March 8, 1995.

Had Roger lived, he would have learned more about the killer's history; he would have discovered that he was wrong about why his son and daughter-in-law's heads had been covered with the bedspread. It wasn't remorse. The last time the killer bludgeoned a couple to death, it had been messy: he didn't want Keith and Patty's blood on him.

One Sunday morning in 1962, a British paperboy found a dead cat on the side of the road. The twelve-year-old put the cat in his bag and brought it home with him. This was in Luton, a town thirty miles north of London. With some time to kill before lunch, the boy placed the cat on the dining room table and began to dissect it with a homemade kit, which included a scalpel fashioned from a flattened pin. A foul odor spread through the house, displeasing the boy's family. Had the cat been alive when it was eviscerated, this anecdote might belong to Ted Bundy's life story. As it happens, the boy in question, a budding scientist, would become serial killers' biggest adversary, the creator of their kryptonite. His name is Alec Jeffreys. In September 1984, Jeffreys discovered DNA fingerprinting; in doing so, he changed forensic science and criminal justice forever.

The first generation of DNA technology compared to current technique is like the difference between a Commodore 64 computer and a smartphone. When the Orange County Crime Lab began incorporating DNA testing in the early 1990s, it would take up to four weeks for a criminalist to work one case. The biological sample being tested needed to be sizable—a bloodstain the size of a quarter, for example—and in good shape. Now a smattering of skin cells can reveal someone's genetic fingerprint in a matter of hours.

The DNA Identification Act of 1994 established the FBI's authority to maintain a national database, and CODIS (Combined DNA Index System) was born. The best way to explain how CODIS operates today is to imagine it as the top of a vast forensic science pyramid. At the bottom of the pyramid are hundreds of local crime labs throughout the country. The labs take unknown DNA samples from crime scenes, along with certain suspect samples that have been collected, and input them into their state databases; in California, the inputted samples are automatically uploaded every Tuesday. The state is also responsible for DNA collection from jails and courthouses. State databases then take all the collected samples and run them through a verification process and an intrastate comparison. After that, the samples are bumped up the national ladder to CODIS.

Speedy. Efficient. Thorough. Not so in the mid-1990s, when the databases were first being developed. Crime labs relied then on RFLP (pronounced "rif-lip," short for restriction fragment length polymorphism) analysis for DNA profiling, a laborious process that eventually went the way of the beeper. But the Orange County lab always had a reputation for being ahead of the pack. A December 20, 1995, article in the *Orange County Register*, "DA's Target: Ghosts of Murders Past," explained that local prosecutors, in coordination with detectives and criminalists, were for the first time submitting DNA evidence from old unsolved cases to the California Department of Justice's new lab in Berkeley, where four thousand DNA profiles of known violent criminals, many of them sex offenders, were filed. California's DNA database was in its infancy, and Orange County was helping it grow.

Six months later, in June 1996, Orange County got its first "cold hit," a match between crime-scene DNA evidence and the

DNA of a known felon in the database. The first cold hit was an extraordinary one; it identified a prison inmate named Gerald Parker as the serial killer of five women. A sixth victim of Parker's was pregnant and survived her attack, but her full-term fetus did not. The husband of the pregnant victim, whose injuries resulted in severe memory loss, had spent sixteen years in prison for her attack. He was immediately exonerated. Parker was a month away from being released when the cold hit was made.

The Orange County Sheriff's Department and Crime Lab staff was stunned. The first time they submit DNA to the fledgling state database, they solve six murders! It seemed that the weather in the Property Room, always an oppressive gray, had lifted and light beamed down on the monotony of cardboard boxes. Old evidence had languished there for decades undisturbed. Each box was a time capsule. Fringed purse. Embroidered tunic. Items from lives defined by violent death. The unsolved section of a Property Room is tainted with disappointment. It's the to-do list that's never done.

Now everyone basked in the possibilities. It was a heady feeling, the idea that one could conjure a man from a stain on a calico patchwork quilt from 1978, that one could reverse the flow of power. If you commit murder and then vanish, what you leave behind isn't just pain but absence, a supreme blankness that triumphs over everything else. The unidentified murderer is always twisting a doorknob behind a door that never opens. But his power evaporates the moment we know him. We learn his banal secrets. We watch as he's led, shackled and sweaty, into a brightly lit courtroom as someone seated several feet higher peers down unsmiling, raps a gavel, and speaks, at long last, every syllable of his birth name.

Names. The Sheriff's Department needed names. The abandoned boxes in the Property Room were packed tight with stuff. Q-tip swabs preserved in tubes. Underwear. Cheap white sheets. Every inch of fabric and millimeter of cotton tip held promise. There were other possibilities besides making immediate arrests. DNA profiles that were developed from evidence might not match a known felon in the database, but profiles from different cases might match each other, uncovering a serial killer. That information could focus an investigation. Energize it. They had to get going.

The crime lab staff crunched the numbers. Between 1972 and 1994, Orange County investigated 2,479 homicides and cleared 1,591, leaving nearly 900 unsolved cases. A strategy was developed for reexamining cold cases. Homicides involving sexual assaults would be prioritized, as those killers tend to be repeat offenders and leave behind the kind of biological material that lends itself to DNA typing.

Mary Hong was one of the criminalists tasked with concentrating on cold cases. Jim White took her aside. Fifteen years later, he hadn't forgotten his old suspicion.

"Harrington," he said. "Witthuhn."

The names didn't mean anything to Hong, who hadn't worked at the lab at the time of the murders. White encouraged her to prioritize those two cases. "I always thought it was the same guy," he told her.

A BRIEF, NONTECHNICAL EXPLANATION OF DNA TYPING MIGHT BE helpful. DNA, or deoxyribonucleic acid, is the molecular sequence that defines each human being as unique. Every cell in your body (except red blood cells) has a nucleus that contains your DNA. A forensic scientist working to develop a genetic profile will first extract available DNA from a biological sample—semen, blood, hair—then isolate, amplify, and analyze it. DNA consists of four repeating units, and it's the precise sequence of the units that differentiates us from one another. Think of it as a human bar code. The numbers on the bar code represent genetic markers. In the early days of DNA typing, only a few markers could be developed and analyzed. Today, there are thirteen standard CODIS markers. The likelihood of any two individuals (except identical twins) having the same human bar code is roughly one in a billion.

In late 1996, when Mary Hong went to retrieve the Harrington and Witthuhn rape kits from the Property Room, DNA typing was experiencing exciting changes. The traditional process, RFLP, was still used by the state database, but it required ample DNA that couldn't be degraded in any way. It wasn't ideal for cold cases. But the Orange County Crime Lab had recently integrated a new technique, PCR-STR (polymerase chain reaction with short tandem repeat analysis), which was much faster than RFLP and is the backbone of forensic testing today. The difference between RFLP and PCR-STR is like copying down numbers in longhand versus using a high-speed Xerox machine. PCR-STR worked particularly well for cold cases, in which DNA samples might be minuscule or degraded by time.

One of the first examples of forensic science solving a murder appears in a book called *The Washing Away of Wrongs*, published in 1247 by Song Ci, a Chinese coroner and detective. The author relates a story about a peasant found brutally hacked to death with a hand sickle. The local magistrate, unable to make headway in the investigation, calls for all the village men to assemble outside with their sickles; they're instructed to place their sickles on the ground and then take a few steps back. The hot sun beats down. A buzz is heard. Metallic green flies descend in a chaotic swarm and then, as if collectively alerted, land on one sickle, crawling all over it as the other sickles lie undisturbed. The magistrate knew traces of blood and human tissue attract blowflies. The owner of the fly-covered sickle hung his head in shame. The case was solved.

Methods are no longer so rudimentary. Centrifuge and microscope have replaced insects. The unidentified male DNA that was extracted from the Harrington and Witthuhn rape kits was subjected to the crime lab's most sensitive tools: restriction enzymes, fluorescent dyes, thermal cyclers. But forensic science advancements are really just about finding the latest way to draw a blowfly to a bloody sickle. The goal is the same as it was in thirteenth-century rural China: cellular certainty establishing guilt.

Hong appeared in Jim White's doorway. He was at his desk.

"Harrington," she said. "Witthuhn."

He looked up expectantly. Criminalists like Hong and White are methodical people. They have to be. Their work is always being torn apart by defense attorneys in court. They often keep their conclusions broad ("blunt object"), which can cause tension with cops, who accuse them of being too self-defensively cautious. Cops and criminalists need each other but are temperamentally very different. Cops thrive on action. They are knee jigglers with paper-strewn desks they avoid. They want to be out there. Badguy behavior they know as muscle memory; if they approach a guy and he abruptly turns to the right, for instance, he's probably concealing a gun. They know which drug leaves burn marks on fingerprints (crack) and about how long someone can survive without a pulse (four minutes.) They slog through chaos inured to bullshit and squalor. The job inflicts lacerations. In turn, the cop becomes lacerating. At his most lacerating, when the darkness has gone through him like dye through water, he'll be called upon to comfort the parents of a dead girl. For some cops, the pivot from chaos to comfort becomes harder and harder to do, and they abandon the compassion part altogether.

Criminalists orbit the chaos from a latex-sheathed remove. The crime lab is arid and rigorously maintained. There's no hard-edged banter. Cops wrestle up close with life's messiness; criminalists quantify it. But they're also human beings. Details from cases they worked stay with them. Patty Harrington's baby blanket, for example. Even as an adult she slept with the little white blanket every night, rubbing its silk edges for security. The baby blanket was found between her and Keith.

"Same guy," Hong said.

Jim White allowed himself a smile before getting back to work.

A FEW WEEKS LATER, AS 1996 CAME TO A CLOSE, HONG WAS AT her desk scanning an Excel spreadsheet on her computer. The spreadsheet was a compilation of the twenty or so unsolved cases in which DNA profiles had been successfully developed. The chart cross-referenced case numbers and victims' names with the profiles, which consisted of five PCR loci, or markers, that were then in use for typing. For example, under the marker "THO1" you might see the result "8, 7" and so forth. Hong knew the Harrington and Witthuhn profiles matched. But as her eyes swept over the spreadsheet, another profile stopped her cold. She read over the sequence several times and compared it to Harrington and Witthuhn to be certain. She wasn't imagining it. It was the same.

The victim was an eighteen-year-old named Janelle Cruz whose body had been discovered in her family's Irvine home on May 5, 1986. No one had ever proposed that Cruz could be connected to Harrington or Witthuhn, even though Cruz lived in Northwood, the same subdivision as Witthuhn, and their houses were just two miles apart. It wasn't just the five-year-plus time span. Or that Janelle was a decade younger than Patty Harrington and Manuela Witthuhn. She was different.

IRVINE, 1986

[EDITOR'S NOTE: The following chapter was pieced together from Michelle's notes.]

THE BRIEF LIFE OF JANELLE CRUZ WAS NO LESS TRAGIC THAN HER death. Her biological father was long out of the picture. She'd suffered a string of stepfathers and stand-ins, most of whom abused her in various ways. Her mother was more committed to partying and doing drugs than raising her—or at least that's how Janelle saw it.

She moved around a lot: from New Jersey to Tustin to Lake Arrowhead to Newport Beach and finally to Irvine.

When she was fifteen, she was drugged and raped by the father of her best friend while at their house for a sleepover. Janelle told her family, and they confronted the man, who was a soldier at the nearby marine base. He denied it. When Janelle's family pressed, he sicced some fellow soldiers on them to intimidate them into letting the matter drop. The crime went unreported.

In the years that followed, Janelle began rebelling. She dressed in black. She withdrew. She started cutting herself. She used cocaine—less for recreational purposes than for weight loss. Her mother sent her away to various places, ranging from YMCA camp to Job Corps in Utah to a short-term psychiatric hospital.

She earned her high school diploma from Job Corps and returned to Irvine, where she enrolled in classes at the local college while cultivating a rotating menu of sex partners, mostly men a few years her senior. She began working as a hostess for Bullwinkle's Restaurant, a Chuck E. Cheese–style family eatery named after the titular moose from *Rocky and Bullwinkle and Friends*.

Irvine's motto, goes the joke, is "sixteen zip codes, six floor plans." Or "Irvine: we have sixty-two words for beige." Janelle roved in her monochrome tract in a kind of fitful, searching daze. The jolt she sought, the love, never came.

On May 3, 1986, her mother and stepfather left for a vacation to Cancún.

The following evening, a male co-worker from Bullwinkle's hung out with Janelle after she told him she was lonely with her parents out of town. They sat on her bedroom floor; she read him some of her poems. His hopeful romantic interest kept him there as she played a forty-five-minute tape recording of a counseling session in which she railed against her messed-up family. A noise outside, like a gate or door closing, startled them. Janelle peeked out her window and closed the shutters. "I think it's just the cats," Janelle said while peering through the window. Sometime later, the noise recurred, this time from the direction of the garage.

Janelle again dismissed it. "It's just the washing machine."

The teenage workmate, recalling that it was a school night, left a short time later. Janelle gave him a friendly hug good-bye.

———

LINDA SHEEN* LEFT HER DESK AT TARBELL REALTY ON THE AFTER-noon of May 5 to visit a home in Irvine for a prospective buyer. The property, located at 13 Encina, was a three-bedroom, two-bath single-story house that had been on the market for several months.

———

* Pseudonym

It was still inhabited by its owner, along with her four children—including two grown daughters—and her husband. It was a house that looked virtually indistinguishable from so many others in the Northwood community, including the one at 35 Columbus, a mile away, where a twenty-nine-year-old housewife had been bludgeoned to death in her bed five years earlier in an unsolved crime that was quickly forgotten.

The house at 13 Encina backed up to a park and was the second-to-last house at the end of a cul-de-sac, sealed by a hedge wall with a break in the middle that led to undeveloped property that marked the end of civilization: miles of orange groves and open fields insulated Northwood from nearby Tustin and Santa Ana. Only ten years earlier, those same orange groves had tiled the land on which 13 Encina and its surrounding neighborhood now stood. Two decades later, the remaining groves gave way almost completely to urbanization, with a mammoth strip mall and uniform housing developments paving the entire distance to those other cities.

Sheen arrived at 13 Encina and rang the doorbell. Although there was a beige Chevette parked in the driveway, nothing inside the house stirred, so she rang again. Still silence, much like earlier in the afternoon when she'd phoned the home and received no answer. She proceeded to the lockbox and retrieved the key, letting herself in.

She looked around and noticed that the dining room light was on. In the kitchen, a carton of milk stood on the breakfast table. A newspaper was open to the Employment section. She put her business card on the dining table and walked to the family room, peering through the sliding glass door into the backyard. She saw several lawn chairs and a lounge chair with a towel draped over it. She went to the master bedroom and turned the doorknob, but it was locked. The second bedroom looked like that of a child, and as Sheen entered the last bedroom at the end of the hall, she saw the body of a young woman lying motionless in the bed, with a blanket covering her head.

A jolt of fear surged through Linda Sheen. She felt she might not be alone in the house. She might be in the wrong place at the wrong time, seeing something she shouldn't be seeing. The woman appeared not to be sleeping but either unconscious— perhaps from a drug overdose—or dead. Sheen bolted from 13 Encina and returned to her office, where she told her boss, Norm Prato,* of her discovery. He told her to phone the residence again. She did—twice. No one answered.

Linda and Norm relayed the situation to colleagues Arthur Hogue* and Carol Nosler* at Century 21, which was handling the sale of the home. The pair skeptically swung by 13 Encina and entered to indeed find the body of a young woman, unquestionably dead. Hogue called the police and told them he found a young lady with her head caved in.

Irvine PD officer Barry Aninag was the first to respond to the scene. As he entered the home, he was immediately approached by Arthur Hogue, who emerged from the kitchen and urgently reported, "There's a dead body in the bedroom. There's a dead body in the bedroom."

He repeated this a few more times as Aninag made his way to the last bedroom down the hall. On the bed was the nude body of a young woman who would later be identified as Janelle Cruz. She was cold to the touch and had no pulse. The body was lying face up, with the chest and face covered by a blanket that featured a large, dark stain over where the victim's head would probably be. Aninag slowly peeled away the blanket that was stubbornly adhering to the victim's face, revealing a massive wound to her forehead, bruising on her nose, and a veritable mask of blood.

---

* Pseudonym

Three of her teeth had been knocked out. Two of them were found in her hair.

Between her legs were flakes of dried fluid, which lab analysis would reveal to be semen. Tufts of blue fibers were found on her body, suggesting that a fabric had been ripped apart by someone as they stood over her.

Tennis shoe prints were found on the east side of the house. No ligatures or weapons were found at the scene.

A heavy red pipe wrench that had been in the backyard was missing, it was later determined.

Police canvassing the neighborhood gleaned little in the way of useful leads. A door-to-door solicitor from a window-washing company had been passing out yellow flyers the night before the murder. A neighborhood kid said he'd heard the girl at 13 Encina had been beaten to death and alerted the cops to a broken baseball bat he spotted in a nearby field. They followed him to the site. A snail oozed its way across the surface of the bat, which was mostly intact. Grass was growing on it. Clearly it had been languishing there for some time.

One neighbor heard Janelle's Chevette, with its distinctively loud muffler, pulling in at around eleven fifteen p.m.—about half an hour after her co-worker would have left the residence. He heard the engine turn off and one of the doors slam shut.

At four a.m. and five thirty a.m. that morning, two different neighbors respectively observed "an inordinate amount of light" emanating from the residence.

Janelle's sister, Michelle, was vacationing in Mammoth when she received the call: "Janelle has been murdered."

The connection was not pristine. Michelle repeated what she thought she heard in utter disbelief: "Janelle got *married*?!"

The words were clearer the second time around.

Lead investigator Larry Montgomery and his colleagues began

scrutinizing Janelle's activities, uncovering a litany of young men who wandered through her life in the days before her murder. There was Randy Gill,* from YMCA camp, who'd been having sex with Janelle and phoned her the night she was killed. He reputedly had a drinking problem. Janelle broke up with him two weeks before her murder. There was Martin Gomez,* an ex-convict who met Janelle at a previous workplace and eased into a sexual relationship with her that she eventually broke off after he became obsessive and controlling. And Philip Michaels,* a lifeguard Janelle had just begun dating, who hung out with her the day before she was murdered. He was also sleeping with Janelle— though he initially denied it.

And then, the Davids: David Decker,* who met Janelle at the YMCA camp when he was a counselor and she was a camper, and had last seen her two days before she died; David Thompson* (not to be confused with Ron Thomsen*—the last boy to see her alive), who also worked with her at Bullwinkle's; and Dave Kowalski,* another boyfriend, who'd visited Janelle at her home the day of her death and told her he loved her. He gave her a Seiko wristwatch as a token of his feelings. It was found next to her body.

There were also the weirdos and outliers like Bruce Wendt,* an oddball who'd been to Janelle's house shortly before the murder. His entry in Janelle's address book was accompanied by a handwritten notation: "Fuckhead, jerk, asshole, faggot."

And then there was the one who confessed.

———

TOM HICKEL* WAS IN HIS VAN, DRIVING HOME FROM THE MOVIES with his friend Mike Martinez* in the passenger seat. Midway through the drive, Martinez suddenly turned to him and said, "I

———

* Pseudonym

have to get something off of my chest." Hickel didn't brace himself hard enough for what followed.

"I killed her." Martinez spoke as if unloading a burden. "I killed Janelle."

He looked dead serious.

"You know that steel thing I have?"

"I don't know what steel 'thing' you're talking about," Hickel replied.

"Never mind," Martinez continued. "I just wanted to see if I had the guts to kill. It started in the bathroom and I fought with her first. I hit her with this steel thing."

Hickel asked him how it felt.

Martinez told him, "It feels like nothing. It feels normal." Hickel tried to hide his goosebumps.

"I wanted to know if I had the guts to kill Jennifer,"* Martinez explained. Jennifer was his girlfriend. "I don't care if I'm put in jail for twenty-five years. They don't have the death penalty here. I killed Janelle, and I will pay for it."

Martinez told Hickel that he'd been over at Janelle's house the week before she died. He met her parents. He learned they were going to be out of town and Janelle would be home alone.

"I purchased a single-shot shotgun from Big Five," Martinez confided. "I'm going to use it to blow Jenny away, because she needs to die."

Hickel continued trying his damnedest to not react.

"I'll turn myself in to the cops after I do it," he promised. "I'm going to do it on Saturday." He didn't say which Saturday.

Before they parted ways, Martinez told Hickel that he was just kidding about killing Janelle.

"I just wanted to see what you'd do."

What Hickel did was, he went to the police—to whom Mike

---

* Pseudonym

Martinez was certainly no stranger. He had prior arrests for attempted marijuana possession, commercial burglary, residential burglary, assault and battery, and he had twice attempted suicide—once by drinking Drano. The residential burglary charge and one of the assault-and-battery charges stemmed from an incident with Jenny, the girlfriend Martinez intended to kill.

And it turned out, Martinez repeated this sequence of crimes—the very night before Janelle was murdered. At one a.m., Martinez drunkenly broke into Jennifer's apartment through the sliding glass door and confronted her, demanding to know why she'd ignored him when they'd crossed paths at a Carl's Jr. a week before. With glazed eyes and unsteady footing, Martinez professed his love for Jennifer and in the same breath attacked her religious beliefs. She pleaded with him to leave. He ignored her. His blank expression betrayed no evidence that he even heard her talking to him.

"Why didn't you call me?" he kept asking.

He then left the room. Thinking he was gone, Jennifer cautiously proceeded downstairs, only to find Martinez in the kitchen. He had a kitchen knife and was cutting a towel into strips. Anticipating that he was about to tie her up, she began screaming. He grabbed her and muzzled her with his hand, dragging her into the bedroom and onto the bed. She screamed and fought, driving him out of the apartment. But only for a moment.

When he returned to look for his keys, Jennifer resumed screaming, ordering him to leave. He knocked her against the couch and punched her twice in the mouth and once in the head. Finally, he left for good.

On June 21, Mike Martinez was arrested near his home in Garden Grove.

In the police cruiser en route to the station, Martinez insisted: "I would have turned myself in. Tom set me up. I didn't do it. It's not fair! Why me?"

He began ranting. "Do you guys have enough evidence right

now to put me away or what? I don't think you do, because I didn't . . . I have not seen Janelle in three years."

"You probably have enough evidence anyways," Martinez continued. "So I'm Mexican. I don't have any money. I can't afford an attorney. I'll get a public defender. He's going to tell me to settle for fifteen or twenty-five years. I'm probably going to get first-degree murder, premeditated. That's going to be twenty-five years. What are you going to charge me with anyway? First degree or second degree? It's not fair. Why did you pick me up?"

A tape recorder was running. The cops let him ramble. He'd dig his own grave.

"Okay, I'm in this situation, is it something that, it fully looks like first-degree premeditated, doesn't it? A lot of people that are innocent, mostly niggers and Mexicans like myself, are going to take the fall. You should at least take blood. Find out I'm innocent, eventually catch the real guy. If I'm innocent, can I sue Tom? I don't think I'm going to get out of it either. I think that Montgomery is just going to use what he has and that is going to be enough."

Once at the station, a technician from Gold Coast Laboratories took Martinez's blood. A CSI officer assisted in collecting hair samples.

EARLY IN JULY, THE LAB RESULTS FROM MICHAEL MARTINEZ'S blood sample were returned to Montgomery. Martinez was eliminated as a suspect.

The co-worker was eliminated too. DNA profiling was still a year away from its debut appearance on the forensic landscape, but advances in serology—the study of serum and other bodily fluids—provided investigators with some insights.

Janelle's killer possessed a rare genetic makeup. He was a nonsecretor, an individual who doesn't secrete blood-group antigens in other bodily fluids like saliva, semen, etc. Nonsecretors make up about 20 percent of the population. His PGM (phosphoglyc-erate mutase), a protein enzyme, was also an unusual type. An Orange County Crime Lab forensic scientist informed a Cruz in-vestigator that the killer's combination of nonsecretor and PGM type is seen in approximately 1 percent of the population.

It wouldn't influence his physical appearance. His health and behavior wouldn't be affected. He simply possessed rare markers.

Investigators appreciated the forensic results, but they needed a face and name. They felt certain the answer was in Janelle's im-mediate orbit. The theory persisted that one of the young men in her life was responsible.

———

TEN YEARS LATER, MARTINEZ AND ALL THE OTHER BOYFRIENDS AND guy pals who drifted into Janelle's circle were conclusively elimi-nated when the DNA profile of her killer was developed. It matched none of the original suspects. Instead, it matched an unidentified killer responsible for three other murders.

Mary Hong has a scientist's dispassion and isn't easily shocked. But the Harrington/Witthuhn/Cruz match dented her compo-sure. She stared wide-eyed at the spreadsheet.

"That's unbelievable," she said to her computer screen.

VENTURA, 1980

THE SHERIFF'S DEPARTMENT FORMED A SPECIAL COLD-CASE UNIT TO deal with the sudden influx of new leads. Members of the County-wide Law Enforcement Unsolved Element, known as CLUE, began digging through old case files in January 1997. Meanwhile, Mary Hong faxed the Harrington/Witthuhn/Cruz DNA profile to hundreds of crime labs throughout the country. There was no response.

Investigator Larry Pool transferred into CLUE from the sex-crimes unit in February 1998. Pool is an air force vet with a stiff bearing. His moral perspective lacks gray. He loves God and abhors cursing. When cops are asked about their favorite part of the job, most reminisce about times they got to work undercover, the adrenaline that comes with unleashing your dodgy id with no idea of what's coming around the corner. Pool never worked undercover. It's hard to imagine that he ever could. He once interrogated a serial killer on death row in another state about a missing woman in Southern California police suspected him of killing. Pool suggested that the killer tell him where to find the body. It was the right thing to do. For his conscience. For the woman's family. The killer began mild negotiations, remarking about the better conditions in California prisons. Maybe a transfer could be negotiated in exchange for information?

Pool organized his paperwork and stood from the table.

"You'll die here," he said and walked out the door.

Cold cases suited him. They were blanks that edgier cops, the ones itching to kick in a door, might never fill in. Pool could. He was an insomniac who liked to "launch a command" in his brain, mull an investigative challenge in the background of his mind, until sometime later, maybe brushing his teeth or getting into his car, an answer came to him. Streetwise cops could sit down with a father who'd just set his family on fire and talk with him as though they were buddies sharing beers at a baseball game; they'd accept a degree of moral ambiguity, or at least pretend they did. For someone like Pool, who couldn't fake it, cold cases were perfect. He was a twelve-year veteran at the Sheriff's Department but relatively fresh at homicide investigation. A cardboard box containing three cases (Harrington, Witthuhn, and Cruz) was his new assignment. Inside were four stolen lives. One featureless monster. Pool told himself he would launch commands until he found him.

Pool noticed a Ventura Police Department case number scribbled in the margin of one of the reports in the Harrington file. He called and inquired. That's the Lyman and Charlene Smith murders, he was told. Notorious case in Ventura. Lyman was a well-known attorney. He was on the verge of a superior court judgeship. Charlene was his knockout former secretary–turned–second wife. On Sunday, March 16, 1980, Gary Smith, Lyman's twelve-year-old son from his first marriage, biked over to his father's house to mow the lawn. The front door was unlocked. An alarm clock buzzing drew him tentatively to the master bedroom. Bark fragments were scattered across the gold carpet. A narrow log lay at the foot of the bed. Two shapes under the covers were the bodies of his father and stepmother.

Investigators were deluged with leads. The Smiths' hilltop home overlooking Ventura Harbor was a slick sheen obscuring instability and drama. Affairs. Less-than-squeaky-clean business deals. They quickly zeroed in on a friend and former business partner of Lyman's named Joe Alsip. Alsip had visited the Smiths the night before their murders; his fingerprint was on a wine goblet. Worse, his minister told police that Alsip had essentially confessed to him. Alsip was arrested. The police and prosecution entered the preliminary hearing braying with confidence. They were especially pleased to see that Alsip's defense attorney was Richard Hanawalt. Hanawalt was best known to them for successfully defending drunk drivers. He was partial to mixed metaphors and non sequiturs.

"Briefly during the lunch hour I wondered what the definition of 'strong' was," he announced to the Alsip courtroom one day. About the opposing narratives in the case, he said, "Little by little it begins to unroll like a long carpet in front of a hotel."

What they thought were Hanawalt's fumbling antics hid a bombshell. Anonymous tipsters had encouraged him to investigate the minister's past. He found a decades-long history, spanning the country from Indiana to Washington, of the minister bizarrely seeking police protection and trying to insert himself into investigations. Sergeant Gary Adkinson, one of the lead investigators on the Smith case, had quietly anticipated the minister's unraveling and cringed when Hanawalt gleefully began to dismantle his story. The chief had given the minister a police radio after he insisted that he'd received threats on his life after turning in Alsip. One afternoon the minister's terrified voice came panting over the radio. "He's here! He's coming at me!" he shouted. Adkinson happened to be at the intersection of Telegraph and Victoria, just a block from the minister's house, and he raced over. The minister stood inside the front door, holding the radio dumbly to his chest, looking devastated to see Adkinson so soon.

"He's gone," he said quietly.

In his closing argument, Hanawalt also succeeded in painting the crime scene as an eerie tableau that felt like the work of a stranger psychopath rather than someone known to the Smiths.

There was the binding with drapery cord, the devastating blows to their heads with the log, the lack of any lights on in the house, which suggested that the violent encounter may have happened in complete darkness. And the bathroom window. Someone standing there had a clear view into the bedroom. A few yards from the window was the firewood pile, where the killer grabbed the twenty-one-inch piece of wood.

After the preliminary hearing, the Ventura County district attorney released Joe Alsip for lack of evidence. The investigative team returned to square one. They were split. Half thought the killer knew the Smiths; the other half thought it was a random, sexually motivated crime. For years the Smith file sat on a shelf in the investigators' bullpen; after a decade, it was relegated to the evidence vault.

Larry Pool explained to Ventura PD that the Orange County Sheriff's Department had an unsolved serial case involving four homicide victims that bore similarities to that of the Smiths. He asked them to send any forensic evidence they still had on Smith over to the Orange County Crime Lab. Mary Hong opened the Ventura PD package; inside were a couple of glass slides. Her heart sank. Q-tip swabs that are routinely taken as part of a rape kit are rubbed against glass slides, as the slides make it easier to look for sperm under a microscope. But usually the swabs are included in the kit too. A criminalist is always looking to work with as much biological material as possible.

On February 17, 1998, Pool received Hong's report. She'd been able to develop a DNA profile from the semen on the slides. Lyman Smith could be eliminated as the source.

The DNA profile matched the Harrington, Witthuhn, and Cruz profiles.

Some of the old guard at the Ventura PD refused to believe it. Detective Russ Hayes, one of the leads on the Smith case, was interviewed for an episode of *Cold Case Files* that aired some years later. "I think you could have knocked me over with a feather," he recalled about the DNA connection. The old-timer's distrust of technology had him shaking his head.

"I couldn't believe it," Hayes said. "Didn't believe it."

Hayes recalled his theory that the killer stood outside the bathroom window at the north side of the house, the portal through which he could see Lyman and Charlene's bedroom, and became enraged at something he saw—an act of intimacy, most likely.

"I thought that it was someone close to them. I thought it was someone who had seen something through that window, looking into the bedroom. And it just infuriated them, causing them to go inside and do what they did."

Hayes was probably right about the position outside the window. And the rage. But not the familiarity. Charlene Smith was just the latest unlucky stand-in for the lustful, sneering women—mother, schoolgirl, ex-wife—who formed a disapproving circle around the killer in his daydreams, their cacophony of disdain forcing him, always, to his knees; the act of grabbing the log was arousal alchemized to hate, a vicious punishment meted out by one judge: his corroded brain.

THE BODY COUNT STOOD AT SIX. NEARLY TWENTY YEARS TOO late, they were learning his methods. How he adapted. And that he was mobile. Mapping the crimes took on a contagionlike feel, a search for victim zero. Where was he before Ventura? Someone dug up the old newspaper articles, the ones questioning whether not only Ventura and Orange were connected but Santa Barbara too. DOUBLE MURDERS MAY BE LINKED, POLICE SAY, read the headline in the July 30, 1981, edition of the *Santa Ana Register*. Nearly twenty years later, the three counties compared information again. There were a few dissimilarities—two of the male Santa Barbara victims had been shot when it appeared they fought back—but too many parallels existed to discount a link. Prowling and peeping. Nighttime attacks on middle-class victims who were sleeping. Bludgeoning. Precut ligatures brought to the scene. Tennis-shoe impressions. Many aspects that were present in a pair of double murders in a town forty miles north.

[EDITOR'S NOTE: The Ventura investigation was unquestionably the most labyrinthine of all the stand-alone investigations. Michelle had planned to cover it at great length, but Ventura is only lightly represented in the book due to her protracted quest to obtain the highly elusive case file.

In 2014 Michelle paid the Ventura County Courthouse $1,400 for hard copies of the transcripts from the Joe Alsip preliminary hearings. All 2,806 pages had to be printed from microfilm. Michelle later recalled the clerk eyeing her with some cocktail of confusion and derision as she handed Michelle the massive volume of freshly printed archive material.

Reading the transcripts, which were full of tantalizing allusions to items more fully documented in the official reports, only made Michelle covet the Ventura file that much more. In January 2016, she finally got her hands on the file when she borrowed three dozen boxes of Golden State Killer material from the Orange County Sheriff's Department. She had read through much of that file—which primarily focused on red herring Joe Alsip—by the time of her death, but she did not have time to weave it into the narrative.

For a more complete account of the Smith investigation and the case against Joe Alsip, Colleen Cason's series "The Silent Witness," published in the Ventura County Star *in November 2002, is an excellent reference.]*

GOLETA, 1979

[EDITOR'S NOTE: Segments of the following chapter have been pieced together from various drafts of "In the Footsteps of a Killer."]

THE MAN APPROACHED LINDA* AS SHE WAS LEAVING FOR WORK IN the morning. "My dog was stabbed in your backyard last night," he said. The man was young, in his early twenties, elfin-featured, and a little hyperactive. He pointed to the footbridge that crossed the creek about two hundred feet from where they stood on Berkeley Road in Goleta. He and his dog, Kimo, had come from there, he explained, Kimo off leash and the man lagging casually behind. The city of Goleta is a bedroom community with a safe reputation, boring even, but few people would brave San Jose Creek alone at night. The narrow gorge winds down from the chaparral-covered mountains through the east side of town and is shrouded in huge, draping trees—sycamore, alder, and eucalyptus, with its papery, cracked bark that looks clawed-at. There are no lights, and the only sounds are the clump and rustling of unseen animals seeking food.

But Kimo was a big, protective dog, a 120-pound German shepherd and Alaskan malamute mix. That something might happen to

---

* Pseudonym

the dog never occurred to the man. When he exited the footbridge into the residential neighborhood, he saw Kimo dart between Linda's house and her next-door neighbor's. Something must have drawn his attention back there. Kimo was nosy. From the man's vantage point, the 5400 block of Berkeley Road was still. Up until the 1960s, Goleta was a sea of walnut groves and lemon orchards, and in certain pockets, especially adjacent to the creek, you could experience what it must have been like back then, no engines revving, no electronics humming; there was just a blanketing, hushed darkness and a scattering of lights from single-story ranch houses. A surfboard atop a VW bus in someone's driveway was the only reminder that this was Southern California suburbia in early fall 1979.

A sharp yelp broke the silence. Moments later Kimo reappeared. The dog made his way unsteadily to the sidewalk and collapsed at the man's feet. The man turned him over. Blood oozed from a long cut to his belly.

Kimo survived. After frantically knocking at several houses, the man was finally able to find a phone and called for help. An urgent care veterinarian closed the wound with seventy stitches, leaving a scar that stretched from Kimo's sternum to the end of his belly. But the man remained puzzled about the source of the injury. Linda understood. Work could wait. She enlisted the help of her next-door neighbor, and together the three of them carefully scoured the side and back yards for sharp objects, like a lawnmower blade or piece of torn fence, which might have cut the dog. They found nothing. It was strange. Also odd was Linda's flooded front lawn. Around the same time Kimo was hurt, someone had apparently turned on her hose and left it running.

Linda never learned the dog owner's name. He thanked her politely and left. She mostly forgot about the incident until another man approached her outside her house with a question in July 1981. A lot had changed in the year and a half since Kimo was injured. Yellow crime-scene tape had gone up three times in the neighborhood, unusual for an area so small—less than two square miles—and so homey that deputies affectionately nick-named the teenagers they regularly ran out of the avocado groves for smoking weed the red-eye gang.

This was Santa Barbara County, home to President Reagan's 688-acre vacation ranch and also a popular retreat for moneyed dilettantes with a hippie bent, where you could wear flip-flops all day or playact in a staged rodeo, where you could enjoy histori-cally preserved Spanish architecture unsullied by garish billboards (a ban won after a multiyear campaign waged by aesthetically inclined civic leaders). From 1950 until 1991, the only stops on Highway 101 between an otherwise open 435 miles from Los Angeles to San Francisco were four traffic lights in Santa Bar-bara; depending on whom you believe, this was because locals feared that a freeway would block their ocean view, or because they wanted tourists to patronize local businesses, or because they felt people should be encouraged to pause and contemplate life, and what better place to do this than in Santa Barbara, America's Riviera, ensconced between a rugged mountain range and the Pacific Ocean? Who didn't want to idle at a stoplight in paradise? The answer, eventually, was no one. The accidents were legion, weekend traffic was a gridlock, and pollution from idling cars became immense.

INVESTIGATORS FELT THEY KNEW THE NIGHT HE LEARNED HE HAD to be careful. They knew the night that changed him. The first crime they could connect him to, where their rewinding stopped: October 1, 1979. Less than a week after Kimo was stabbed. That was the night a Goleta couple on Queen Ann Lane awakened to a blinding flashlight and a young man's clenched-teeth whisper. The woman was ordered to tie up her boyfriend. Then the in-truder tied her. He rummaged around, opening and slamming drawers. Cursing. Threatening. Asking for money but not focused on it. He led the woman into the living room and made her lie face down on the floor, throwing a pair of tennis shorts over her head as a blindfold. She heard him enter their kitchen. She heard him chanting to himself.

"I'll kill 'em, I'll kill 'em, I'll kill 'em."

A surge of adrenaline allowed the woman to escape her bindings and flee out the front door screaming. Her boyfriend, bound in the bedroom, was able to hop into the backyard. When he heard the intruder coming, he dropped and rolled behind an orange tree, narrowly eluding the searching beam of the flashlight.

The couple's next-door neighbor was an FBI agent. Alerted by the woman's scream, he came outside just in time to see a man furiously pedal past on a stolen silver Nishiki ten-speed. Pendleton shirt. Jeans. Knife holster. Tennis shoes. A blur of brown hair. The agent gave chase in his car; his headlights connected with the biker a few blocks later on San Patricio Drive. When the headlights hit him, the suspect dropped the bike and hopped the fence between two houses.

The couple could give only a general description. White male. Dark hair above the collar. Five ten or five eleven. Around twenty-five, they guessed.

After that, none of his victims ever lived to describe him again.

———

THE BODIES WERE IN THE BEDROOM.

On the morning of December 30, 1979, Santa Barbara County Sheriff's deputies responded to a call at 767 Avenida Pequena, the condominium of osteopathic surgeon Dr. Robert Offerman. Offerman's good friends Peter and Marlene Brady* had arrived

———

* Pseudonyms

for a scheduled tennis game with him and his new girlfriend, Alexandria Manning, and found a sliding glass door open at the condo. They stepped inside and called out to Offerman but got no response. Peter crossed the living room and peered down the hallway toward the bedroom.

There's a "girl lying on the bed naked," he reported back to his wife.

"Let's go," Marlene said, not wanting to interrupt. They began to leave.

But after a few paces, Peter stopped. Something wasn't right. Hadn't he called out to Offerman loudly? He pivoted and returned to the bedroom to take a closer look.

When the deputies arrived, Marlene Brady was standing out front crying.

"There are two people dead inside," she said.

Debra Alexandria Manning lay on the right side of the waterbed, her head turned to the left, her wrists bound behind her with white nylon twine. Offerman was on his knees at the foot of the bed; he clutched a length of the same twine in his hand. Pry marks indicated that the offender used a screwdriver to force his way inside the home, probably in the middle of the night when the couple was asleep. Flashing a gun, he may have suggested he was there to rob them: two rings belonging to Manning were found hidden between the mattress and bed frame.

The attacker most likely tossed the twine at Manning and demanded she tie up Offerman, which she did, but not tightly. Investigators believe at some point, perhaps after the offender was finished tying Manning's wrists, Offerman broke free from his bindings in an attempt to fight back.

Neighbors reported that at around three a.m. they heard a burst of gunfire, which was followed by a pause and then another shot. Offerman was shot three times in the back and chest. Manning's single wound was to the upper left back of her head.

The book on Offerman's nightstand was *Your Perfect Right: A Guide to Assertive Behavior*, by Robert E. Alberti. It was the holidays. A green wreath with red flowers hung on the front door. There was a pine tree in a bucket in the entryway. As authorities processed the crime scene, they stepped around a turkey carcass wrapped in cellophane that had been discarded on the patio. They concluded that at some point the killer had opened the refrigerator and helped himself to Dr. Offerman's leftover Christmas dinner.

Whoever the killer was, he'd been on a restless hunt that night. Investigators could track the star-shaped pattern from his Adidas running shoes as he circled Offerman's condo. They noted the trampled flowerbed at 769 Avenida Pequena, the vacant condo next door. Inside was evidence of squatting, most notably in the bathroom, where a length of nylon twine was left behind.

Reports came in of ransackings and break-ins in the neighborhood in the hours before the murders. When a couple who lived on Windsor Court, a half mile from Offerman's condo, pulled up to their house at around ten fifteen p.m., they spotted a man running through their living room toward the back door. As they came inside they heard him jump the rear fence. A white male in a dark fisherman's hat and dark jacket was all they could say for sure. He'd brutally punched their poodle in the eye.

In the days after the murders, investigators continued to discover pieces of nylon twine dropped in various locations: on a dirt trail alongside San Jose Creek, on a lawn on Queen Ann Lane. They couldn't be certain when the Queen Ann Lane twine had been left, though; a few doors down lived the couple who had narrowly escaped Offerman and Manning's fate just two months before. It was all there in the police reports. Nylon twine. Pry marks. Adidas running-shoe impressions.

GOLETA, 1981

WHAT DEBBI DOMINGO REMEMBERS MOST ABOUT THE LAST TIME
she talked with her mother, Cheri, is that they didn't talk. They
screamed. It was Sunday, July 26, 1981, high summer in Santa Barbara. The coastal fog, with its smell of damp eucalyptus, was gone.
The Pacific Ocean was warming up, an inviting churn of whitecaps
making its way toward soft sand and an endless line of hundred-
foot palm trees. Golden teenage boys with lank hair and effortless
muscles headed for the water with their boards in a gait the locals
called the surfer bounce. This was Santa Barbara's magic time, and
when she wasn't at her part-time job at the Granada Theater, Debbi
wanted to bask in it. She loved the energy of East Beach, especially
its volleyball scene. There was one hitch, which is why Debbi hit
the brakes on her ten-speed in front of a pay phone on State Street
that afternoon. She dug coins from the pocket of her denim cutoffs.
Her mother picked up. Debbi got right to the point.

"I need to come get my swimsuit," she said.

Her mother's stony reply surprised her.

"No," Cheri said.

A spike of rage torched Debbi behind the eyes. She gripped the
phone and dug in. Mother and daughter were back where they'd
left off.

That was four days earlier and around the corner at 1311
Anacapa Street, in an unassuming little house that was the headquarters of Klein Bottle Crisis Shelter, an organization for troubled

teens. Debbi had shown up there in the middle of July, a runaway on a bike with one hastily packed bag and a well-honed detection system for rules and how to flout them. But Klein Bottle was hardly a stern lockdown facility. The abundance of ferns hanging in macramé planters told you that. This was the peak era of Alice Miller's *The Drama of the Gifted Child*, a self-help bestseller that aimed to expose the subtle bad parenting that lurks in even the most functional-seeming families. Miller urged her readers to "find their own truth" about possible childhood abuse; in doing so, she helped ignite the talk therapy craze. Klein Bottle counselors drank tea from earthenware mugs and assured inarticulate adolescents that no feeling was too banal or shameful to share.

In addition to assigned chores, there was one house rule: the kids could come and go as they pleased, but they had to sign an agreement to participate in therapy sessions. The staff arranged for Cheri and Debbi to meet together with a counselor to help resolve their problems.

The Domingos must have seemed like an optimal case for mediation. Neither was a dull-eyed drug abuser exhibiting the ravages of stress and neglect. Far from it. Mother and daughter were both delicate-featured beauties. They sported matching beach-casual styles: easy on the makeup, huarache sandals, print tops, and jeans. Debbi adorned her hair with the occasional braid or side barrette. Cheri was thirty-five, a pin-thin Natalie Wood lookalike with a no-nonsense, pleasant demeanor, the result of working as an office manager. Debbi was more voluptuously built; her wide, blue eyes were attuned, as most teenagers are, to the short stretch rather than the long term. Both radiated good health and a core of self-assured calm.

The meeting time arrived. Cursory pleasantries were exchanged as everyone took a seat. As soon as Debbi and Cheri touched down on the couch, alighting like two birds on a wire, they erupted. Their battles were by then front-loaded with fury, a miserable lockstep in which the only changes in position were who was incredulous and who was aggrieved. They needed no coaxing. Boundaries. Rules. Boyfriends. Disrespect. Debbi can't remember if the counselor was a man or a woman. She only remembers shouting and a vague third presence in the room; someone who'd presumably seen it all but who exuded dumbstruck ineffectualness. In the end, Debbi fled abruptly, as she had before, a dark-haired storm of a girl pedaling away with her belongings crammed into a bag. In two weeks she'd turn sixteen.

Cheri watched the city swallow her daughter and worried. Santa Barbara beguiled. It deceived. The promise of romance reigned, and the potential for danger was obscured. After a nineteen-second earthquake shattered much of downtown Santa Barbara in 1925, the city was rebuilt in a unified Spanish Colonial style—white plaster walls, low-pitched red tile roofs, wrought iron. Preservation-minded civic leaders continued to keep buildings low and billboards out. There was a gentle small-town feel to the place. Every day for thirty-two years, a Greek immigrant, "the popcorn man," sold pinwheels and popcorn from his station wagon at the foot of Stearns Wharf. The smell of night-blossoming jasmine drifted in through open windows on hot evenings. The roar of the ocean rocked people to sleep.

But instability lurked. A raggedy undercurrent roiled. The recession had gutted a lot of downtown businesses. There was not yet an open-container law on lower State Street; at night weaving drunks shouted at each other between breaks to piss and puke. The music clubs were changing. Folk and disco were out, replaced by angrier punk. The local papers were reporting that an anonymous male caller was telling children ages eleven to fifteen who answered the phone that they were going to die. Another caller, maybe the same man, was telling women that he'd hurt their husbands if they didn't comply with his demands. Local cops nicknamed the unidentified creep "our breather."

There was a stoplight at State Street and Highway 101, one of the main north-south routes spanning California, and for more than a decade a colorful parade of hippies held up signs there asking for rides to places like San Diego or Eureka. It was such a Santa Barbara tradition that the Texaco gas station kept felt-tip markers for the hitchhikers to use on their cardboard signs.

But lately it was hard not to notice that, despite their Summer of Love robes and tambourines, the hippies weren't young anymore. Up close, you could see they'd weathered not just wind and sun but gradations of defeat that had turned the light off in their eyes. There were fewer signs marked with destination requests. Some just paced in circles all day.

Santa Barbara's magenta bougainvillea could distract you from its hairline cracks. Cheri hoped no harm would come to Debbi out there. Every mother's brain cycles through the litany of terrible things that might befall her child. Rarely does the reverse occur. Why should it? Especially for teenagers, who between seeing their parents as God and then as human view them temporarily as an obstacle, a particularly cumbersome door that won't quite budge.

No, it was Debbi who was, in the parlance of Klein Bottle, "at risk." The story rarely ends well for the beautiful teenage runaway. This time it did.

Not being home saved Debbi Domingo's life.

CHERI KNEW THAT HER DIFFICULTIES WITH DEBBI WERE JUST A rough spot, a bump in the road, and they would patch things up eventually. They'd laugh about it when Debbi had a teenager of her own. But in the meantime, she needed solutions. She was an office manager everyone described as a "mother hen," who, it seemed, could neither mother nor manage her own daughter.

"How do you do it?" Cheri asked her best friend, Ellen,* as they sat in Ellen's Jacuzzi in the backyard drinking wine. Ellen had three foster girls, all teenagers, living with her and her husband. Girls born drug-addicted. Abandoned on doorsteps. Cheri marveled at how well behaved they were.

"Discipline," Ellen said.

The way Ellen saw it, Cheri's attempt at disciplining Debbi had come too late. She'd been too permissive. Ellen demanded to know where her girls were at all times. The girls knew that if they cut class, either Ellen or her husband, Hank, would show up at school wearing a placard identifying themselves as the truant's babysitter. The risk of social mortification kept them in line.

Cheri, on the other hand, had given Debbi a long leash. She was patient when Debbi broke curfew or didn't check in. Cheri was by nature an optimistic, level-headed person; she believed Debbi was engaging in typical teenage behavior and was reluctant to bring the hammer down. The phase would pass, she said. Cheri was just nineteen when Debbi was born, and in happier times, when mother and daughter tried on clothes together at the mall or had lunch at their favorite restaurant, Pancho Villa, they delighted when strangers took them for sisters. They'd giggle at the assumption. The strangers would realize their mistake. Of course these two weren't sisters. They were friends.

Which is why, in the months of escalating tension when Debbi would scream, "I don't care about your rules! You're ruining my life!" Cheri's reply, while true, had a meek, uncertain tenor to it: "But I'm the mom."

The starting pistol that began the collision course was the divorce. Cheryl Grace Smith met Roger Dean Domingo, an electronics technician in the coast guard two years her senior, when she was in high school. They married shortly after Cheri turned

---

* Pseudonym

eighteen, on September 19, 1964, in San Diego. Debbi was born
the following August. Almost exactly a year later, a son, David,
arrived. Roger left the coast guard and became a Methodist minister, then a middle-school teacher. In 1975 the family moved to
Santa Barbara.

Debbi remembers the first twelve years of her life in a warm
amber light. Cheri doling out home-baked sugar cookies. Picnic
lunches at Nojoqui Falls Park. She loved having young parents,
the kind who didn't watch you from the park bench but hoisted
you onto the monkey bars and scrambled up the rocks after you at
the beach. Cheri and Roger were physically fit people raised in the
sun, and their demeanor showed it. "I didn't know what cynicism
was until I hit junior high," Debbi says.

A strain developed between Cheri and Roger somewhere along
the line. There exists a 1,157-page Santa Barbara County Sheriff's
Department report, much of it dedicated to the details of Cheri's
life; on page 130, Roger is questioned about their marriage, in
particular their social life in Santa Barbara. He recalls outdoor
picnics. They liked to visit Solvang, he says, a quaint Danish-
themed village nearby. Midinterview he switches pronouns from
"we" to "she." Cheri liked to dance. She liked to "party." It's unclear if the quotations are Roger's or the interviewer's. But they
hang there accusingly. Cheri wasn't a drug abuser or hard drinker;
the word "party" likely reveals more about inclination. Roger was
content with a wicker basket and a blanket on the grass; at some
point Cheri wanted more. They separated in December 1976.

Roger moved back to San Diego, and Debbi and David split
their time between the two cities. Debbi recognized an opportunity in the family splinter. She began playing her parents against
each other. She tested limits. Ignored house rules. At the slightest
hint of pushback she'd pack her bag and announce she was going
to live with the other parent. She ping-ponged this way for several years, shuttling back and forth between San Diego and Santa

Barbara, switching schools at least a half-dozen times, sometimes midyear. By July 1981, her once good grades had taken a dive. She was hung up on an older boyfriend in San Diego whom Cheri and Roger, who rarely were in accord on anything, agreed was bad news.

A defiant teenager in full rebellious bloom can rattle the most stable of families, so it didn't help matters that Cheri's life was in flux and under stress too. In June, with the economy tanking, she and Ellen were laid off from their jobs at Trimm Industries, a small firm that manufactured computer furniture. Cheri spearheaded their search for new employment by renting an IBM Selectric typewriter and polishing their résumés. Then, on top of everything else, she decided to move.

For several years, Cheri and the kids, when they weren't in San Diego with their dad, lived in a rented guesthouse in Montecito. But in May Cheri's father's cousin, known to the family as Aunt Barbara, called to say she was putting her house in Goleta on the market and moving to Fresno. Aunt Barbara didn't want the house to be empty while it was for sale. Would Cheri and the kids like to house-sit?

Aunt Barbara lived on Toltec Way, a cul-de-sac in a quiet, leafy pocket of northeast Goleta, adjacent to San Jose Creek. The wood-shingled Cape Cod–style house had a second-story addition over the garage and shuttered windows. To the neighbors, it was "the big red barn." What sealed the deal for Cheri was that by sheer coincidence Ellen lived catercorner on Toltec Drive.

In early June, Cheri and the kids, with the help of a moving company, hauled their belongings into 449 Toltec Way. Eucalyptus draped heavily here. The quiet seemed not so much peaceful as mandated by nature, but the stillness didn't still Debbi. The action was in the Mesa area of Santa Barbara or back with her friends in Montecito. Everything felt provisional. Temporary. A Realtor would be conducting open houses. A sign on their lawn read SANTANA PROPERTIES / FOR SALE. Debbi missed the bad-influence boyfriend in San Diego and racked up enormous phone bills calling him. A few weeks after moving in, after an explosive blowout with Cheri, she shoved what she could into a bag, hopped on her bike, and took off.

Most nights Cheri walked across the street to Ellen's, and the friends opened a bottle of wine and hopped into the Jacuzzi. They talked about Cheri's fight with Roger over child support. Job searches. Love. Cheri had started experimenting with personal ads and professional dating services. There'd been a few stilted dates at downtown restaurants. One man had called the office for Cheri and mysteriously left his name as "Marco Polo." Cheri laughed when she took the message but revealed nothing. Ellen knew that Cheri wanted to marry again, that her friend, a little surprisingly for a divorcée, was an old-fashioned romantic who yearned for the gauzy postcard image of love—the radiant couple walking hand in hand on the beach at sunset.

Cheri was circumspect about the one man who'd come closest to winning her heart since the divorce. Ellen never met him because the relationship predated Ellen's friendship with Cheri, but she spied him once slipping into Cheri's office at work. He was much younger than Cheri, gorgeous, tall, and immaculately put together, with thick dark hair. All Ellen knew was that they'd had an on-and-off relationship for years, but Cheri had recently decided it was over. Time to move on.

Mostly the two women talked about Cheri's problems with Debbi. Tough love, Ellen said. Consequences.

"Put your foot down," she advised.

WHICH IS EXACTLY WHAT CHERI DID WHEN DEBBI CALLED HER four days after their clash at Klein Bottle. Debbi had one thing on her mind, and it wasn't an apology or an olive branch, but a swimsuit. She'd left it behind at the Toltec house.

"I need to come get my swimsuit," she said.

"No," Cheri said.

"What?"

"I said no," Cheri said.

"It's my swimsuit!"

"It's my house!"

Debbi howled angrily into the phone. Cheri howled back. People on State Street slowed, sensing a scene. Debbi didn't care what the gawkers thought. Her body quaked with rage. The worst thing she could think to say spouted forth from her mouth with wild force.

"Why don't you just get the hell out of my life!" she screamed. She slammed down the phone.

The next day around two thirty p.m., Debbi got a call at the friend's house where she was crashing. The caller was a co-worker of Debbi's from the Granada Theater. Her mother's friend Ellen had phoned the theater looking for Debbi and left word that Debbi should call her immediately. Debbi steeled herself for the inevitable guilt trip Ellen would unload on her about how she was treating her mother. Ellen's first words didn't surprise Debbi at all. She could imagine Ellen standing there, hand on hip, lips pursed in judgment.

"You need to come home," Ellen said.

"I'm not coming home," Debbi said. "No way."

Ellen and Debbi have different memories of what exactly was said next, but both agree Debbi quickly understood she needed to come right away. That it was urgent. Debbi sat in the front seat of her friend's Volkswagen bus on the ride there, her mind racing with possibilities. What she remembers most about pulling up to Toltec Way was the yellow crime-scene tape, how it cordoned off not only the street itself but also the second house on the west side of the street. The big red barn. Aunt Barbara's house.

How strange it was to see dozens of people swarming the

normally empty cul-de-sac. Uniformed officers. Detectives in suits. The media. The din had the pitch of stress and confusion. People moved quickly, coming together and then pivoting, seekers of information with strained expressions. Somehow Debbi was led under the tape. She walked in a daze through the clamor.

Why don't you just get the hell out of my life!

Her heart leaped when she spotted her mother's car, a brown Datsun 280ZX, parked in the driveway.

And then she recognized another car, a white Camaro with two black racing stripes, parked in front of the house.

"Where's Greg?" Debbi asked no one in particular. She looked around for him, her voice rising. "I want to talk to Greg!"

The swarm in the cul-de-sac froze and turned toward her in unison, a mob of raised eyebrows. They repeated two words as they closed in on her—an odd, needling harmony that contributed to the dreamlike trance Debbi floated through as she made her way toward the place she hoped her mother would be.

"Greg who? Greg who? Greg who?"

———

[EDITOR'S NOTE: The following section has been reconstructed from Michelle's notes and a "Writer's Cut" piece she published in the digital edition of Los Angeles *magazine as a follow-up to the "In the Footsteps of a Killer" article.]*

GREG WAS GREGORY SANCHEZ, A TWENTY-SEVEN-YEAR-OLD COMputer programmer who first met Cheri Domingo in the late 1970s while both were employed at the Burroughs Corporation. They dated on and off from 1977 through 1981, and they were on and off and on again so many times that, when they finally ended it, Debbi just assumed they were on another break.

Greg was eight years Cheri's junior, and sometimes it showed.

He was a man preoccupied with being a man. He rode a motorcycle. He drove a Camaro with racing stripes. He coached Little
League and Pop Warner football, and he had the spare bedroom
of his apartment outfitted with every high-end stereo component
imaginable. Greg was in shape and always dressed well. Like
Cheri, he took good care of himself. They shared a certain metic-
ulousness. Neither had grown up with a lot and took great care of
what they had. For four years, their relationship trajectory was a
decidedly circular one. She waited for him to grow up. He waited
for her to chill out. Finally, they'd had enough. Both began seeing
other people.

In June of 1981, the Burroughs Corporation announced it
was shutting down its Santa Barbara division. Sanchez planned a
trip to the East Coast to explore job opportunities at their Florida
branch. The following month, while Debbi was living at the Klein
Bottle shelter, Greg got in touch and invited her out to lunch.

Greg and Debbi had been close. He was like family. Not quite
a father figure, as his age fell somewhere in the middle between
Cheri's and Debbi's, he was something in the realm of an older
brother. He was fun and he treated her well. He liked to call her
Debra D.

"Greg, my name's not Debra," she'd remind him.

"That's alright, Debra D," he'd tease. "Don't worry about it."

Over hamburgers that afternoon in mid-July, Greg broke the
news to Debbi that he was moving to Florida. He explained that
he wanted her to hear it from him, rather than learning about it
after the fact—which he knew would shatter her. She was not
much less crestfallen hearing it directly from the source.

"I've proposed to your mom so many times," he said resignedly.
"She'll never marry me." Cheri felt she was too old for Greg, a
rationale Debbi thought was ridiculous.

What Debbi didn't know was that Greg was already seeing
someone else.

He had met Tabitha Silver* in May. Both lived in the same apartment complex, and Greg had dated her close friend Cynthia.* Cynthia remained friends with Greg and ultimately introduced him to Tabitha. They began going out, and their relationship deepened quickly. Not even three weeks in, Greg was marveling—with some degree of alarm—at the speed with which things had turned serious.

But the timing was off. Both their lives were in states of flux. Tabitha was starting dental school at UCLA in the fall, and in the interim, she'd left Santa Barbara and moved back home to San Diego for the summer. Greg's job status was in limbo and he was considering relocating to Florida.

"This is not the time in my life to get involved," Greg told her.

"When is the time going to be?" Tabitha retorted. "When you're six feet under?"

Greg returned from Florida on July 23 and immediately phoned Tabitha. He was going to remain in California after all, he'd decided. Florida was too far away from his friends and family. With her birthday only days away, he invited her to Santa Barbara for the weekend.

She drove up that Saturday and they spent the day together. He hinted at a marriage proposal. The following night, she appeared at the door of his apartment. He surprised her with a last-minute change of plans: he was going to spend the evening with a friend instead.

That friend was Cheri Domingo.

A NEIGHBOR OF CHERI DOMINGO'S HEARD A GUNSHOT, FOL-lowed by a voice in the middle of the night—a woman speaking to someone in a controlled, unemotional way, something along

---

* Pseudonym

Manuela Witthuhn, who was murdered on
February 5, 1981, in Irvine, California.

Classmates.com

Keith and Patrice Harrington, who were murdered in Dana Point, California on August 19,
1981. The couple had been married for three months when Keith's father discovered the bodies
in his home, where they had been staying.

Orange County Sheriff's Department

Golden State Killer victim Janelle Cruz in happier times, at the Bluff Lake YMCA camp (circa 1981).

Courtesy of Michelle White

Charlene and Lyman Smith, who were murdered on March 13, 1980, in their Ventura home.

Classmates.com

Debra Alexandria Manning, who was murdered alongside Robert Offerman in his Goleta condominium on December 30, 1979.

Santa Barbara County Sheriff's Office / Orange County Sheriff's Department

An undated photo of osteopathic surgeon Robert Offerman, who was shot to death on December 30, 1979.

Santa Barbara County Sheriff's Office / Orange County Sheriff's Department

Cheri Domingo and Gregory Sanchez, who
were murdered by an intruder on July 27,
1981, in Goleta.
Courtesy of Debbi Domingo

Debbi Domingo, daughter of victim Cheri
Domingo, had run away from home; she last
talked to her mother by phone the day before her
murder. Debbi's final words to her were "Why
don't you just get the hell out of my life!"
Courtesy of Debbi Domingo

Crime-scene tape cordons off Toltec Way,
the quiet Santa Barbara cul-de-sac where
Cheri Domingo and Gregory Sanchez
were murdered. Thirty years later, DNA
from the crime scene connected the double
homicide to the Golden State Killer.
*Santa Barbara County Sheriff's Office / Orange
County Sheriff's Department*

Brian Maggiore and his wife, Katie, were shot to death by an unknown assailant while walking their dog in Rancho Cordova, on February 2, 1978. The crime is now suspected to have been perpetrated by the Golden State Killer.

Classmates.com

Investigators process the Rancho Cordova backyard where Brian and Katie Maggiore were found shot to death after attempting to flee their assailant.

Sacramento County Sheriff's Department / Orange County Sheriff's Department

Mad is the word, the word that reminds me of 6th grade. I hated that year.

I wish I had know what was going to be going on during my 6th grade year, the last and worst year of elementary school. Mad is the word that remains in my head about the my hateful year as a 6th grader. My madness was one that was caused by disapointments that hurt me very much. Disapointment that were planed, then canceled. My 6th grade teacher gave me a lot of disapointments which made me very mad and moe me built a state of hatel in my heart, no one ever let mes down that hard befor and I never "hated" anyone as much as I did him. Disapointment wasint the only reason that made me mad in my 6th grade class, another was getting in twoble at school especially talking thats what really bugged me was writing sentances, those awful sentance that my teacher made me write, hours and hours I'd sit and write 50-100-150 sentence day and night I write those dreadful to paragraphs which embarrased me and more important it made me ashamed of myself which in turn; deepdown inside made me realize that writing sentance wasn't fair it wasn't fair to make me suffer like that, it just wasn't fair to make me sit and wraight until my bones aked, until my hand felt every horrid pain of ever had and as I wrote, I got madder and madder until I cried, I cried because I was ashamed I cried because I was discusted, I cried because I was mad, and I cried for myself, kid who kept on having to write those blame sentances. My angryness from sixth grade will scar my memory for life and I will be ashamed for my sixth grade year forever

"Mad is the word." A piece of paper torn from a spiral notebook found after a nearby East Area Rapist (EAR) attack. It was bundled with other materials discovered on a trail sniffed out by bloodhounds along a railroad right-of-way in Danville, California. The handwritten contents appear to be a journal entry in which the author vents about a disciplinarian sixth-grade teacher.

Contra Costa County Sheriff's Office

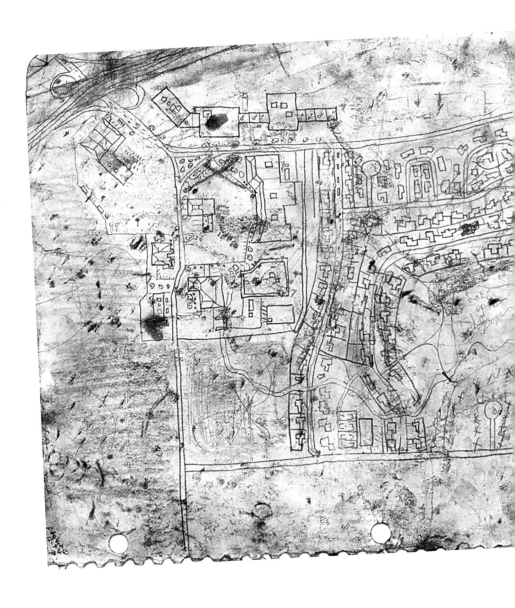

A hand-drawn map found with the "Mad is the word" journal entry. The area depicted is unclear, but Contra Costa criminalist Paul Holes believes the map exhibits the sophistication of someone who works in or around landscape architecture or development. On the flipside of the map are doodles, including the word "punishment," intensely scrawled.

Contra Costa County Sheriff's Office

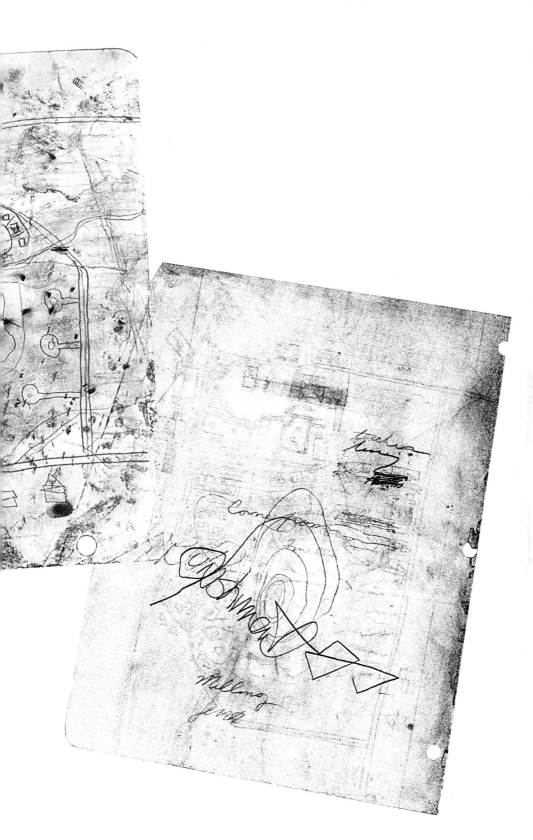

A shoe impression found by detectives investigating the October 1, 1979, attack in Goleta.
Santa Barbara County Sheriff's Office / Orange County Sheriff's Department

A sketch depicting a masked burglar, believed to have been the East Area Rapist, who was scared off by a light-sleeping Danville resident on July 5, 1979.
Tom Macris / Contra Costa County Sheriff's Office

A sketch of a prowler and would-be intruder, observed by a teenage girl as he attempted to enter her San Ramon house while she was home alone on August 8, 1979. The incident occurred fewer than eight hundred feet away from the scene of an earlier EAR attack. When he realized he'd been observed, the prowler fled into the same Christmas tree farm used as an escape route in that previous attack.

Tom Macris / Contra Costa County Sheriff's Office

A facial composite of the prowler suspected of shooting Douglas Moore* on February 16, 1977.

Sacramento County Sheriff's Department

* pseudonym

Contacted victim ▮▮▮▮ at her residence for the purpose of asking a series of questions pertaining to the attack on the victim on 10/5/76.

1. Victim received 2 suspicious phone calls (no answer when victim answered phone) about 2 weeks prior to the attack. She further stated that she was the victim of a Burglary 2 weeks prior to the attack.

2. Victim stated that the house accross the street from her residence was for sale at the time of the attack. The house was listed by Century 21 ▮▮▮▮▮▮▮▮▮▮▮▮▮▮ and the house has no swimming pool.

3. ▮▮▮▮▮ stated that she did not notice any unusual actions on the part of the suspect as she was blindfolded immediately.

4. The victim has no idea if the suspect was Right or Left handed.

5. The victim cannot recall if she made any purchases or gave name, address and phone number to anyone just prior to the

6. The victim owns a ▮▮▮▮▮▮▮▮▮▮▮▮▮ and a ▮▮▮▮▮

7. Her phone was listed under the name of ▮▮▮▮▮▮▮.

8. The only contact with door to door salesmen was the Fuller Brush man but he is an elderly man.

9. The victim has a personal checking account with her name, address and phone number printed on the checks.

End of interview.

	BADGE	DIV	HAS THIS PAGE BEEN CODED?	APPROVING SUPERVISOR	PAGE
VINS	31	Det	☐ YES ☒ NO		

Murder links investigated

Investigators from three counties are probing a possible link between four double murders, including the bludgeoning murder of a young couple near Laguna Beach last year as they slept.

Although Orange County sheriff's investigators "have looked into" a possible connection between the county murders and murders in Ventura and Santa Barbara, Lt. Andy Romero said there has been no proof that the murders are related.

Dubbed the "night stalker" by some police detectives after a couple was killed in Santa Barbara, an FBI psychological profile suggested the murderer was a "psychopath who would strike again."

Some investigators believe he may have indeed struck again, but few clues have been found at the scene of each murder. No weapon has been found in connection with any of the murders.

According to Santa Barbara County public information officer Russ Birchim, the killer first appeared in Oct. 1979 when he terrorized a Santa Barbara couple in their home. The knife-wielding assailant fled after one victim escaped. No injuries were reported.

Two months later, in the same neighborhood, Dr. Robert Offerman, 44, and his girlfriend, Debra Manning, 35, were shot to death late at night in a bedroom of Offerman's condominium.

March 16, 1980, a Ventura couple was found dead in the bedroom of their home. Police believe a log from the fireplace may have been used by the murderer to bludgeon to death attor-ney Lyman Smith and his wife, Charlene. The weapon has not been found.

Keith Eli Harrington, 24, and his wife of four months, Patty, 27, were bludgeoned to death Aug. 19 or 20 as they slept in a bedroom of Harrington's father's home in Niguel Shores, south of Laguna Beach. Harrington was a Phi Betta Kappa medical student at UCI and his wife was a nurse.

The most recent murder occurred Sunday or Monday in the Santa Barbara suburb of Goleta and about five blocks from the scene of the first murder.

Greg Sanchez, 28, and an ex-girlfriend, Cheri Domingo, 35, died of massive head wounds. Sanchez, a computer technician, was also shot once but police said the wound was only "a contributing factor to death."

Double murders may be linked, police say

By Keith Easthouse
Register staff writer

A possible link between the murder of a sleeping young couple in an exclusive South Laguna community last summer and three similar double murders that have occurred in Southern California during the past 18 months is being investigated by Santa Barbara County detectives.

Public information officer Russ Birchim said that striking similarities between the four double slayings have led investigators to believe that one man – dubbed the "night stalker" – is responsible for all eight deaths.

The two most recent victims were bludgeoned to death in the bedroom of a suburban Santa Barbara home sometime Sunday night or Monday morning. Birchim said.

Investigators from the Orange County Sheriff's Department "have looked into" the three other sets of murders – one in Ventura County and two in Santa Barbara County – but have found no proof of a connection, according to Lt. Andy Romero.

Neither have Ventura city police, according to spokesman Larry White, who added that his department has had no contact with investigators from Orange and Santa Barbara counties concerning the slayings.

Nonetheless, the similarities between the four cases are startling:

● All the victims were relatively young couples killed in bed late at night as they slept.

● All were professional, middle- to upper-middle class people who lived in expensive homes.

● Six of the eight victims were bludgeoned to death. The other two were shot.

● In none of the four cases were there any signs of resistance, was a weapon recovered, or was anything stolen from the homes.

According to Birchim, investigators believe the killer first appeared in October of 1979, when an unidentified couple were terrorized in their suburban Santa Barbara home late at night by a knife-wielding assailant.

Birchim said the couple probably escaped death when the assailant fled after one of them escaped.

The first killings took place in the same wealthy neighborhood on December 30, 1979. Both Dr. Robert Offerman, 44, and his girlfriend, Debra Manning, 35, a Santa Maria psychologist, were shot to death in the bedroom after some person – or persons – broke into Offerman's condominium late at night.

Birchim said a psychological profile done after the murders by the FBI at the request of the Sheriff's Department suggested that the man responsible was a "psychopath who would strike again."

Three months later, on Sunday, March 16, 1980, another couple was found dead in their bedroom in a plush Ventura hillside home.

The victims, Lyman Smith, a prominent attorney, and his wife, Charlene, 33, were bludgeoned to death sometime late that Saturday night or early Sunday morning, according to police.

Police believe a log from the house's fireplace was used as a weapon, but there was not able to prove it. There was no sign of forced entry.

Four months later, either on the evening of August 19, or Wednesday morning, August 20, Keith Eli Harrington, 24, and his wife of four months, Patty, 27, died of massive head injuries inflicted by a blunt instrument. They were killed as they slept in the bedroom of Harrington's father's exclusive home in Niguel Shores, south of Laguna Beach.

Harrington was a Phi Beta Kappa medical student from UC Irvine and his wife was a nurse. As with the Ventura killings, there was no sign of a forced entry.

And almost a year later, on a Sunday night or early Monday morning, yet another young couple was killed in a bedroom.

This time the killings took place back in the same suburb of Santa Barbara – Goleta – not more than five blocks from the site of the first murders.

The victims, Greg Sanchez, 28, and his ex-girlfriend, Cheri Domingo, 35, also died of massive head injuries, just like the Smiths and the Harringtons. Sanchez, who was a computer technician, was also shot once, but Birchim of the sheriff's department said the wound was only "a contributing factor to death."

Like the first killings, but unlike the other two, whoever killed Sanchez and Domingo had broken into the home.

Sheriff Appeals for Information in Dual Slayings

The Orange County Sheriff's Department has appealed for information regarding the unsolved August, 1980, double-murder of Laguna Niguel newlyweds Keith and Patti Harrington.

Families of the slain couple have offered a $25,000 reward for information leading to the conviction of the killer or killers in the bludgeoning death of the couple on Aug. 19, 1980, in their home.

Keith Harrington was a 24-year-old medical student at UC Irvine and his wife Patti, 27, was a registered nurse.

People with information concerning the murders may call 834-3000. All tips will be kept confidential, a Sheriff's Department spokesman said.

Probe of Niguel Shores murders reaches dead end

By Anita Snow
Register staff writer

On Aug. 19, 1980, medical student Keith Harrington and his wife, Patty, a registered nurse, were bludgeoned to death as they lay in bed in a Niguel Shores home.

Almost two years later, Orange County sheriff's deputies have completed the last of almost 250 interviews in connection with the case. No arrests have been made and detectives say they're run out of clues.

"All we can do now is re-evaluate the information we've collected and begin re-contacting some of the people we've already interviewed," sheriff's spokesman Lt. Wyatt Hart said Monday.

Hart said the sheriff's department is asking that anyone who has information about the case, no matter how little, contact the department.

Members of the victim's families are reminding the public that they still offer a $25,000 reward for any information that leads to conviction of the person or persons responsible for the killings.

"We think there are people out there that know something about the killings," Hart said. "We're hoping we can jog some memories."

At the time of his death, Keith Harrington, 24, was a fourth-year student at University of California, Irvine, Medical School. His wife of four months, Patty, 27, was a registered nurse.

The Harringtons were killed in Keith's father's home at 33381 Cockleshell Drive, Niguel Shores, an exclusive, guarded community north of Dana Point.

Sheriff's detectives say nothing was taken from the house. There was no sign of forced entry.

Since the murders, Hart said, investigators have interviewed "everyone the Harringtons knew," including friends and family members.

Investigators also have looked into other similar double homicides throughout the country, hoping to make some kind of link, Hart said.

But they've come up empty-handed.

Hart stressed that the sheriff's department will keep confidential the identities of any persons who provide information about the slayings.

He urged that those with information about the Harrington murders call (714) 834-3000, which is a 24-hour hotline.

Newspaper clippings archived by the Orange County Sheriff's Department. Although the possibility of a link between some of the crimes was considered at the time, the presence of a serial killer in the region largely went undetected.

Anaheim Bulletin / Orange County Sheriff's Department; Orange County Register / Orange County Sheriff's Department; Orange County Register / Los Angeles Times / Orange County Sheriff's Department

LEFT: A typical page from Sacramento County's massive body of documentation on the East Area Rapist crimes.

Sacramento County Sheriff's Department

Sacramento County Sheriff's Department organized an EAR–focused community meeting on November 8, 1977, at Mira Loma High School in Sacramento, where frightened residents voiced their concerns.

Sacramento County Sheriff's Department

Sergeant Larry Crompton of the EAR Task Force in Contra Costa County, pouring plaster to create a cast of a footwear impression.

Courtesy of Larry Crompton

Paul Holes, early in his career as a criminalist at the Contra Costa County Sheriff's Office.

Courtesy of Paul Holes

Detective Richard Shelby, the original lead investigator in the EAR series, types a report at the Sacramento County Sheriff's Department.

Courtesy of Richard Shelby

Detective William McGowen, Visalia Police Department.

Courtesy of Mary Lou McGowen

Larry Pool, in a photo taken during his swearing-in as a Senior Investigator at the Riverside County District Attorney's Office in August 2017.

Courtesy of Larry Pool

Michelle McNamara, conducting research for *I'll Be Gone in the Dark*. Also on the couch, Michelle's daughter, Alice, who is "double-checking" her mother's work.

Courtesy of Patton Oswalt

Michelle McNamara hard at work in her preferred writing environment.

Courtesy of Patton Oswalt

the lines of "Take it easy." That was probably the last thing Domingo ever said.

Investigators later theorized that the conspicuous scraping sound the bedroom door made against the shag rug had alerted Sanchez to an intruder. It appeared he'd fought with the killer.

One detective familiar with the case recalled the woman's voice, steadying and deflective, overheard by the neighbor. "She pissed him off," he said.

This time the killer took the ligatures with him. He was adapting, eliminating evidence.

ON MONDAY MORNING, A REALTOR ARRIVED AT 449 TOLTEC WAY to show the property to a prospective buyer and his family. He let himself into the house and, upon entering the master bedroom, discovered the bodies of a male and a female. He immediately whisked his clients out of the house and called the police.

Both victims were nude. Sanchez's body was half inside the closet in a prone position. The killer had covered his head with a pile of clothing pulled down from the rack above. Near the body was a flashlight—the batteries had Sanchez's fingerprints on them, indicating it came from the house.

Sanchez had been shot in the cheek, probably while struggling with or resisting the perpetrator. That wound was not fatal. The twenty-four blunt-force wounds, inflicted by an unknown instrument, were. Domingo was face down on the bed in a pool of blood. She had been bludgeoned to death with the same instrument. Draped over her was a bedspread that matched the wallpaper. Her hands were crossed behind her back as though they'd been bound. Ligature marks on her wrists supported this notion.

Investigators found a small window open in the downstairs

guest bathroom. The window screen had been removed and hidden in the bushes behind a juniper tree. Though the window was too small for an adult male to enter, they deduced that the perpetrator had reached through the window and unlocked the outside bathroom door.

Officers processing the crime scene noticed outlines of two tools that had been recently removed from a dusty gardening shelf in the hallway. One clearly belonged to a pipe wrench. The missing tool responsible for the other outline was later identified by Cheri's ex-husband as likely having been a gardening instrument called a turf plugger. Neither the turf plugger nor the pipe wrench was ever located.

The police went door to door, canvassing the neighborhood. The next-door neighbor reported having been awakened at approximately two fifteen a.m. by barking dogs. He and his wife looked out the window. They observed nothing of concern and returned to bed.

Two thirteen-year-old boys told police they had been walking in the neighborhood at about nine forty-five p.m. when they saw someone standing behind a large tree a block over from the crime scene. They thought the individual was male, but couldn't be sure; in the shadows, it was merely a blank silhouette.

Len and Carol Goldschein* reported that they'd gone out for a walk that night and had a strange encounter. At approximately ten thirty p.m., as they were heading westward on University Drive, they noticed that an unfamiliar man appeared to be following them, and was gaining on them. As they turned onto Berkeley Road, the subject crossed the street and continued walking parallel to them.

The man was white, in his late teens or maybe early twenties, about five eleven, with a slender build and very blond, straight

---

* Pseudonyms

hair that reached his neck. He was clean-shaven. He was wearing an Ocean Pacific–type shirt with light blue trousers, corduroy or maybe denim.

At around eleven p.m. that same night, Tammy Straub* and her daughter Carla* were jogging on Merida Way when they spotted a suspicious young male with a German shepherd gazing toward the garage of one of the houses. He stood completely still, his back to them, as though he were frozen. The man appeared to be in his twenties or early thirties, five ten and well built. His hair was blond, and he was wearing white or beige tennis shorts and a light-colored T-shirt. A composite sketch was later made.

Detectives learned that, on the afternoon before the murders, Realtor Cami Bardo* had been conducting an open house at the big red barn. While she was engaged with another party, a white male between thirty-five and forty years old walked in and, without saying a word, began exploring the house. Before she was able to break free from her conversation, the man left.

When the viewing was over, Bardo inspected the house and noticed some metal fragments in the kitchen. In retrospect, she realized that they looked consistent with a locking device from the rear door of the house.

Bardo described the strange open-house visitor as having bright blue eyes and short, light-brown hair that was curly and sun-streaked. He was tan, stood about five nine, and was wearing a green alligator shirt and faded Levi's. She met with the Santa Barbara Sheriff's sketch artist and a composite was drawn.

Initially, police considered the possibility that drug dealers had broken into the home and killed the couple, but those close to the victims dismissed this idea as ludicrous. Neither one did drugs. Detectives then focused their crosshairs on Cheri's ex-husband. After grilling him relentlessly, they vetted his alibi. It checked out.

---

* Pseudonym

Over the years, locals dubbed the phantom responsible for the thwarted attack and two double murders the Creek Killer. Because all three couples targeted were unmarried, some speculated that the killer was a religious zealot who sought to punish those he deemed to be living in sin. Meanwhile, Santa Barbara investigators remained convinced that their killer was a local punk named Brett Glasby.

First eyed by Santa Barbara investigators as a potential suspect in 1980, Glasby was a local hood well known for his nastiness and violent temper. No one had a kind word to say about him. He was a mean bastard. An accomplished burglar, Glasby was tangentially connected to victim Robert Offerman: he and some thugs he ran with were the prime suspects in the savage beating of a janitor who worked in Offerman's office building. Glasby lived in the target area and also had access to a .38 Smith & Wesson— the same type of gun used in the Offerman/Manning homicides. But ballistics tests ruled the gun out, and no physical evidence ever connected Glasby to any of the crimes.

Brett Glasby himself was murdered, alongside his brother Brian, in 1982. The two were vacationing in Mexico when they headed to the beach in San Juan de Alima for what they thought was a drug deal. Once there, they were robbed and shot to death in what turned out to be a setup. The Santa Barbara Sheriff's Department maintained that Glasby was likely responsible for the Offerman/Manning and Sanchez/Domingo double homicides, and they stuck to this conclusion even after Orange County's cold-case unit linked the crimes by m.o. to the Original Night Stalker—whose last known crime was committed in 1986, four years after Glasby's death.

In 2011, years after previous failed attempts, a DNA profile was successfully developed from degraded genetic material recovered from a blanket at the Sanchez/Domingo crime scene. It conclusively linked the Goleta cases to the East Area Rapist/Original Night Stalker.

Like Joe Alsip, Brett Glasby turned out to be just another red herring.

———————

NO ONE EVER TOLD DEBBI DOMINGO THAT HER MOTHER'S KILLER might have claimed other victims. She found out only in the early 2000s, when cable true-crime programs began profiling the Original Night Stalker cases. By that time, Debbi was working as a prison guard in Texas, seven years clean after nearly a decade of addiction to methamphetamines. Her life had been thoroughly derailed after her mother's murder.

On that day in July, when fifteen-year-old Debbi had first learned of her mother's death, she called her grandmother and told her that her mother was dead.

"Debbi," her grandmother replied, "it's not nice of you to joke like that."

She moved to San Diego almost immediately after. Her mother's side of the family gradually receded from her life. Shortly after her mother's death, she'd overheard a family exchange that would haunt her. "Linda," her grandmother told her aunt. "I'm so glad it wasn't you. I don't know what I would do if it had been you."

Over the years, Debbi has reached out to her grandmother and to her aunt, hoping to rekindle a connection. They've never responded.

ORANGE COUNTY, 2000

OLD-TIMERS AT THE ORANGE COUNTY SHERIFF'S DEPARTMENT WOULD see Larry Pool's furrowed brow, the victims' photos pinned to the board above his cubicle, the binders accumulating around him like a dreary fortress.

"Guy's dead," they'd tell Pool flatly, as if repeating a basketball score from last night's game. "Or a lifer. Those guys never stop."

"Those guys" were psychopaths, serial killers, monsters. Whatever you called them, the conventional wisdom was that extremely violent serial offenders didn't stop killing until they were forced to by death, disability, or imprisonment. Pool's target had last struck in 1986. It was 2000.

"So why do you care?" The old-timers would needle Pool. The attitude rankled him. It ignited his rectitude and made him double down on a belief he kept to himself: he was going to catch the guy.

Santa Barbara didn't yet have DNA, but the m.o. was strong enough that Pool included it in the series of murders along with Cruz. October 1, 1979, to May 5, 1986. Ten bodies. Two survivors. The scope of the case gave investigators a lot to work with. They decided to hold off contacting the media until they'd exhausted leads. They didn't want to tip the killer off. Pool agreed with the old-timers that a guy this prolifically violent might be doing time somewhere on a serious charge. He scoured arrest records. Peepers. Prowlers. Burglars. Rapists. They exhumed an ex-con's body in Baltimore. Zip. Nothing.

Pool kept the search command roving in his brain. One day he flashed back on the first autopsy he ever witnessed, near the end of Police Academy training. The body was removed from the bag and laid onto the steel table. The deceased male was five eleven, with dark hair, brawny. And hog-tied. He was wearing women's shoes, hosiery, panties, and a stuffed bra. The cause of death was toluene poisoning; he'd been sniffing glue out of a sock while indulging in some kind of autoerotic experience. Pool could see ejaculate on the panties. The sight made an impression on the straitlaced Pool. Looking back, he wondered if maybe their killer sometimes experimented with binding himself when he didn't have a victim. He thought back and placed the autopsy in October 1986, five months after the last murder.

He dug up the hog-tied guy's history. There was no criminal record; no link to the other crime locations. He'd been cremated. *If he was their guy*, Pool thought, *we're toast*. Pool gathered coroners' reports from May 5 through December 31, 1986, in every county in Southern California and began combing through them. Leads failed to develop. After a while, going to the media didn't sound so bad.

The October 1, 2000, edition of the *Orange County Register* ran the first article about the DNA link: "DNA May Point to Serial Killer in the Area." Pool was described as having ninety-three binders of material on the case in his office.

"Our killer is the original 'Night Stalker,'" Pool said.

His intention was only to point out that their killer's crimes predated those of Richard Ramirez, aka the Night Stalker, who terrorized Southern California from 1984 to 1985, but much to his chagrin the confusing nickname stuck. It was the Original Night Stalker from then on.

The article opened with speculation about where the killer could be. Dead. Behind bars. Plotting his next murder. There was no speculation about his past. Privately many of the Orange

County investigators suspected the killer came from Goleta, as that's where the murders started. One of Pool's colleagues, Larry Montgomery, even drove up there and spent a few days asking elementary-school teachers, active and retired, from the neighborhood around San José Creek if they recalled any troubled young boys they taught in the midsixties, boys who worried them in an abusing-small-animals sort of way. He returned with a few names, but they checked out and had grown up okay.

The October 1, 1979, attack did possess some juvenile elements that suggested maybe a local punk. The stolen ten-speed. The steak knife grabbed from inside the house. But other clues, passed over at the time, suggested experience honed somewhere else, not in the dope haze of cliquey surfers who were long on talk and short on misdemeanors, but in isolation, solitary but compulsive—alienation channeled into raw criminal skill. He didn't just jimmy a lock at the couple's house that night. He pulled the doorframe off and threw it over the fence.

The fact, too, that he was able, on a ten-speed, to evade an armed FBI agent pursuing him in a car, with a fleet of sheriff's deputies on their way? Stan Los, the FBI agent who chased him, would later catch shit from local cops about why he didn't shoot the guy. Los bristled at the taunt but remained resolute about his decision. All he had was a woman screaming and an ordinary white male on a bike who accelerated every time Los hollered or honked at him. He lacked the necessary context to shoot.

Los wasn't a fortune-teller. He couldn't have predicted, when the guy threw the bike on the sidewalk and sprinted between 5417 and 5423 San Patricio Drive, hopping the fence, that the next time he'd emerge, he'd be coarsened, his knots tighter, no longer in need of chants to pump himself up; he'd be a full-blown killer. The night of the pursuit, he was pedaling away from Los to escape, obviously, but he was also running toward something else, a state of mind, one where trivial everyday matters disappeared and the compulsive fantasies, lapping at the edges of his thoughts, blew open and took force.

Los couldn't have taken a shot. Not that he doesn't occasionally reconstruct the events of that night, the lost seconds restarting his car, the U-turn, the figure on the bike about fifty yards away, merging with the right edge of his lights, how the headlights acted as a kind of command. Bike dropped. Man running. Had Los the power to foresee what the man would become, he would have taken aim with his .38 special and brought him down right there.

Everyone agreed that October 1, 1979, was the precipice, the night a would-be killer crossed over.

The mystery prowler would ultimately target a northeast neighborhood around the intersection of Cathedral Oaks and Patterson, within a two-mile-square radius. All three Santa Barbara attacks would be adjacent to San Jose Creek, a stream that begins in the laurel-covered mountains and meanders down through east Goleta before emptying into the Pacific. The creek's suburban stretch is a Huckleberry Finn dream of moss-covered rocks and rope swings and delinquents' cigarette butts shrouded by a canopy of trees. Looking at the crime locations on a Goleta map, Pool was struck by the way the killer hewed to the creek like an umbilical cord.

The Goleta attacks were noteworthy for another reason. Control was this offender's chosen language. It was in the bindings. The blitz attacks. He might be a forgettable loser in the daytime, but he ruled in the houses he sneaked into, a static mask imposing horror. He sometimes left milk and bread out in the kitchen, the psychopath communicating confident leisure.

Yet this master criminal always lost control in Goleta. Three times he hit there; three times he was thwarted. He was never able to sexually assault the female victims; in the first attack she got away, and in the second and third, the males resisted and were shot to death. He was probably concerned that the gunshots would attract police, so he quickly killed the female victims and fled.

Tracking back the killer's predatory development was like watching a horror movie in reverse, but rewinding was important. "A criminal is more vulnerable in his history than his future," writes David Canter, a leading British crime psychologist, in his book *Criminal Shadows.* Canter believes the key to solving a series of crimes is to find out what happened before the first crime rather than establishing where the offender went after the most recent one. "Before he committed the crime he may not have known himself that he would do it," writes Canter, "so he may not have been so careful before as afterwards."

That he was careful later there was no doubt. He was a watcher. Calculating. Take, for example, Ventura. He hit multiple times in Santa Barbara and Orange Counties, but only once in Ventura. Why? Joe Alsip's arrest for the Smith murders was huge news. Why risk committing another double homicide in Ventura, raising doubts about Alsip's guilt, when the sucker was about to take the fall for you?

THE FACT THAT THE THREE HOME INVASIONS OCCURRED IN GO-leta, Santa Barbara's more recently developed and less genteel neighbor to the west, didn't stop the Sheriff's Office from trying to keep the crimes under wraps. Like most longtime institutions, the Santa Barbara Sheriff's Office had developed an organizational culture, and its reputation was for insularity and secretiveness. Hair on the back of a detective's neck might be raised by what he saw at a crime scene, but his job required that he remain poker-faced to the public. That's certainly the impression Sheriff's Detective O. B. Thomas was trying to convey on the afternoon of Friday, July 31, 1981, when he began canvassing the neighborhood around 449 Toltec Way, five days after he was the first officer to arrive in response to an emergency call there. Canvassing consists of knocking on neighbors' doors and asking them about any unusual or suspicious sightings or incidents. There was no need to panic the public. Thomas asked the questions but revealed little about what had happened. You wouldn't know from his face what he'd seen.

Linda lived just a block from Toltec Way. When Detective Thomas knocked on her door and took out his notepad, he triggered a memory. She remembered the wounded dog, her flooded lawn, and the curious absence of any sharp objects in either her or her neighbor's backyard that could have cut the animal. She told Detective Thomas the story. He asked her if she could remember the date of the incident. Linda thought back, and then consulted her diary. September 24, 1979, she said.

The date's significance was clear to them immediately. That was a week before the first attack. Detectives knew very little about the suspect they sought other than what a witness who glimpsed him fleeing in the dark told them: he was an adult white male. They didn't know what drew him to this sleepy pocket of tract homes, but they knew some things. He carried a knife—he'd dropped one running from the first scene. He was a night prowler; they'd followed his shoe impressions as he crept from house to house searching for victims. And he liked the creek. Maybe he used the undergrowth and canopy of trees to move about undetected. Maybe he had history there, had played as a kid among the moss-covered rocks and rope swings. Whatever the reason, shoe prints and precut ligatures he'd dropped signaled his presence there. And all three houses he invaded shared one characteristic: they were close to the creek.

From where they stood, Linda and Detective Thomas could see the tangle of trees and the low white wooden fence that paralleled the creek. There was the footbridge that Kimo had emerged from that night, his radar alerted to something moving in the dark that shouldn't be. It was becoming clear what had probably happened next. The dog peeled off between the houses to nose around, and the prowler, startled and no doubt annoyed, gutted him to keep him away. Maybe he got Kimo's blood on him and used Linda's hose to wash it off. There were often signs of his presence in a neighborhood before he struck, small, disquieting details only understood in retrospect.

Years later, after the invention of Google Earth, cold-case investigators created a digital map and time line detailing the suspect's violent trail across California. Bright yellow pushpin icons along San Jose Creek represent the locations where he hit in northeast Goleta. The neighborhood hasn't changed much in thirty-five years. Zoom in further and there's the backyard where his presence was first signaled by a dog's yelp in the night. The depth of his shoe impressions shows that he often remained in one position for long periods of time, pressed against a wall or crouching in a garden. It's easy to imagine him standing in the dark backyard as Kimo whimpers out front, as his owner knocks on doors, and then a car rumbles up to take them away. Quiet settles over the night again. He creeps between the houses, turns on the hose to wash the splatter from his shoes, and sneaks away, rivulets of watery blood disappearing into the grass behind him.

CONTRA COSTA, 1997

John Murdock was taken aback for a moment. He hadn't heard the acronym in years.

"Why?" Murdock asked.

They were sitting across the aisle from each other on a flight to a California Association of Criminalists conference. It was 1997. Murdock had recently retired as the chief of the Contra Costa County Sheriff's crime lab. His specialty was firearms and tool marks. Holes, in his late twenties, had landed a job as a deputy sheriff criminalist soon after graduating from UC-Davis with a major in biochemistry. He started in forensic toxicology but soon realized that his passion was CSI. Then his curiosity outgrew the microscope. He began going around with the investigators; he was a cold-case investigator trapped in a crime lab. He enjoyed wandering the Property Room, pulling out boxes of old unsolved cases. What he found there were stories. Statements. Photographs. Incomplete thoughts scribbled in the margins by a distracted investigator. Ambiguities don't exist in the lab. Old case files teem with them. The puzzles beckoned.

"Paul, that's not your job," more than one fellow criminalist scolded him. He didn't care. He possessed the handsome Eagle Scout's talent for remaining convivial while doing exactly what he wanted. What he wanted, he realized, was to be an investigator. He was angling to make the move to that division when the chance arose.

Despite their age difference, Murdock and Holes recognized that they had something in common: they excelled at science, but it was stories that pulled them in. Every day after he finished his lab work, Holes would sit down with old case files, appalled and fascinated by the dark off-roads of human behavior. Cold cases stayed with him. He had the scientist's intolerance for uncertainty. After devouring boxes of old unsolved cases, he noticed a pattern; the same person always signed the most meticulous crime-scene reports: John Murdock.

"I saw EAR marked in big red letters on some folders set aside in a filing cabinet," Holes explained to Murdock. Holes hadn't delved into the files yet, but he could tell that they had been set aside in a special, almost hallowed way.

"EAR stands for East Area Rapist," Murdock said. The name was clearly cataloged in his head, its significance not dimmed by time.

"I don't know that one," Holes said.

For the rest of the flight, thirty thousand feet up in the air, Murdock told Holes the story.

He was a hot prowler. He barely registered with the cops at first. In mid-June 1976, he appeared in a young woman's bedroom in east Sacramento doing "the no-pants dance," wearing a T-shirt and nothing else. Knife in hand. Whispered threats. Ransacking. He raped her. It was rough, but Sacramento in 1976 had an abundance of predatory creeps. Ski mask and gloves suggested some intelligence, but no-pants dancers are usually rum-dum teenagers whose mothers turn them in by the scruff of the neck.

That never happened. More rapes did. Twenty-two in eleven months. His methods were distinct and unwavering. An initial just-a-robber ruse to secure compliance. Females as gagged objects, moved to his specifications. Their hands and feet tied and retied, often with shoelaces. Sexual assault that curiously avoided breasts and kissing. Ransacking as stimulation. Gleefully raising the stakes as east Sacramento entered full-blown panic. Taking on sleeping couples. Stacking dishes on the bound man's back, threatening to kill his wife or girlfriend if he heard the dishes fall. The East Area Rapist was the bogeyman in the bedroom, the stranger who knew too much—layouts of homes, number of children, work schedules. The ski mask and raspy, faked voice suggested an alter ego, but from whom was he altering?

The Sacramento County Sheriff's Department hit walls. Hit walls hard. The same young white males were stopped repeatedly. The right one wasn't. Or maybe he was. That was the problem. All EAR Task Force investigators had their own mental impression of the suspect's face, but none were the same. He was a blond stoner in an army jacket. A Mormon on a bike. A slick, olive-skinned Realtor.

Carol Daly was the lead female investigator on the task force. By the twenty-second rape, after another three a.m. trip to the hospital with a distraught victim, she surprised herself with a dark thought. *I love my husband. I hate men.*

What kept investigator Richard Shelby up at night were the repeated credible reports called in of a suspicious prowler who, once spotted, walked away "at a leisurely pace."

The creep of a bitch was an ambler.

The community began to glimpse fear in the sheriff's deputies' eyes. The EAR was stalking their heads. All their heads. Sundown produced collective dread. It seemed impossible that he'd never be caught. The law of chance would get him eventually, but who wanted to be the schmuck waiting around for that?

Then, as mysteriously as he'd appeared in east Sacramento, he was gone, after a two-year reign of terror, from 1976 to 1978.

"Wow," said Holes. "What happened then?"

Murdock remembered that Holes was a ten-year-old at the time, unaware of the mass paralysis the case caused, its twists, false hopes, and dead ends. His connection to the case came only from spotting files labeled EAR in red.

"He resurfaced in the East Bay," Murdock said. "He came to us."

Holes began asking older friends and colleagues about the EAR and was surprised at how pervasive the case had been. Everyone had a story. His undersheriff remembered the helicopters whirling overhead, the roving spotlights darting through the quiet subdivisions. A UC-Davis professor said his first date with his wife had been taking part in one of the nightly rape patrols. One of his co-workers quietly confided in Holes that his sister was one of the victims.

Between October 1978 and July 1979, after which he vanished from Northern California, there were eleven EAR cases in the greater East Bay area, including two in San Jose and one in Fremont. Trying to make headway twenty years later was daunting. Local police departments handled some of the cases. All of the agencies, including Sacramento County, had destroyed their evidence. It was routine Property Room procedure. The cases were past the statute of limitations. Fortunately CCCSO (Contra Costa County Sheriff's Office), where Holes worked, had kept its evidence. The set-aside red EAR files weren't a fluke; demoralized CCCSO deputies back in the day assured that it would stay that way. It was the opposite of hanging a police commendation plaque. The EAR was their failure. If the human brain was, as experts allege, the best computer in the world, the old guard wanted their conspicuous EAR files to lure one of those young, inquiring computers in, fast and deep. Sometimes the tough cases were just a relay race.

"We always catch the dumb ones," cops like to say. They could tick off ninety-nine out of a hundred boxes with these kinds of arrests. That one unchecked box though. It could vex you into early death.

IN JULY 1997, HOLES BEGAN PULLING THE EAR RAPE KITS FROM Property and seeing what evidence might be coaxed from them. The CCCSO crime lab wasn't as advanced as other California labs. Their DNA program was relatively new. Still, it looked as though three kits would yield material for a rudimentary profile. Holes figured that, even though the EAR's m.o. was distinctive and there was little doubt the Northern California attacks were connected, if he could conclude with scientific certainty that one man was responsible for CCCSO's three EAR-suspected cases, that could resurrect the investigation. They could dig up old suspects and swab them.

The DNA-amplification process took a while, but when the results developed, they confirmed the match. The same man, as predicted, was responsible for the three Contra Costa County cases. Holes now had a basic DNA profile of the EAR that would grow more advanced when the lab acquired better equipment. He began delving into the case files themselves, something he'd put aside while he concentrated on the science. He picked up on the EAR's patterns. Choosing neighborhoods to prowl for information gathering. Phoning victims. Tactically preparing.

Holes compiled a list of old suspect names and then tracked down retired detective Larry Crompton. Crompton had been a member of the CCCSO's EAR Task Force at the height of the series. Holes could tell from the number of times Crompton's name appeared in the reports that he was the de facto leader. He'd either been a worker bee or taken the cases to heart.

Calling up retired detectives about an old case is a mixed bag.

Some are flattered. A lot are mildly annoyed. They're in line at the pharmacy waiting for their heart medication. They're installing garboard drain plugs on their fishing boats. Your polite enthusiasm represents lost minutes of their day.

Crompton answered Holes's call as if he'd just been talking about the EAR that moment, had possibly been talking about the EAR for years, and this unexpected, welcome call was a natural continuation of an ongoing conversation in the Crompton household.

Crompton was born in Nova Scotia and looks like the kind of tall, lean, honest-faced rancher John Wayne would have trusted in one of his Westerns. He's got a slightly odd, breathless way of speaking; never hesitant, just brief, confident declarations that could use a little more air.

Holes wanted to know if Crompton remembered any old suspects who stood out and should be reexamined. He did, and unenthusiastically fed Holes some names. Crompton's real wish, it turned out, was for Holes to follow up on an old hunch of his that the bosses had prevented him from pursuing at the time.

Jurisdictional cooperation is spotty at best now but was downright dismal back in the late 1970s. Police Teletype and the gossip mill were the only ways cops heard about cases in other agencies. The EAR disappeared from the East Bay in the summer of 1979. Crompton's bosses nearly danced with relief. Crompton was panicked. He could tell the guy was escalating, that he was requiring more terror in his victims' eyes to get off; his threats about killing his victims, previously stilted in manner, were more severe but also looser, like someone shedding his inhibitions. Crompton worried. Inhibition shedding was not what the EAR needed.

In early 1980, Crompton got a call from Jim Bevins, a Sacramento Sheriff's investigator he'd become close to through their work on the EAR Task Force. Bevins was trying to step away from the case. Its hold over him broke up his marriage. But he wanted to tell Crompton that he was hearing rumors that Santa Barbara had a couple of cases, one a homicide, that felt like the EAR. Crompton called down there.

They stonewalled. "Nothing like that here," he was told.

Several months later at a statewide training conference, Crompton was seated by chance next to a Santa Barbara County Sheriff's investigator. Small talk ensued. Crompton played dumb. Pretended he wanted to talk shop.

"What about that double homicide not too long ago?" he asked.

He never let his face reveal the chill he felt as he listened to the details.

"I'm telling you, Paul," Crompton said. "Call down south. Start with Santa Barbara. I heard there was something like five bodies down there."

"I will," Holes promised.

"I *know* it's him," Crompton said, and hung up.

TWENTY YEARS LATER, HOLES CALLED SANTA BARBARA AND GOT shut down too. The Sheriff's Department denied having any cases that resembled what he was talking about. But near the end of the conversation, the detective on the other end either recalled something or had a change of heart about obfuscating.

"Try Irvine," he said. "They have something like that, I think."

Holes's call to Irvine led him to the Orange County Sheriff's Department, which put him in touch with criminalist Mary Hong at the crime lab. Holes explained that he'd recently developed a DNA profile for an unidentified white male known as the East Area Rapist, or EAR, who'd committed fifty sexual assaults in Northern California from 1976 to 1979. EAR investigators always suspected he'd headed south and committed more crimes there. Holes rattled off a quick description of his m.o. Middle- to upper-middle-class single-story homes. Nighttime home invasions. Sleeping couples. Binding. Female raped. Occasional theft, mostly personalized jewelry that meant something to victim over more valuable items. Ski mask made physical identification difficult but evidence indicated a size 9 shoe, blood type A, nonsecretor.

"Sounds a lot like our cases," Hong said.

At the time Holes and Hong talked, their labs were using different DNA-typing techniques, OC being an early adopter of STR typing. They could compare one gene, DQA1, which matched, but that's all they had to compare. The Contra Costa lab also wasn't CODIS-eligible yet, meaning they couldn't link into the state or national databases. Hong and Holes agreed to keep in touch and update each other when the Contra Costa lab was up and running.

GOVERNMENT-FUNDED CRIME LABS EXPERIENCE ALL THE USUAL economic vagaries one would expect. Elected officials know it's not popular to reduce the police force, so job cuts often fall on less conspicuous positions, like forensic scientists. Lab equipment isn't cheap, and lab directors often have to make repeated requests to get what they need.

Which in part explains why the Contra Costa lab, historically lean, needed about a year and a half to catch up with Orange County. In January 2001, when Contra Costa got its STR typing up and running, Holes asked one of his colleagues, Dave Stockwell, to rerun the DNA extracts from the EAR case to see if the three cases still had the same offender profile. Stockwell reported back they did.

"Call Mary Hong in Orange County," Holes told him. "We've got the same technology now. Check it against hers."

Over the phone, Stockwell and Hong read off the markers to each other.

"Yes," Hong said when Stockwell read one of the EAR markers.

"Yes," Stockwell said in reply to one of hers.

Stockwell came into Holes's office.

"Perfect match."

The news hit the media on April 4, 2001. DNA Links '70s Rapes to Serial Slaying Cases read the *San Francisco Chronicle* headline. No one had warned the surviving rape victims that the story was coming out, so many of them got a shock picking up the morning paper at the breakfast table. There it was on the front page of the *Sacramento Bee*: New Lead Found in Serial Rapes: After Decades, DNA Links the East Area Rapist to Crimes in Orange County.

Even more unreal for many of them was the sight of the detectives on the front page of the *Bee*. Richard Shelby and Jim Bevins. Shelby, tall, gruff, coarse, the guy with the impeccable memory and miserable social skills whom fellow officers tried to keep from interacting with people. And Jim Bevins—Puddin' Eyes, his cop buddies called him teasingly. No one was liked more than Bevins. Even when he was striding toward you from fifty yards away, you could see that he was the guy sent to deescalate and make everything right.

And here they were on the front page, old men now. Twenty-five years is a long time in cop years. The high mileage showed. Their expressions hinted at something. Sheepishness? Shame? They speculated on what their nemesis was doing now. Shelby voted loony bin. Bevins guessed dead.

Holes fielded reporters' calls and enjoyed the excitement for a few days. But even though privately he still felt investigative work was his calling, he'd been promoted to criminalist supervisor.

Commitments beckoned. He was married with two young kids. He didn't have the time to dedicate himself to the ten thousand pages of case files that the new DNA connection unified. It was an unheard-of amount of evidence. Optimism among those who worked the case ran sky high. DNA profile? Sixty cases spanning the state of California? They fought over who would interrogate him first when they got him in the room.

Larry Pool in Orange County was the designated point man. For Pool the news of the DNA connection was great but daunting, as if he'd spent the last couple of years in a small, familiar room only to discover that it was an annex to a warehouse.

He continued to bat away contempt from hardened cops who kept insisting that the monster was dead. Sexually motivated serial killers don't stop killing unless they're stopped; maybe some righteous homeowner shot him dead during a burglary. Don't waste your time, they said.

Seven months later, Pool would be vindicated by some news from the Pacific Northwest. In November 2001, the media's attention turned to another unidentified serial killer who'd been dormant for nearly two decades and presumed by some to be long dead: Washington's Green River Killer. As it turned out, this prolific slayer of prostitutes was very much alive and well and living in suburban Seattle. His reason for slowing down? He'd gotten married.

"Technology got me," Gary Ridgway told cops, the verbal equivalent of an upturned middle finger. He was right. He fooled the cops for years by slackening his face and dimming the light in his eyes. No way this half-wit is a diabolical serial killer, they thought, and always, despite mounting evidence, they let him go.

On April 6, 2001, two days after the news linking the East Area Rapist and the Original Night Stalker hit the media, the phone rang in a house on Thornwood Drive in east Sacramento.

A woman in her early sixties answered. She'd lived in the house for nearly thirty years, though her last name had changed.

"Hello?"

The voice was low. He spoke slowly. She recognized it immediately.

"Remember when we played?"

PART TWO

SACRAMENTO, 2012

[EDITOR'S NOTE: The following section is an excerpt from an early draft of Michelle's article "In the Footsteps of a Killer."]

THE WOMAN WHO SAT ACROSS FROM ME IN THE CRAMPED OFFICE at a troubled high school in east Sacramento was a stranger. But you wouldn't have known that from the conversational shorthand we used with each other from the moment we met, the EAR-ONS version of Klingon.

"Dog beating burglary in '74?" I asked.

The woman, I'll call her the Social Worker, retied her thick ponytail and took a sip from a can of Rockstar. She's "almost sixty," with large, penetrating green eyes and a smoky voice. She greeted me in the parking lot by waving her arms wildly overhead. I liked her right away.

"I don't believe it's related," she said.

The '74 burglary in Rancho Cordova is the kind of recently un-covered incident members of "the board," that is A&E's *Cold Case Files* message board on EAR-ONS, of which the Social Worker is one of the de facto leaders, thrive on analyzing. I've come to ap-preciate their thoroughness about the case, but at first I was simply daunted. There are over one thousand topics and twenty thousand posts.

I found my way to the board about a year and a half ago after devouring, practically in one sitting, Larry Crompton's book *Sudden Terror*, which is an unvarnished avalanche of case details, full of 1970s political incorrectness and strangely moving in its depiction of one matter-of-fact cop's haunting regret. The abundance of information available on the case astounded me. More than a dozen books are dedicated to December 25, 1996, the night Jon-Benet Ramsey was murdered. But EAR-ONS? Here was a case that spanned a decade, an entire state, changed DNA law in California[†], included sixty victims, a collection of strange utterances from the suspect at crime scenes ("I'll kill you like I did some people in Bakersfield"), a poem he allegedly wrote ("Excitement's Crave"), even his voice on tape (a brief, whispery taunt recorded by a device the police put on a victim's phone), yet there was only a single self-published, hard-to-find book written about it.

When I logged on to the EAR-ONS board for the first time, I was immediately struck by the capable, exhaustive crowdsourcing being done there. Yes, cranks exist, including one well-meaning guy who insists that Ted Kaczynski, the Unabomber, is EAR-ONS (he's not). But much of the analysis is first-rate. A frequent poster named PortofLeith, for instance, helped uncover the fact that California State University–Sacramento's academic calendar from the years the EAR was active there correlates with his crimes. There are member-made maps detailing everything from crime-scene locations to witness sightings to the spot where he dropped a bloody motocross glove in Dana Point. Hundreds of posts dissect his possible connections to the military, real estate, and medicine.

The EAR-ONS sleuths have skills, and they're serious about

---

† This case inspired California Proposition 69, approved in 2004, which mandated DNA collection from all felons, and from adults and juveniles charged with certain crimes (e.g., sex offenses, murder, arson). Keith Harrington's brother Bruce sponsored the campaign, pledging nearly $2 million to fund it.

using those skills to catch him. I met with a computer-science graduate student at a Los Angeles Starbucks to discuss his person of interest. Before we met, I received a seven-page dossier, which included footnotes, maps, and yearbook photos of the suspect. I agreed that the suspect looked promising. One unknown detail that niggled at the grad student was his suspect's shoe size (at 9 or 9½, the EAR's shoe size is slightly smaller than the average man's).

Message board members tend to be a paranoid bunch, pseudonym heavy, and perhaps unsurprisingly for people who spend a great deal of time on the Internet discussing serial murder, there are personality conflicts. The Social Worker operates as a kind of gatekeeper between Sacramento investigators and the board community. This irks some posters, who accuse her of hinting at confidential information but then shutting down when asked to share.

That she occasionally has new information to share is not in dispute. On July 2, 2011, the Social Worker posted a drawing of a decal that she said was seen on a suspicious vehicle near the scene of one of the Sacramento rapes.

"It is possibly from NAS [Naval Air Station] North Island, but unconfirmed and has no record. Is it familiar to anyone on the board? Hoping we may find where it is from."

We. The curious but unmistakable presence of law enforcement became apparent the more I got sucked into the board. The Web detectives, drawn to a decades-old cold case for their own private, idiosyncratic reasons, were the ones hunting the killer with their laptops, but the investigators were subtly steering them.

The Social Worker took me on a driving tour of EAR hot spots, around the maze of modest ranch houses abutting the old Mather Air Force Base, through the larger, leafier neighborhoods of Arden-Arcade and Del Dayo. She began working informally with Sacramento investigators about five years ago, she told me.

"I lived here through the height of it," she said. She was a young mom then and remembers the terror reaching a nearly debilitating peak around rape number fifteen.

The east Sacramento neighborhoods EAR-ONS preyed on were not built for excitement. I counted an entire block of unbroken beige. The tamped-down cautiousness belies the terrible things that happened here. We turned onto Malaga Way, where on August 29, 1976, the clanging of her wind chimes and the strong smell of aftershave awakened a twelve-year-old girl. A masked man stood at her bedroom window, prying at the upper left corner of the screen with a knife.

"It's a really dark place, thinking about this stuff," the Social Worker said. So why did she?

She'd been channel surfing one night in bed years ago when she came across the tail end of a *Cold Case Files* episode. She sat up in horrified recognition. *Oh my God*, she thought, *he became a murderer*.

An uneasy memory from that period nagged her, and she reached out to a detective with the Sacramento Police Department to see whether it was all in her mind. It wasn't. He confirmed that, before the EAR's penchant for phoning victims had ever been publicized, she had filed three police reports about an obscene caller, a stalker who, she said, "knew everything about me." She now believes the caller was EAR-ONS.

The American River flashed blue in the distance. She feels "spiritually" called, the Social Worker told me, to help solve the case.

"But I've learned you've got to watch out, to take care of yourself. Or it can consume you."

Can? We'd spent the last four hours talking of nothing else but EAR-ONS. When her husband senses where she's headed at dinner parties, he kicks her under the table and whispers, "Don't start." I once spent an afternoon tracking down every detail I could about a member of the 1972 Rio Americano High School water polo team because in the yearbook photo he appeared lean and to have big calves (at one point a purported EAR-ONS trait). She once dined with a suspect and then bagged his water bottle for DNA. In the police files, suspects' names are often logged last name first, and at my lowest, most dazed point, I actually began looking into one "Lary Burg" before my eyes and brain realigned to recognize *Burglary.*

There's a scream permanently lodged in my throat now. When my husband, trying not to awaken me, tiptoed into our bedroom one night, I leaped out of bed, grabbed my nightstand lamp, and swung it at his head. Luckily, I missed. When I saw the lamp overturned on the bedroom floor in the morning, I remembered what I'd done and winced. Then I felt around the covers for where I'd left my laptop and resumed my Talmudic study of the police reports.

However, I didn't laugh at the Social Worker's gentle warning about not becoming obsessed. I nodded. We're skirting a rabbit hole, I agreed to pretend, rather than deep inside it.

Joining us inside the rabbit hole is a thirty-year-old man from South Florida whom I'll call the Kid. The Kid has a film degree and, he's hinted, a somewhat troubled relationship with his family. Details matter to the Kid. He recently stopped watching a cable broadcast of *Dirty Harry* because "it blew up from [an aspect ratio of] 2.35:1 to 1.78:1 after the opening credits." He's smart, meticulous, and occasionally brusque. He's also, in my opinion, the case's greatest amateur hope.

Most people familiar with the EAR-ONS case agree that one of the best leads is his geographic trail. There are only so many white men born between let's say 1943 and 1959 who lived or worked in Sacramento, Santa Barbara County, and Orange County between 1976 and 1986.

But only the Kid has spent nearly four thousand hours data

mining the possibilities, cold-searching everything from Ancestry
.com to USSearch.com. He owns, courtesy of eBay, a copy of
the R. L. Polk 1977 Sacramento Suburban Directory. He has the
1983 Orange County telephone directory digitized on his hard
drive.

My first inkling that the Kid's work was high quality came at
the beginning of my interest in the case when, after noting from
his posts on the board that he seemed knowledgeable, I e-mailed
him about a possible suspect I'd uncovered. I've now come to
realize that getting excited about a suspect is a lot like that first
surge of stupid love in a relationship, in which, despite vague
alarm bells, you plow forward convinced that he is the One.

I all but had my suspect in handcuffs. But the Kid was about
a year of researching and several databases ahead of me. "Haven't
done anything with that name in a while," he wrote back. Included in the e-mail was the image of a dour nerd in a sweater
vest, my suspect's sophomore year picture. "Not in my top tier,"
wrote the Kid.

He later underscored how tricky suspect assessment is by
pointing out that just based on geographic history and physical
description a good EAR-ONS suspect would be Tom Hanks.
(Who, it should be emphasized, can be eliminated by the shooting schedule of *Bosom Buddies* alone).

I was vacationing last spring in Florida with my family and
made arrangements to meet the Kid in person at a coffee shop.
He's attractive, clean-cut with sandy brown hair, and articulate,
an altogether unlikely candidate for compulsive data miner of
cold cases he has no connection to. He declined coffee but chain-
smoked Camel Lights. We talked for a bit about California and
the movie business; he told me he once traveled to Los Angeles
just to see the director's cut of his favorite film, Wim Wenders's
Until the End of the World.

Mostly we discussed our common obsession. The case is so

complex and difficult to distill to people that I always find it something of a relief to be in the presence of someone who knows the shorthand. We both seemed a little mystified and self-conscious about our preoccupation. At a wedding reception recently, the groom interrupted a conversation between his mother and the Kid, who is an old friend. "Tell her about your serial killer!" the groom suggested to the Kid before moving on.

What I always think about, I told him, are experiments that show that animals in captivity would rather have to search for their food than have it given to them. Seeking is the lever that tips our dopamine gush. What I don't mention is the uneasy realization I've had about how much our frenetic searching mirrors the compulsive behavior—the trampled flowerbeds, scratch marks on window screens, crank calls—of the one we seek.

Something Jeff Klapakis, a detective with the Santa Barbara County Sheriff's Department, said offhand finally made me feel less strange about my fascination. We were sitting in his and his partner's EAR-ONS "war room," a back office teeming with plastic bins stacked with old file folders. Over his right shoulder hung a poster-size Google Earth map of Goleta with the sites of the double homicides marked, nineteen months between them but only 0.6 miles apart. The San Jose Creek curved down the middle of the map, its massive, draping trees providing EAR-ONS with cover.

I asked Klapakis what made him come out of retirement to work on the case. He shrugged.

"I love puzzles," he said.

The Kid was getting at the same thing when he wrote a brief explanation for any investigators who might come across his research. His interest, he wrote using the third person, is "inexplicable in short form, except to say that it's a big question with a simple answer, and he's compelled to know the answer."

The Kid eventually shared with me his pièce de résistance,

which he calls "The Master List," a 118-page document with some two thousand men's names and their information, including dates of birth, address histories, criminal records, and even photos when available. His thoroughness—it has an index—left me agape. There are notations under some men's names ("dedicated cycling advocate" and "Relative: Bonnie") that seem nonsensical unless you know, as we do, far too much about a possibly dead serial killer who was last active when Reagan was president.

"At some point, I'll have to walk away from all this and move on with my life," the Kid wrote me in an e-mail. "The irony has been that, the more time and money I invest into this very impractical (and to most, inexplicable) endeavor, the more apt I am to continue doing so, so that I may perhaps identify this fucker and thus justify my investment."

Not everyone admires the board sleuths or their efforts. One agitator came on recently to rant about what he characterized as wannabe cops with a twisted, pathetic obsession. He accused them of being untrained meddlers with an unhealthy interest in rape and murder.

"WALTER MITTY DETECTIVE," he wrote.

By then I was convinced one of the Mittys was probably going to solve this thing.

EAST SACRAMENTO, 2012

THE THINGS THEY SEE: HEADLIGHTS IN AN EMPTY FIELD BEHIND their house where a car shouldn't be. A man in a white shirt and dark pants climbing through a hole in a neighbor's fence at three a.m. Jimmied doors. A flashlight beam in their bedroom window. A man emerging from a drainage ditch and sneaking into the backyard next door. Gates previously closed now open. A dark-haired man in a blue leisure suit standing under a tree across the street, staring at them. Mysterious footprints in the yard. A man bursting forth from the bushes and hopping on a bicycle. More flashlights in bedroom windows. The lower half of a man dressed in brown corduroys and tennis shoes running alongside the house and hiding behind a planter. A census worker at the front door wanting to know how many people live in the house in a year the census isn't being taken. Their neighbor, a thirty-four-year-old man stumbling out of his house in his underwear, arms and legs bound, screaming for help at two in the morning.

The things they hear: Dogs barking. Heavy footsteps on the lava rock path. Someone cutting through the window screen. A thump against the air conditioner. Tampering with the sliding glass door. Scratching at the side of the house. A call for help. A scuffle. Gunshots. A woman's long scream.

No one calls the police.

The police canvasses net these after-the-fact observations. Occasionally, when the police stop by neighbors' homes to ask questions, they're shown a slashed screen or vandalized porch light. Reading through the police reports, I found the neighbors' inaction peculiar at first. Eventually I became borderline obsessed. Some of the unreported suspicious behavior occurred at the height of the East Area Rapist panic in Sacramento.

"He was prowling these neighborhoods constantly. Why didn't more people call in?" I asked Richard Shelby. At first glance, Shelby is rough-looking, as a retired cop in his midseventies living out in the sticks of Placer County might be. ("We live so far out in the country we keep our gas in jerricans," he told me). He's tall and wary. He's got a W. C. Fields nose and, of course, he's missing half of his left ring finger, that injury that almost kept him off the force. But there's a softness there, in his light blue shirt, in his extremely soft voice I could barely hear, and in the way, when the waitress at lunch told him they were out of lemonade, he didn't scowl but smiled, softly, and murmured, "Iced tea, then." Shelby, who had what he admits was a rocky career with the Sacramento Sheriff's Department, came on the case early, in fall 1976, and was among the first to make the connection that they had a serial rapist on their hands.

"Call in what?" Shelby asked. "It's night. He's dressed all in black. Creeping along the hedges. What's to see?"

"I mean what came out during the police canvasses. What the neighbors full-on admitted they saw and heard," I said.

A line jotted down during a police canvass of the area around Malaga Road and El Caprice in Rancho Cordova on September 1, 1976, after the third rape, particularly haunted me. "Several of the neighbors stated they heard the screaming, but did not look outside."

In January 1977, a man who lived just south of the American River and whose home had recently been burglarized glimpsed a young guy peeping into his next-door neighbor's window. He coughed to let the peeper know he'd been spotted; the stranger ran. The gesture seemed almost polite. A week later a twenty-five-year-old woman living one block north became victim eleven. She was five months pregnant at the time.

Maybe the reluctance to call police was emblematic of the seventies, I suggested to Shelby. I started in on something about post-Vietnam rootlessness, but Shelby shook his head. He didn't have an answer, but that wasn't it. For him, the neighbors' passivity was just one failure in a case plagued with them, from superiors preoccupied with bullshit politics to a couple of crucial wrong turns Shelby admits he made in his own patrol car to a dispatcher's instruction to a family calling about a cloth bag they'd found hidden in their hedges that contained a flashlight, ski mask, and gloves: "Throw it away."

Shelby lives about thirty miles north of Sacramento now, in the country, where he can do, as he put it, "manly farmer things." But we'd met for lunch in his old stomping grounds, in the neighborhood where thirty-six years ago he patrolled the twisty streets buffeting the river, his dashboard lights dimmed, directed only by radio sputter and the hope that he'd make the right turn and his headlight beams would land on a young man about five nine in a ski mask. Shelby never encountered another offender like the East Area Rapist in his career. Up on rooftops, they kept finding small items he'd stolen from victims. For some reason, he was tossing them up there. Then, after enough people called in about strange thumps on their roofs, Shelby realized that the stolen items weren't being tossed but were falling out of his pocket; he was crawling around up there.

Shelby's one of those proudly blunt people whose eyes flick away the moment before they say something hard, a giveaway to softness churning underneath. He'd picked the lunch spot, but I could tell that for him this neighborhood would always be the place where he was thwarted by the stutter steps of an opponent, "that sociopathic bastard," whose voyeur's lair, indicated by a heap of cigarette butts and zigzag shoe tracks, he once found under a dense tree off Northwood Drive. Another vague presence noted by neighbors but never called in.

"People say he was so smart," Shelby said. His eyes flicked away. "Truth is, he didn't always need to be."

EARLY IN MY REPORTING FOR AN EAR-ONS STORY I HAD PITCHED to *Los Angeles* magazine, while in Sacramento, I came into possession of a flash drive containing over four thousand pages of digitized old police reports. I acquired the flash drive in an old-fashioned trade, the kind in which neither party really trusts the other and so, arms extended and eyes locked, we agree to simultaneously release our goods for the other to grab. I had in my possession a rarely seen disc of a two-hour videotaped interview with a peripheral but important person connected to one of the Southern California homicides. I gave it away without a second thought; I had a copy at home.

These underground trades, the result of furtive alliances forged from a shared obsession with a faceless serial killer, were common. Online sleuthers, retired detectives, and active detectives—everyone participated. I received more than one e-mail with the subject line "quid pro quo." I believed, as they did, that I and I alone was going to spot what no else could see. In order to do that, I needed to see everything.

The grandiose seeker in me couldn't wait to insert the flash drive into my laptop back at my hotel. At every stoplight, I touched the top pocket in my backpack to make sure the tiny rectangle was still there. I was staying at the Citizen Hotel on J Street downtown. The photos online, of lead-paned windows and mustard-colored striped wallpaper, had appealed to me. The check-in area had built-in bookshelves for walls. The front desk was ornate and painted Chinese red.

"How would you describe the style here?" I asked the front-desk clerk when I was checking in.

"Law library meets bordello," he said.

I later learned that the building's architect, George Sellon, had also designed San Quentin.

Once in my room, I immediately changed into the crisp white hotel bathrobe. I lowered the shades and turned off my phone. I dumped a bag of minibar gummy bears into a glass and set it next to me on the bed, where I sat cross-legged in front of my laptop. Ahead of me was a rare twenty-four-hour stretch without interference or distraction—no tiny hands slick with paint asking to be washed, no preoccupied hungry husband appearing in the kitchen to inquire about dinner. I inserted the flash drive. My mind in mail-sorter mode, my index finger on the down arrow key, I began to not so much read as devour.

Police reports read like stories told by robots. They're terse and demarcated, with little space for judgment or emotion. Initially the sparseness appealed to me. Scrubbed of extraneous detail, I felt sure his name would gleam. I misjudged. The concise format of the reports is deceiving. Absorbed cumulatively, even the most clipped details began to swarm into an indistinguishable mass. Some moments separated from the pack, imparting jolts of powerful feeling I didn't always see coming—the recently separated thirty-eight-year-old mother who scoots across the floor in the dark to find her son's toy saw and tries in vain to use it to cut the bindings from her swollen hands; the thirteen-year-old girl tied up in bed who asks her beloved dog after the rapist has left the room, "You dummy, why didn't you do anything?" The dog nudges her with his nose. She tells him to lie down and go to sleep. He does.

Hours vanished. The gummy bears were gone. My room was on the tenth floor, right above a tent hosting a wedding reception. I'd sidestepped the bridesmaids in sea-foam green posing for pictures in the hallway on my way in, and now the music started up. It was loud. I picked up the phone to call the front desk. What was I going to say? "Keep the joy down"? I hung up. The truth was, I was jittery from sugar, hunger, and spending too much time alone in the dark absorbing a fifty-chapter horror story narrated in the kind of dead voice used by desk clerks at the DMV. My eyes were stripped by computer glare and as devoid of moisture as if they'd been vacuumed clean by an airplane toilet. Kool and the Gang's "Celebration" wasn't the soundtrack for my frame of mind.

The city of Sacramento is located at the north end of California's Central Valley, at the confluence of the Sacramento River and the American River, and was designed with drainage in mind. The idea is that excess water, from mountain runoff or rainfall, will flow downriver toward the California Delta and into the ocean. I know this only because drainage ditches and cement-lined canals come up frequently in the police reports. It's clear from the start, from footprints, evidence, suspicious sightings, and even bringing one victim down there, that the East Area Rapist traveled this way, that like a subterranean creature, he bided his time belowground until dark. I was reminded of an iconic scene from *The Creature from the Black Lagoon*, when the marine biologist Kay, played by the beautiful actress Julie Adams, dives from the expedition ship into the black lagoon, and from an underwater point of view we watch as the terrifying humanoid Creature emerges from a tangle of seaweed to glide underneath her, mirroring her, mesmerized. You keep waiting for her to see him and thrash with panic, but he goes undetected, except for the moment when he brushes a scaly webbed claw against her foot and she jerks a little, unnerved.

The East Area Rapist stalked individuals, but it was clear after reading the police reports that he stalked neighborhoods too, often by traversing Sacramento's underground maze of canals and drainage ditches. He preferred single-story houses, usually second from the corner, near a greenbelt area—an open field, a park. Before an attack, there'd be evidence of prowling and illegal entries in the homes around the victim's. Small, inexpensive, sometimes personal items would go missing. Incidents of hang-up phone calls rose sharply in the four- or five-block radius just before an attack. He was doing reconnaissance. He was studying people, learning when they were home. His method appeared to be to pick a neighborhood, target a half-dozen possible victims, and maybe even prioritize them. He maximized options and laid groundwork; that way, when mission night arrived, his urge never went unfulfilled.

That means that women exist who, because of change of schedule, or luck, were never victims, but like the Creature's shapely object of obsession treading in the lagoon, they felt something terrifying brush against them.

The neighbors, in the scant five or six lines allotted them in the canvass reports, offer evocative haikus of a certain time and place. When questioned, they're on their way back from the disco club, or a double feature of *Earthquake* and *Airport '77* at the drive-in, or the Jack LaLanne gym. They report missing two size 5 women's jackets, one brown suede, the other leather. A girl saw a suspicious man with a "Wolfman Jack" look. Door-to-door solicitors— sprinklers, Fuller Brush, personal photography, painters—were a near-constant presence back then. In one neighborhood, everyone seemed to be heading for work at five a.m. These people took special notice of newer model, "shiny" cars. In other neighborhoods, mostly north of the American River, the only person home to answer the officer's questions might be the live-in babysitter. These neighbors were suspicious of "dirty" cars, cars with side dents that were "a heap" or "in bad shape."

In April 1977, a boy hoisted his younger sister onto his shoulders. From her higher vantage point, she suddenly saw a prowler in her neighbor's yard, a white man in dark clothing crouching in the bushes. When the prowler realized he'd been spotted, he took off running and hurdled several fences. A month later, that neighbor, a young waitress, woke her husband at four a.m. "I hear something. I hear something," she said. A flashlight lit up their bedroom doorway. She later told police that she believed the EAR when he threatened to kill her, and she lay there, bound in the dark, wondering what it would feel like to have a bullet go through her.

————

READING THROUGH THE SACRAMENTO REPORTS, YOU CAN TRACK public awareness that there's a serial rapist at large. It's zero to dim in the first dozen or so attacks; then the media runs with the story, and chatter and paranoia build. By a year into the attacks, victims recount being awakened by flashlight and thinking, *Oh shit! It's him.* They behaved in certain ways, they told investigators, based on gossip they'd heard about the East Area Rapist, cowering, for instance, because they'd been told he liked his victims terrified. It's around a year in that the source of neighbors' inaction is no longer unawareness or inertia but a fortress mentality. They see something, and they lock their doors, turn off the lights, and retreat to their bedroom, hoping he doesn't come for them. "I was afraid," one woman admitted. Then why not call the police? My imagination burbled with what-ifs.

They weren't thinking of their neighbors, but he was. Part of the thrill of the game for him, I believe, was a kind of connect-the-dots puzzle he played with people. He stole two packs of Winston cigarettes from the first victim, for instance, and left them outside the fourth victim's house. Junk jewelry stolen from a neighbor two weeks earlier was left at the fifth victim's house. Victim twenty-one lived within shouting distance of a water treatment plant; a worker there who lived eight miles away became the next victim. Pills or bullets stolen from a victim would later be found in a neighbor's yard. Some victims shared surnames or jobs.

It was a power play, a signal of ubiquity. I am both nowhere and everywhere. You may not think you have something in common with your neighbor, but you do: me. I'm the barely spotted presence, the dark-haired, blond-haired, stocky, slight, seen from the back, glimpsed in half-light thread that will continue to connect you even as you fail to look out for each other.

I left Sacramento in a bad mood. I hadn't slept well. The hungover wedding party crowded the front door of the hotel as I tried to make my way out. At the airport, I walked past a giant red rabbit sculpture I somehow had been too preoccupied to notice when I flew in. I don't know how I missed it before. The fifty-six-foot-long, ten-thousand-pound aluminum rabbit is suspended by cables and appears to be diving toward the baggage claim area. I searched the term "Sac airport rabbit" on my iPhone while waiting to board my plane. An Associated Press article said that artist Lawrence Argent had been commissioned to create an iconic piece for the new terminal, which was unveiled in October 2011.

"I wanted to play around with the idea that something has come from the outside and leapt into the building," Argent said.

THE CUFF-LINKS CODA

[EDITOR'S NOTE: The following section is an excerpt from an early draft of Michelle's article "In the Footsteps of a Killer."]

THE DAY AFTER I PLACED THE ORDER FOR THE CUFF LINKS, I CALLED the Kid. I told him I was having the cuff links shipped overnight to me.

"To a P.O. box?" the Kid asked. Well no, I admitted. A ludicrous scenario flashed through my mind: EAR-ONS reselling the cuff links to the store where he happened to work inputting customer addresses; he'd no doubt be suspicious of someone who paid forty dollars for next-day delivery of his eight-dollar cuff links.

The best thing to do, I knew, was to turn over the cuff links to EAR-ONS investigators. The risk was that they'd be angry I'd taken this kind of unauthorized initiative. Coincidentally, I had recently scheduled my very first interview with Larry Pool in Orange County. I decided that if I felt the interview was going well, I'd explain the story and hand over the tiny gold cuff links in their square Ziploc bag.

The problem was, of all the investigators, the prospect of meeting with Pool was the most intimidating to me. He'd been described as inaccessible and a little remote. I knew he'd been working on the case for the last fourteen years. He'd been instrumental, along with victim Keith Harrington's attorney brother, Bruce, in the passage of Proposition 69—the DNA Fingerprint, Unsolved Crime and Innocence Protection Act, which in 2004 established an all-felon DNA database in California. The California Department of Justice now has the largest working DNA data bank in the country.

Pool and Harrington felt that by expanding the DNA database they'd surely net EAR-ONS. The disappointment when that didn't happen, it was suggested to me, was sharp. I had imagined Larry Pool as a steely, impassive cop locked away in a dimly lit room, the walls plastered with EAR-ONS composites.

A pleasant but somewhat formal man in wire-rim glasses and a red checkered shirt greeted me in the lobby of the Orange County Regional Computer Forensics Laboratory. We sat in a conference room. He was duty officer for the computer lab that day, and when the occasional colleague poked their head in and said something, Pool would respond with a clipped "Copy that."

I found him a thoughtful, measured speaker, the kind of person whose stoic exterior masks how generous they're being with their insights. When I met with Larry Crompton, it was clear that the retired detective took his failure to solve the case personally. It kept him up at night, Crompton confessed, and he always asked himself, "What did I miss?"

Pool didn't present the same sort of anguish. At first I took this as cockiness. Later I realized it was hope. He's not nearly done yet.

We were wrapping up our conversation. I pegged him as someone who prioritizes procedure and decided he wouldn't like the cuff-links story. But at the very end, I caved; I don't know why. I began speaking way too fast and rustling around in my backpack. Pool listened but his face revealed nothing. I nudged the cuff links across the conference table at him. He took the bag and examined it very carefully.

"For me?" he asked, stone-faced.

"Yes," I said.

He allowed the slightest hint of a smile.

"I think I love you," he said.

———

BY THE TIME I RETURNED HOME TO LOS ANGELES, POOL HAD tracked down the victims and sent them a high-resolution image of the cuff links by e-mail. The cuff links had originally belonged to a deceased family member, and the victims had had them in their possession only a short while before they were stolen. They *looked* like the cuff links, but the victims were cautious about merely "wanting them to be them." They got in touch with another family member who was more familiar with the jewelry. A couple of days later, Pool called me with the news: not the same cuff links.

I was disappointed; Pool seemed unfazed. "I don't get excited like I used to," he'd told me earlier. A decade ago, when the shock of the DNA match between the EAR and the ONS was still fresh, he had every investigative resource at his disposal. An Orange County Sheriff's Department helicopter once flew to Santa Barbara just to pick up a suspect's DNA swab. The suspect was under active surveillance at the time. Pool traveled to Baltimore to exhume a body. This was before 9/11, and he recalls that parts of the suspect were packed in his carry-on.

Eventually cold-case funding dried up. Investigators got reassigned. And Pool got less emotionally invested in every new development. Even the composite of EAR-ONS that hangs above Pool's desk is deliberate and matter-of-fact—it shows the suspect in a ski mask.

"Is it of any value?" Pool said. "No. But we know he looked like that."

He showed me the stack of mail he continues to get with tips from the public, including one piece of paper with a photocopy of a man's driver's license photo and the words "This is EAR ONS." (The man is far too young to be a viable suspect.)

Eight thousand suspects have been examined over the years, Pool estimates; several hundred have had their DNA run. They conducted a DNA test on one suspect in a southern state twice when they weren't satisfied with the quality of retrieval the first time. When Pool comes across an especially intriguing suspect, his curt response is always the same.

"Gotta eliminate him."

Despite his reserve, Pool has reason to be optimistic about the case; in fact, everyone who's weathered the ups and downs of the EAR-ONS mystery agrees that the pendulum is currently swinging in an upward direction.

LOS ANGELES, 2012

I WAS IN A PANIC. WE WERE HOSTING, AS WE HAD FOR YEARS, ABOUT a dozen adults and four kids under the age of ten, and the second draft of my seven-thousand-word story was due Tuesday. A few days before, I'd sent out SOS e-mails, brief and frank pleas for help that I hoped would be understood. "Dinner rolls. Butter." Thanksgiving always makes me nostalgic for the Midwest. But the day was sunny and unusually brisk, the kind of California autumn afternoon when, if you concentrate on your friend's gray cardigan and the forkful of pumpkin pie in your mouth and the snippet of NFL commentary running in the background, you can forget the bougainvillea and the wet swimsuits drying over the backyard chairs; you can imagine that you live somewhere where the seasons actually change. I wasn't myself though. Impatience roiled. I made a bigger deal than I needed to that Patton bought an undersize turkey. When we went around the table and said what we were thankful for, I forgot the holiday for a moment and shut my eyes, thinking about a wish. After dinner the kids piled together on the couch and watched *The Wizard of Oz*. I stayed out of the room. Little kids have big emotions, and mine needed reining in.

That Saturday Patton took Alice for the day, and I hunkered down in my office on the second floor to revise and write. About four o'clock in the afternoon, the front doorbell rang. We get a lot of deliveries, and I had in fact already answered the door a couple of times that day and signed for packages. I was irritated at yet another interruption. Normally I'd ignore it and let them leave the package at the door. Usually, just to be sure, I walk over to our bedroom window and peek out, and yes, there's the back of the Fed Ex deliveryman, our front gate closing behind him.

I'm not sure what made me get up this time, but I walked a few steps down our curving staircase and called out, "Who is it?" No one replied. I went to our bedroom window and peeked out. A slim, young African American kid in a pink shirt and tie was walking away from our house. I had the strong sense he was a teenager; maybe I saw him in profile for a moment. I guessed he was selling magazine subscriptions door to door, and let the drape fall. I went back to work and didn't think more about it.

About forty-five minutes later, I got up and grabbed my car keys. I'd made plans to meet Patton and Alice for an early dinner at one of our favorite restaurants in the neighborhood. I made sure the doors were locked and headed out to my car parked on the street. When I was about halfway down our walk I saw out of the corner of my eye the figure of a young man off to my left, walking very slowly with his back to me in front of my next-door neighbor's house.

I'm not sure I would have noted him if his body language hadn't been so unusual. He froze completely when I came bounding out of the house. He was a young African American kid, not the same kid who'd rung our door, but similarly dressed in a pastel blue shirt and tie. He kept his body still and craned his neck ever so slightly in my direction. I hesitated. I thought again about teenagers selling magazine subscriptions, and wondered if he was gauging me as a possible customer. But I knew it was weirder than that. His body language was so off. I got into my car and drove away, and as I did I picked up my phone to call the police. I pressed 9 and 1. But what was I going to say? Suspicious young black kid? That felt racist and like an overreaction. I canceled the call. They weren't doing anything overtly criminal. Still, I hit the brakes and yanked the wheel to the left, making a quick U-turn back to our house. It couldn't have been more than forty-five seconds, but neither kid was on the street. Dusk was making it harder to see. I figured they'd rung someone's bell, begun the magazine pitch, and been invited in. I headed to the restaurant.

The following night, I was upstairs when I heard the doorbell ring and Patton greet someone at the front door. "Michelle!" he called. I came down. Our next-door neighbor, Tony, was standing there.

Tony was the first neighbor we'd met when we'd bought our house two and a half years earlier. We hadn't moved in yet, and I was at the house with our contractor, talking about renovations, when an attractive man in his forties peeked in at the front door and introduced himself. My memory is that he was gregarious and a little self-effacing. The previous owner had been a recluse, and Tony had never seen the inside of the house. He was curious. I told him go ahead, walk around. I thought from his outgoing demeanor that we'd end up being friends, the way you imagine things when you're picturing your life in a new space. He told me he was recently divorced, and his teenage daughter was going to live with him and attend the local all-girls Catholic high school. He was renting the house next door.

But our relationship, while always friendly, never blossomed into a real friendship. We waved and made occasional small talk. When we first moved in, Patton and I talked about how we should have a get-together in our backyard and meet all the neighbors. Our intentions were good. We kept talking about it but then getting waylaid. The house was always being worked on, or one of us was traveling. But when Alice's ball flew over the fence into their yard, Tony and his daughter always graciously returned it. When I found a motherless baby pigeon on the curb in front of their house and fashioned a nest from a wicker basket and leaves and fastened it to a tree branch, Tony came out and smiled at me.

"You're a good person," he said. I liked him. But our interactions were relegated to comings and goings, to moments between dog walking and toddler wrangling.

My second-floor office faces their house; a distance of only about fifteen feet separates us. I've become accustomed to the rhythms of their lives. In the late afternoons I hear their front door slam, and Tony's daughter, who has a beautiful voice, begins to sing. I always mean to tell her what a beautiful voice she has. I always forget.

Tony was at our front door because he wanted to tell us that they'd been robbed yesterday.

"I think I know what happened," I said, and motioned for him to sit down on our living room couch. I explained the doorbell and no answer, and what I saw. He nodded; the elderly couple that lived on the other side of Tony had seen the same kids hauling bags out of Tony's house. They got in through the kitchen window and completely ransacked the place. The cops told him it's a common ruse used by teams of petty thieves on holiday weekends. Ring and see if anyone's home; if no one answers, break in.

"It's just iPads and computers," Tony said. "But I keep thinking, what if my daughter had been home alone? What might have happened then?"

At the word "daughter" his voice quavered. His eyes welled. So did mine.

"You don't have to explain," I said. "It's such a violation." I reached out and put my hand on his.

"Michelle's a crime writer," Patton said.

Tony looked surprised.

"I don't even know what you do," he said.

From now on, the three of us told each other, we'll look out for each other. We'd alert each other when we were going out of town. We'd be better neighbors, we promised.

Later that night, I kept going over the events of the last few days in my head. I thought about the intimacy of that moment in the living room, the unexpected surge of emotion we shared with Tony.

"We don't even know his last name," I said to Patton.

I HAVE A NIGHTLY RITUAL WITH ALICE, WHO IS A TROUBLED SLEEPER and has terrifying dreams. Every night before falling asleep, she'll call out for me to come into her bedroom.

"I don't want to have a dream," she says. I brush her sandy hair back, put my hand on her forehead, and look straight into her big brown eyes.

"You are not going to have a dream," I tell her, with crisp, confident enunciation. Her body releases its tension, and she goes to sleep. I leave the room, hoping that what I promised but have no control over will be true.

That's what we do. All of us. We make well-intentioned promises of protection we can't always keep.

I'll look out for you.

But then you hear a scream and you decide it's some teenagers playing around. A young man jumping a fence is taking a shortcut. The gunshot at three a.m. is a firecracker or a car backfiring. You sit up in bed for a startled moment. Awaiting you is the cold, hard floor and a conversation that may lead nowhere; you collapse onto your warm pillow, and turn back to sleep.

Sirens wake you later.

I saw Tony walking his big white dog this afternoon and waved at him from outside my car, in between fumbling for my keys and remembering something I had to do.

I still don't know his last name.

CONTRA COSTA, 2013

CONCORD

The history of Concord, California, involves Satan and a series of misunderstandings. Legend has it that in 1805 Spanish soldiers in pursuit of a band of reluctantly missionized Native Americans cornered their quarry near a willow thicket in what is present-day Concord. The natives took cover in the dense trees, but when the soldiers charged in to seize them, the natives were gone. The spooked Spaniards dubbed the area Monte del Diablo—thicket of the devil—the archaic definition of the word "*monte*" translating loosely into "woods." Over the years, it morphed into the more conventional "mountain" or "mount," and English-speaking new-comers transferred the name to the nearby 3,848-foot peak that dominates the East Bay landscape, and it became Mount Diablo. Devil Mountain. In 2009 a local man named Arthur Mijares filed federal paperwork to try to change the name to Mount Reagan. He found the Devil name offensive.

"I just happen to be an ordinary man that worships God," he told the *Los Angeles Times*. Mijares wasn't successful, but he needn't have worried. Concord is thirty-one miles east of San Francisco and feels every mile of it. Whatever sinister wilderness existed has been bulldozed and replaced with enthusiastically bland retail hubs. Across from my hotel is the Willows Shopping Center, a sprawl of worrisomely underattended chain stores and restaurants: Old Navy,

Pier One Imports, and Fuddruckers. Nearly everyone I ask about Concord mentions the convenience of its BART stop, East Bay's subway system. "Twenty minutes to Berkeley," they say.

Paul Holes and I have agreed that he'll pick me up outside my hotel at nine a.m. He's taking me on a tour of the Contra Costa County crime scenes. By morning the temperature is already in the eighties, a blazing day in what will be the hottest month of the year in the East Bay. A silver Taurus pulls up right on time, and a fit, neatly dressed man with short blond hair and a hint of summer tan gets out and calls my name. I've never met Holes in person. During our last phone conversation, he cheerfully complained that his family's golden retriever puppy was keeping him up at night, but he looks as if he's never had a worry in the world. He's in his midforties and has a calm, easygoing face and a jock's gait. He smiles warmly and gives me a firm handshake. We'll spend the next eight hours talking about rape and murder.

Of course, Holes isn't technically a cop; he's a criminalist, chief of the County Sheriff's crime lab, but I've been spending a lot of time with cops, and he reminds me of them. When I say cops I mean specifically detectives. After spending enough hours with them, I've noticed a few things about detectives. They all smell vaguely of soap. I've never met a detective with greasy hair. They excel at eye contact and have enviable posture. Irony is never their go-to tone. Wordplay makes them uneasy. The good ones create long conversational vacuums that you reflexively fill, an interrogation strategy that proved to me through my own regrettable prattle how easily confessions can be elicited. They lack facial elasticity; or rather, they contain it. I've never met a detective who pulled a face. They don't recoil or go wide-eyed. I'm a face maker. I married a comedian. Many of my friends are in show business. I'm constantly surrounded by big expressions, which is why I immediately noticed the lack of them in detectives. They maintain a pleasant but vigorous blankness that I admire. I've tried to imitate it, but I can't. I came to recognize subtle but discernible shifts in the blankness—a narrowing of the eyes, a jaw squeeze, usually in response to hearing a theory they've long since eliminated. A veil comes down. But they'll never tip their hand. They'll never tell you, "We already looked into that angle ages ago." Instead they'll just absorb it and leave you with a polite "Huh."

In their reserve and in virtually every other way, detectives differ from show-biz folks. Detectives listen. They're getting a read. Entertainers get a read only to gauge their influence on a room. Detectives deal in concrete tasks. I once spent an hour listening to an actress friend analyze a three-line text that hurt her feelings. Eventually I'll see the cracks in a detective's veneer, but in the beginning their company is an unexpected relief, like fleeing a moodily lit cast party loud with competitive chatter and joining a meeting of determined Eagle Scouts awaiting their next challenge. I wasn't a native in the land of the literal-minded, but I enjoyed my time there.

The EAR's first attack in the East Bay took place in Concord and is just a 10-minute drive from my hotel. Holes and I dispense with small talk and dive right into discussing the case. The most obvious first question is, what brought him here? Why did he stop attacking in Sacramento and, in October 1978, embark on a nearly yearlong spree in the East Bay? I know the most common theory. Holes does too. He doesn't buy it.

"I don't think he got scared out of Sacramento," he says.

Proponents of the "scared away" theory point to the fact that on April 16, 1978, two days after the EAR attacked a fifteen-year-old babysitter in Sacramento, police released enhanced composite sketches of two possible suspects in the Maggiore homicide—an unsolved case in which a young couple was mysteriously gunned down while out walking their dog. After the sketches were released, the EAR stopped attacking in Sacramento; only one more rape in Sacramento County would be attributed to him, and it wasn't until a year later. One of the Maggiore sketches, the thinking goes, must have been uncomfortably accurate.

Holes is unconvinced. He has studied and is well versed in geographic profiling, a type of analytic crime mapping that tries to determine the most likely area of offender residence. In the late seventies, cops might stand around a map with pins stuck in it and idly speculate. Today, geographic profiling is its own specialty, with algorithms and software. In predatory crimes there is usually a "buffer zone" around a criminal's residence; targets within the zone are less desirable because of the perceived level of risk associated with operating too close to home. In serial crimes, geographic profilers analyze attack locations in an attempt to home in on the buffer zone, the ring around the bull's-eye where the criminal lives, because offenders, like everyone, move in predictable and routine ways.

"I've read a lot of studies about how serial offenders do their victim selection," Holes says. "It's during their normal course of living. Say you're a serial burglar and you drive to work like a normal person every day. You've got an anchor point at home and an anchor point at work. But they're paying attention. They're sitting like we are here"—Holes gestures at the intersection we've stopped at—"and they're noticing, you know, that might be a good apartment complex over there."

The geographic distribution of attacks in Sacramento follows a completely different pattern than in the East Bay, Holes says, and that's significant.

"In Sacramento, he's crisscrossing but he's staying within that northeast, east suburban area. Geographic profilers call him a 'marauder.' He's branching out at an anchor point. But once he moves down here, he's becoming a commuter. It's obvious he's traveling up and down the 680 corridor."

Interstate 680 is a seventy-mile north-south highway that cuts through central Contra Costa County. Most of the EAR's attacks in the East Bay occurred close to I-680, half of them a mile or less from an exit. On a professionally prepared geo-profile map, I saw the East Bay cases represented by a series of small red circles, almost all just right, or east, of 680, red drops cleaving to a yellow vein.

"You'll get a feel for it as we drive up and down 680," says Holes. "I think he's branching out because he's got a change in life circumstances. It wouldn't surprise me if he's still living in Sacramento but now commuting for work and taking advantage of being out of his jurisdiction and attacking."

At the word "work" I perk up. I've sensed from our recent e-mail correspondence that Holes is onto something regarding the EAR's possible line of work, but he remains oblique about the specifics. Even now, he waves me off, anticipating my question.

"We'll get to that."

Holes didn't grow up here. He was just a kid in 1978. But he's worked for the Contra Costa County Sheriff's Office for twenty-three years and has visited the crime scenes countless times. He's also dug into what the area looked like back then. He's pulled permits. Studied aerial photographs. Talked to locals. He possesses a mental map of the area circa October 1978, which he overlays over the current one as we drive. He slows and points to a cul-de-sac. The homes are located just behind the house where the EAR's first attack in Concord took place.

"These weren't here then," says Holes. "It was a vacant field."

We pull up and park at a corner house in a quiet residential neighborhood. A photo attached to the first East Bay file shows an attractive couple with their one-year-old daughter; the little girl wears a polka-dotted birthday hat and a summer dress, and the parents each have a hand on a ball they're holding up in front of her, presumably one of her gifts. The baby is smiling at the photographer, the parents at the camera. A month and a half after the photo was taken, on October 7, 1978, the husband was awakened by something touching his feet. He opened his eyes, startled to see a figure in a dark ski mask looming over him.

"I just want money and food, that's all. I'll kill you if you don't do what I say." The intruder held a flashlight in his left hand and a revolver in his right.

Holes points to the dining room window where thirty-five years ago the EAR slithered in and made his way to the foot of the couple's bed. The little girl wasn't bothered and slept through the ordeal.

The house was built in 1972 and is single-story, L-shaped, occupying roughly the same quarter acre as the other houses on the block. I'm struck by how much the house resembles the other crime-scene locations I've seen. You could pick it up and drop it in any of the other neighborhoods.

"Definitely the same kind of house," I say. Holes nods.

"Very few neighborhoods he attacked in had two-story houses," he says. "Makes a lot of sense if you know your victims are sleeping. In two stories there's a single way upstairs and single way downstairs. You're more likely to be cornered in that situation. Also it's easier to determine what's going on inside a single-story house, going from window to window. And if you're prowling, jumping fences, and going through yards, somebody can have a vantage point to see you from a second floor versus downstairs."

The husband, under hypnosis, remembered that when he and his wife pulled up around eleven fifteen p.m. on the evening of the attack, he saw a young man standing near a parked van on the side street next to their house. The van was box-shaped and two-tone in color, white over aqua green. The young man appeared to be in his twenties and was white with dark hair, of average height and weight, and he was standing near the right back corner of the van, stooped over, as if checking out a tire. A fragment of an image, one of hundreds half-absorbed peripherally every day. I imagine the husband in a chair, summoning and parsing a snapshot made retrospectively crucial. Or not. That was the madness of the case: the uncertain weight of every clue.

"In this case, what's striking is the sophistication of how he broke in," Holes says. "It looks like he tried the side door. He's cutting near the doorknob. He abandons that effort for whatever reason. He comes out front. There's a window on the dining room. He punches out a small hole in the window so he can push the latch and then gets in that way."

"I know nothing about burglaries. Was he good?"

"He was good," says Holes.

We sit in the hot car and list the ways he was strategically good. Bloodhounds, shoe impressions, and tire tracks showed investigators he was canny about the routes he took. If there was a construction site nearby, he'd park there, as the transient vehicle population allowed him to hide in plain view; people would assume he was associated with the job. He'd approach a house one way but take a different route to escape, so that he wasn't seen coming and going, and was therefore less likely to be remembered.

Dogs that normally barked didn't bark at him, suggesting he may have been preconditioning them with food. He had the unusual habit of throwing a blanket over a lamp or a muted TV when he brought his female victims into living rooms, which allowed him enough light to see but not so much that it would raise notice from outside. And his preplanning. The corner-house couple said that when they returned home, they noticed the husband's study door was closed, which was unusual, and the front door wasn't locked, as they believed they'd left it. They wondered if he was already in the house then, maybe hiding among the coats in the hall closet, waiting for their murmurs to grow softer and the bar of light at his feet to go out.

There's a pause in my conversation with Holes, one I've come to anticipate in discussions about the case. It's knockdown time. The verbal pivot is akin to the moment when you've talked too much about an ex, catch yourself, and stop to emphasize that the ex in question is, of course, a worthless piece of shit.

"He's very good at committing *his* crime," Holes says, "but he's not rappelling down the side of a building. He's not doing anything that suggests he has any specialized training."

Holes's parents are from Minnesota, and he retains a chipper midwestern rhythm to his speech, but when he says the EAR wasn't particularly skillful, his voice loses momentum, and he sounds unconvincing and unconvinced. On to the next recognizable stage in case analysis: self-debate.

"It's ballsy. The EAR. That's the thing," Holes says, his jaw uncharacteristically clenched. "What sets him apart from other offenders is going into a house. The Zodiac, for instance. In many ways his crimes were kind of cowardly. Lovers' lanes. From a distance. You step it up when you go inside. You step it up further when there's a male in that house."

We talk about how the male victims are overlooked. He tells me a story about a time when he needed to question a female victim in Stockton who'd been attacked with her husband. Holes decided to contact the husband first, figuring he'd be better able to handle the cold call. The husband politely told Holes he didn't think his wife wanted to talk about the attack. She'd buried it. She didn't want to revisit the experience; nevertheless, the husband reluctantly said, he'd pass Holes's questions on to his wife. Holes didn't hear anything. He figured it was a lost cause. Several months later, the wife finally got in touch. She answered Holes's questions. She was willing to help him, she said. She was willing to remember. Her husband wasn't.

"He's the one who's having the problems," she confided.

The male victims were born in the forties and fifties, a generation for whom therapy was mostly an alien concept. In the police files, gender roles are rigid and unambiguous. Detectives ask the women where they shop and the men about the locking mechanisms on the doors and windows. They drape blankets over the women's shoulders and ferry them to the hospital. The men are asked what they saw, not what they felt. Many of the male victims had military experience. They had toolsheds. They were doers and protectors who'd been robbed of their ability to do and protect. Their rage is in the details: one husband chewed the bindings off his wife's feet.

"So much trauma exists to this day," Holes says, starting the car. He pulls away from the curb. The corner house recedes from view. There's a brief handwritten note in the file from the female victim, the pretty young mother of the darling little birthday girl, to the lead detective, dated five months after their attack.

> *Rod,*
> *Enclosed please find*
> *a. missing property list and*
> *b. list of checks written for July–August.*
> *All jewelry was taken from either our bedroom chest drawer or the top of dresser. Other items are appropriately indicated. I do hope this will be all that will be needed as we are desperately trying to get our lives back to normal. I'm sure we both can appreciate each other's positions.*
> *Good luck in the piecing together!*

The tone was reasonable, direct, and resilient. Upbeat even. I found it extraordinary. Some people, I thought when I read it, can endure horrible, traumatic things and move on. A few pages later in the file, there's another short note, handwritten by a sheriff's deputy. This family no longer lives in Contra Costa County, the note says. They've moved to a city hundreds of miles away.

Good luck in the piecing together!

I'd read the exclamation point as optimism. But what it meant was good-bye.

WE HEAD EAST. THE SECOND ATTACK IN CONCORD OCCURRED A week after the first and is located less than a half mile away. Holes slows for a stop sign. He points to the street perpendicular to us, again consulting his mental map of October 1978. "Right in this area there's new construction going on. So people, construction workers, delivery trucks, are coming down this road"—he indicates the one we're on—"or that road, in order to get to the construction location."

Of the two primary thoroughfares someone could take to the construction site in October 1978, Holes says, one route passes the first attack location, and the other passes the second. I remember that Holes said he believed the EAR came to the area for work.

"Building? Construction?" I ask.

"That's the avenue I'm pursuing," he says.

I notice that he says "the" and not "an."

"Do you know who the developer of that construction site was?"

He doesn't answer, but his expression says he does.

We pull up to the second Concord crime scene, another single-story, L-shaped home, this one cream with green trim. A giant oak dominates the small front yard. Nothing about the neighborhood suggests that people with a great deal of weekday leisure time live here. No one ambles by with a dog. No one is speed walking with an iPod. Few cars pass.

In this case, the EAR hinted at a possibility, one that flickers intriguingly throughout the series a handful of times. It was Friday the thirteenth, four thirty a.m. The EAR's psychosexual script that he forced upon his victims with his flashlight and clenched-teeth threats was by now, his thirty-ninth attack, so well established that, reading the police reports, one can be forgiven for missing the clue, the key change of a single word: "I" to "we."

"All we want is food and money, and then we'll get the hell out of here," he ranted at the disoriented couple. "I just want food and money for my girlfriend and me."

Once the couple was restrained and compliant, he began his frenetic ransacking, slamming kitchen cupboards, rummaging through drawers. The female victim was led to the family room. He laid her on the floor.

"You want to live?" he asked her.

"Yes," she said.

He blindfolded her with a bathroom towel.

"This had better be the best fuck I've ever had, or I'm going to kill you."

She told investigators she kept flashing on *In Cold Blood*, on the story of a family annihilated in the middle of the night by fickle killers.

However, what followed, while terrifying for the victim, seemed oddly juvenile and of little interest to her attacker. He quickly and perfunctorily ran his hands over her thighs; she could feel that he was wearing thick leather gloves. He made her masturbate him for a minute, then penetrated her and was done in thirty seconds. He jumped up and began ransacking again. It seemed that the raiding of the house stimulated him more than actual sex.

A door opened and she felt a draft; he was in their attached garage. A trash bag rustled. He seemed to be going back and forth from the house to the garage. She heard him say something, but not to her.

"Here, put this in the car," he whispered.

There was no reply; she heard no footsteps. A vehicle never started up. She never knew how or when he left, just that at some point he did.

It wasn't the only time the EAR suggested he had an accomplice. The first victim heard what she thought were two separate voices in her living room whispering heated, overlapping threats. "Shut up," followed quickly by, "I told *you* to shut up."

Another victim heard a car horn honk four times outside, and then someone began ringing the doorbell. There was knocking at the front window. She heard muffled voices, possibly a woman's. She couldn't tell if the EAR's voice was among them. He left, and the voices went away, but the victim, who was bound and face down on her living room floor, couldn't tell if the events occurred at the same time, or were related at all.

"My buddy is out in the car waiting," he said once.

Was it a lie, a bolstering tactic when he psychologically felt the need for backup? An attempt to misdirect the police? Most of the investigators believe it was a bluff. Holes isn't so sure.

"Does he have someone who's assisting him at times? In the sexual assaults, no, but on the burglary side? Who knows? It happens enough throughout the series, that you go, 'Maybe.' Maybe we have to consider that possibility."

Holes concedes that much of what the EAR said was deflection and misdirection. He ranted about living in his van or at a camp by the river, but he rarely emitted the kind of body odor a transient would. He invented connections to his victims. "I knew when I saw you at the junior prom I had to have you," he whispered to a blindfolded teenager, but she'd heard tape being pulled from her bedroom wall—her junior prom picture coming down. "I've seen you at the lake," he said to a woman with a ski boat in her driveway.

Some of the lies—about killing people in Bakersfield, about being kicked out of the military—probably played into a tough-guy image he nurtured of himself. The fake connections to victims were possibly part of his fantasy or an attempt to unsettle them with opaque familiarity. Holes and I speculate about his other behavior, like the gasping breaths. They were described as huge, gulping intakes of air, bordering on hyperventilation. A criminal profiler who examined the case in the seventies felt that the breathing was a scare tactic, a way to make his victims think he was a lunatic capable of anything. Holes says a fellow investigator who has asthma wondered if it was legitimately respiratory distress; adrenaline can trigger an attack.

The EAR is a card face down on a table. Our speculation is a cul-de-sac. Round and round we go.

"San Ramon?" asks Holes.

SAN RAMON

We head for 680, which will take us seventeen miles south to the next attack, the third that month. October 1978. Carter was president. *Grease* had been the huge summer movie, and John Travolta and Olivia Newton-John's "Summer Nights" was still a radio mainstay, though the Who's "Who Are You" was climbing the charts. The fresh-scrubbed face of thirteen-year-old Brooke Shields stared blankly from the cover of *Seventeen*. The Yankees beat the Dodgers in the World Series. Sid Vicious's girlfriend Nancy Spungen bled to death from a stab wound on a bathroom floor at the Chelsea Hotel. John Paul II was the new pope. Three days before the San Ramon attack, the movie *Halloween* was released.

"What about the crying? Do you think that was real?" I ask Holes.

Nearly a dozen victims reported that he cried. He sobbed, they said. He stumbled and seemed lost. He whimpered in a high-pitched voice like a child. "I'm sorry, Mom," he wept. "Mommy, please help me. I don't want to do this, Mommy."

"I do," says Holes. "Women have good insight into men's behaviors. There are times when the victims say his anger is a put-on, he's acting, but other times, when he's in a corner sobbing uncontrollably, it feels real to them. He's conflicted. The crying is always after the sexual attack. That's when he's sobbing."

There's an exception among the victims who believed the tears were real. The Stockton woman, the one whose husband struggled to come to terms with their attack, didn't buy the crying, Holes tells me.

"She heard those sounds. But she wouldn't attribute them to crying," says Holes.

"What did she think it was?" I ask.

"High-pitched hysteria," Holes says. "Like laughter."

For years no one seems to have noticed that the 911 emergency number didn't work in unincorporated San Ramon, even though the phone company charged residents for the service. A woman who lived at the end of a quiet court discovered the discrepancy. The discordant squawk her receiver emitted indicating a failed call was a jolt she didn't need after two hours of sexual violence at the hands of a stranger. The woman, using the pseudonym Kathy, is quoted in an *Oakland Tribune* article that ran on December 10, 1978, six weeks after her attack. When Kathy awoke the night of her rape, her eyes frantically sought to adjust to the darkness. She could make out only one thing in the pitch-black: a disembodied wild gaze, his " 'little eyes, *just staring.*' "

" 'I just really hate that guy,' " Kathy says matter-of-factly of her unidentified rapist. She explains she's also angry with the phone company for not providing emergency service when they said they did. Of this outrage, Kathy tells the reporter, she can exact some quantifiable justice: she has the 911 charge deducted from her bill now, a savings of twenty-eight cents a month.

Help came after Kathy dialed the Contra Costa County Sheriff's Office directly.

In the wake of the two rapes in Concord the Sheriff's Office had issued an alert to its deputies. Sacramento's warning had proved prescient: The EAR was pressing his ski mask against *their* windows now. Everyone needed to be vigilant. A strike force began identifying neighborhoods where the EAR might hit. License numbers of vehicles parked next to open areas, or otherwise deemed suspicious, were quietly recorded.

Bug-eyed attentive wasn't the San Ramon beat's usual mode. From 1970 to 1980, the city more than quadrupled its population, but it was, and still is, ringed by rolling grasslands studded with oak trees, vast swaths of undeveloped country that suggest space and impose quiet. Police radios lulled with extended silences. Patrol headlights swept over the same detached garages, the same darkened windows on ranch homes occupied by young families. Suspicious figures rarely peeled off from San Ramon's unvarying suburban silhouette; the fence lines were unbroken, the shrubs never shook. Deputies were trained for action but accustomed to stillness.

That changed on October 28 just after five a.m., when dispatch delivered to the graveyard shift a blast of static followed by scant but alarming details. Home-invasion rape and robbery. Montclair Place. A one-man unit was the first to respond to the scene. The victims, Kathy and her husband, David,* calmly met the deputy at the front door. After confirming that the couple didn't need immediate medical care, the deputy's interest was absorbed by the odd scene behind them. The house was almost completely empty. Drawers of the few pieces of furniture were haphazardly pulled open and bare. Closet doors stood open, revealing hanging rods and nothing else. Had they been completely cleaned out by the intruder? No, Kathy and David explained, they were in the process of moving out.

He'd come for them during their last few hours in the house.

---

* Pseudonyms

There was the real estate factor again. And the canny timing that suggested inside knowledge. Kathy and David had a three-year-old son; they pointed out to investigators that the EAR never opened or even approached their son's bedroom door. Other victims with small children noticed the same thing. How he zeroed in on victims and gained knowledge about their lives and the layouts of their homes was a question of endless speculation.

Gary Ridgway, the Green River Killer, called the preattack time he spent casing for victims "patrolling." Banality was his camouflage. He'd back his truck into a 7-Eleven on Pacific Highway South, the gritty stretch around the Seattle-Tacoma airport known for prostitution. Sometimes he'd pop the hood. He was a slight man with a putty-colored face who was preoccupied with engine trouble. His presence never registered. The washed-out gray landscape absorbed him seamlessly. Only a close, patient observer could have picked up on the detail that signaled something was wrong: time didn't concern the man. His pupils flicked like a pendulum, fixing on everything but his engine, a quick-change of hungry considerations tracking as forcefully as a planchette on a Ouija board.

Clank. It was a sound so routine it was lost in the urban noise, in the whoosh of wet tires in light rain and door chimes at the convenience store. It's the scariest sound no one heard—Ridgway closing his hood. Patrolling was over; a new phase had begun.

Initially I felt that the EAR, like Ridgway, must have hidden in plain sight. He seemed to possess information that could only have been gleaned from careful, prolonged observation. But he clearly wasn't an obvious lurker: despite thousands of pages of police reports, including victim statements and neighborhood interviews, no consistent physical description of a suspect emerges. Over the course of fifty rapes, a face should start to cohere, I thought, at the very least an agreed-upon hair color. But none did. Therein lay the puzzle. Chance wins eventually. Luck is unreliable. How did he survey so long without being surveyed?

My mind kept circling back to the image of a man in a uniform, a telephone lineman or a postal worker, an everyday worker bee straight out of Richard Scarry's Busytown, the kind of person whose presence signals that everything is running smoothly. No one fastened on him. He was in a state of constant dissolve. What people bounced past, what they missed in the blur of beige was the devouring force in his angry eyes.

A retired investigator who worked the Irvine homicides tried to dissuade me from my image of a master reconnoiterer. The attacks didn't require a lot of preplanning or inside information in his opinion. He and his partner conducted an experiment one night when they were working the case. They dressed in all black, laced up soft-soled shoes, and prowled the Irvine neighborhoods, following the paths they believed the killer took. They crept along cinder-block walls, peeped over backyard fences, and concealed themselves against tree trunks in the dark.

Rectangles of light drew them closer. Rear windows offered access into dozens of strangers' lives. Sometimes there was only a sliver through a curtain, enough to see the blank face of a woman rinsing and rerinsing a single glass at her kitchen sink. Mostly it was quiet, but occasionally there was a shower of laughter from a TV. A teenager's shoulders inched to her ears as her boyfriend lifted her skirt.

The investigator shook his head at the memory.

"You'd be amazed at what you can see," he told me.

In fact, I asked every investigator I talked to about prowling and got the same response, a succession of head shakes and expressions that all said it's the easiest thing in the world to do.

A compulsive prowler is a quick study of body language, the way a woman home alone might glance out her living room's rear window before turning out the light, or how a teenager moves more quietly when her parents are asleep. After a while, it's pattern recognition. Operation time is cut down considerably.

I ask Holes how methodical he thought the EAR was in selecting victims.

"I think there's evidence of both ways. There are times I think he's done a fair amount of surveillance. He sees somebody. Focuses on them. Follows them. And there are times he's attacking them the first time he sees them."

No one knows how long he was watching Kathy, but they have a good idea from where. The house backed up on a Christmas tree farm. The criminalist noted "zigzag jogging type" shoe impressions on the board fence in the backyard.

Holes turns right and points out where the tree farm used to be behind the house. We go a block or two more and he takes another right, to the 7400 block of Sedgefield Avenue.

"The next day there's a vehicle parked here on the side. There's blood inside."

The car was a Ford Galaxie 500. It had been reported stolen.

"Somebody obviously bleeding, probably with a bloody nose. Then you see the trail of blood as they take off. Evidence from that is long gone, but I've speculated that if you've got somebody escaping through a Christmas tree farm in the middle of the night, what's the likelihood he ran into a tree? And then got into this car that he stole and abandoned? I had a case where somebody was escaping a shooting and ran into a telephone pole. Left a blood trail just like that."

The trail of blood traveled east and over the curb. Some tissues were crumpled up in the gutter. The blood drops grew smaller and disappeared. Like every trail in the case, this one eventually led to a series of blank walls. Nothing ever led to a front door. Every object found in a search could or could not be his and always lacked firm, traceable information. It was a case whose wheels spun endlessly in possibility.

"Everything is a half clue," says Holes.

"What about construction at the time in San Ramon?" I ask.

Holes tells me that Kathy provided them with helpful information.

"She was able to recount multiple active construction sites for new subdivisions going on around her neighborhood at the time of her attack."

It takes me a moment to realize that he means he talked to Kathy personally.

"You talked to her?"

He knows why I'm shocked.

In his book about the case, *Sudden Terror*, Larry Crompton disparages Kathy. He describes her demeanor during the police interview as almost seeming as if she's reliving "the ultimate turn-on." He discloses unflattering details about her life after the attack. He says he feels sorry for her husband and son. I like Crompton but thought he was wrong here. Seriously wrong. He even rates her looks against other victims—favorably, but it's still wrong. His treatment of Kathy is at best wildly tone-deaf and at worst victim blaming. His portrayal assumes that there's only one way to respond to a violent sexual attack. It lacks compassion and understanding. For example, he describes derisively how she told police that she asked for a glass of water first when the EAR demanded that she fellate him, without considering that for a terrified victim a plea for water could be a stalling tactic. And the pseudonym Crompton chose for her, "Sunny," while probably not deliberately malicious, seemed a particularly cruel choice in light of how he depicted her.

Shortly after Crompton's book came out, the Sheriff's Office received an e-mail from Kathy. She was furious about how she was portrayed. They didn't have the authority to put her in touch with Crompton, who was retired, but Holes and a female colleague invited Kathy to meet with them in person at the office.

"She was shaking like a leaf," Holes recalled, in a voice that said he didn't blame her. Kathy barely made eye contact with him in the meeting, something he attributed to her residual trauma. The relationship between victims and cold-case investigators is an odd combination of intimate and remote. Holes was ten years old when a man in a mask put a knife to Kathy's neck and pushed her down on the cold linoleum kitchen floor. Nineteen years later, Holes pulled a Ziploc bag with her case number on it from Property and withdrew a swab from a plastic tube. Kathy was a stranger to him. He'd studied her rapist's sperm cells in a microscope, but he'd never looked her in the eye or shaken her hand.

He asked very few questions in the meeting and let his female colleague take the lead. Then Kathy said something that focused his attention.

She and her husband, David, had long since divorced. Like many couples who were victims of the EAR, their relationship didn't survive. Kathy said that David told her after the attack that he thought he recognized the EAR's voice, but he couldn't quite place it.

What Kathy said was important for two reasons. First, she'd never seen the geo-profile. She didn't know that, while Contra Costa County didn't provide the same obvious living pattern as Sacramento, the geo-profiler had determined that the most likely area of the offender's residence was there anyway: San Ramon. It was central to the East Bay series, and one of the few places he hit only once. As the distance from an offender's residence increases, so do the number of potential targets. But occasionally a predatory offender, either because he's drawn to a particular victim or confident he won't be caught, attacks closer to home.

On the geo-profile map, a blade of red, indicating the peak area for the EAR's likely home base, runs east to west just north of Kathy's house.

Kathy also didn't know that an FBI profiler had presented new findings at a recent EAR Task Force meeting. Something the profiler said resonated with Holes. She said they should consider that in some of the cases the male victim had been the target. In some instances, the EAR may have been exacting revenge on the male for some perceived wrongdoing.

What Kathy told them raised the possibility of a link, a previously overlooked close degree of separation that could lead to the suspect. Many well-known serial cases turn out to possess at least one such connection. An old roommate of Lynda Healy's, a victim of Ted Bundy, was a cousin of Ted's, and investigators later unearthed rosters that showed that Ted and Lynda shared at least three classes. Dennis Rader, the BTK killer, lived six doors down from Marine Hedge, his eighth victim. John Wayne Gacy talked publicly in a store with Robert Piest about hiring him for a construction job shortly before Piest disappeared.

The EAR went to great lengths to hide his identity. He covered his face and suppressed his voice. He blinded his victims with a flashlight and threatened to kill them if they looked at him. But he was also brazen. Barking dogs didn't deter him. Two joggers, a college-age brother and sister, were out running on a foggy night in December 1977 when they spotted a man in a dark ski mask emerging from the hedged walkway of a house on the 3200 block of American River Drive. The man stopped abruptly when he saw the joggers. They continued running. They looked back and saw him quickly climb into an older model step-side pickup truck. Something about the way the man had paused and then moved quickly into the truck made them run faster. They heard the noisy rattle of the truck's engine as the truck sped toward them. They sprinted around the corner; the truck screeched to a stop and backed up haphazardly to where they were. They ran to another house and hid, watching as the truck followed, turning in circles in the street until the man gave up and sped off.

The EAR was extremely careful about self-preservation, but success and the arrogance it breeds punctures holes in master plans. It whispers grandiose persuasions. He'd already defeated a series of mental barriers that would have stopped most of us: rape, breaking into a stranger's home, taking control of a couple rather than a lone female. After dozens of uninterrupted successes, his self-confidence might have adrenalized him to the point where he broke his own rule about targeting only victims to whom he had no connection. A guttural whisper heard in the middle of the night thirty-six years ago may be a clue.

After San Ramon, the EAR hit twice in San Jose, forty miles south. Holes and I decide to skip San Jose to save time.

"I want to show you Davis," he says. "I think Davis is important."

But first we have two more stops. After San Jose, the EAR returned to Contra Costa County, attacking for the first of what would be three times in Danville. Holes and I head north on 680 toward Danville, to the site of the December 9, 1978, attack, which gave him his most promising lead.

DANVILLE

A hundred years ago, the steady drumming of steam trains was the sound of boom time in the broad green valley adjacent to Mount Diablo. Starting in 1891, the Southern Pacific Railroad ferried passengers up and down a twenty-mile route from San Ramon to just north of Concord. Enterprising visitors disembarked, blueprints and dreams in hand. Land was abundant. Parceling and developing commenced. Passenger service eventually disappeared with the invention of the automobile, but the San Ramon Branch Line continued hauling freight—Bartlett pears, gravel, sheep. The railroad tunneled indistinguishably into the landscape. Train whistles marked time. The depots were all painted the same dandelion yellow with brown trim. The tracks ran past Murwood Elementary in Walnut Creek, and at recess the kids, hearing a rumble and feeling the ground vibrate, stopped their hopscotch or dodgeball and waved at the passing crews, receiving a horn blow in reply.

Southern Pacific helped transform the rural valley, but not in a way that kept its trains running. Industrial hubs never materialized. Single-family homes were developed instead. Central Contra Costa County became "the outer East Bay." The completion of I-680 in 1964 represented speed, efficiency, and death for the railway. Moving freight was cheaper by truck. The number of train cars dwindled. And kept dwindling. The sprawling orchards were gone now, and crowds of roofs advanced on either side of the tracks. Southern Pacific finally petitioned the Interstate Commerce Commission to abandon the line. In September 1978, nearly a century after the first track was laid, the line closed for good.

Debate ensued about what to do with the right-of-way. Until a decision was made, the twenty-foot-wide strip of land remained vacant, a shadow corridor bisecting neighborhoods of warmly lit houses. The dead zone didn't inspire dread as much as inattention. This was especially true of the five-mile stretch that ran through Danville, the town just north of San Ramon. Danville lots were larger, the homes older, its residents wealthier and quieter. The deserted tracks lay beyond tidily cordoned-off backyards. The fence lines were essentially drapes. Shorn of its usefulness, the right-of-way was blotted out. Nothing moved. Nothing was heard. That is, until one December morning when a peculiar noise disturbed the silence. The casual listener may not have been concerned at first. The sound was steady, rhythmic, but to the sensitive ear it signaled an evident urgency: a bloodhound galloping, gripped with purpose.

BY EARLY DECEMBER 1978, THERE EXISTED AMONG CONTRA COSTA County residents the hopeful but mostly unspoken feeling that maybe they could relax. In October the East Area Rapist hadn't merely surfaced in their area; he'd inflicted on them something that, in its swiftness and ability to shock, resembled a spree: three attacks in twenty-one days. After the third attack, people spent nights locked inside brightly lit homes, fighting sleep and blinking against muzzy visions of ski masks. But weeks passed without incident. Fresh horrors distracted. News anchors interrupted regular programming on November 18 to announce that more than nine hundred Americans, a third of them children, lay dead in a jungle commune in Guyana after drinking Flavor Aid laced with cyanide at the behest of cult leader Jim Jones. The Peoples Temple, Jones's church, had had its headquarters in San Francisco before relocating to Guyana. The dead included Northern California congressman Leo Ryan, who'd flown there to investigate alleged abuses and was gunned down at an airstrip just before takeoff. The Jonestown Massacre absorbed much of the country's horrified attention, if not the world's, but it particularly rocked the Bay Area.

Thanksgiving weekend came and went peacefully. A new moon lacquered the sky the night of November 30, extinguishing light that shone on even the most desolate hiding spots. The determined concealer was presented with ideal conditions. But December dawned without news of another EAR attack. No one was neglecting to lock up just yet, but reflexes spring-coiled with panicky anticipation slowly began to ease.

It's probably not a coincidence that the EAR stole clock radios from five homes, even when more valuable items were there for the taking. Time was important to him—controlling it, manipulating it. He possessed uncanny instincts about how much time had to pass before precautions weakened. Keeping communities and victims uncertain about his presence gave him a strategic advantage, of course. The blindfolded victim tied up in the dark develops the feral senses of a savannah animal. The sliding glass door quietly shutting registers as a loud, mechanical click. She calculates the distance of ever fainter footsteps. Hope flickers. Still, she waits. Time passes in tense perception. She strains to hear breathing other than her own. Fifteen minutes go by. The dread sense of being watched, of being pinned down by a possessing gaze she can't see, is gone. Thirty minutes. Forty-five. She allows her body to slacken almost imperceptibly. Her shoulders fall. It's then, at the precipice of an exhale, that the nightmare snaps into action again—the knife grazes the skin, and the labored breathing resumes, grows closer, until she feels him settling in next to her, an animal waiting patiently for its half-dying quarry to still.

The illusion of being gone was a cruel and effective trick. The victim on whom the trick was played would wait much longer the next time she thought the EAR left; some victims, catatonic with dread, waited hours, waited until birds chirped and weak sunlight flickered at the edges of their blindfolds. The extra time before the police were called allowed the EAR to put greater distance between him and the crime scene.

By early December, it had been six weeks since the EAR had struck in Contra Costa County. The community was the equivalent of the cautiously hopeful victim who believes he's left her home for good. No one from Sacramento or the East Bay, neither the public nor the investigators, knew at the time that during the EAR's absence from their area he'd committed two rapes forty miles south in San Jose, one in early November and another on December 2. Even if they had known about the San Jose rapes, the EAR's route might have relieved them. He appeared to be following a steady southerly course: first Concord, then eighteen miles down I-680 to San Ramon, and next San Jose, in another county altogether.

As night fell on Friday, December 8, residents of the bedroom communities nestled at the base of Mount Diablo, outer East Bay towns like Concord, Walnut Creek, Danville, and San Ramon, went to bed feeling spared. Common sense suggested that he'd keep moving south and hit in Santa Cruz or Monterey. They were in his rearview mirror, receding targets. The worst was over. Midnight turned to one a.m. Refrigerators hummed in darkened houses. A car occasionally whooshed by, punctuating the quiet. The collective circadian rhythm was in rest mode.

Not everywhere. In Danville, just east of the abandoned railroad tracks, a six-foot wooden fence concealed by large trees buckled under the weight of someone scaling it.

No outdoor lights illuminated the ranch-style house that lay behind the fence. Nighttime was ideal for the fence hopper. Shrouds lured him. He roved in dark clothes, searching for the rare blot among the luminous houses. His black pupils sought shadows.

He crossed the backyard to the patio. No lights were on inside. A woman's purse lay on the kitchen counter. Prying the sliding glass doors required only a small amount of pressure and resulted in little noise. He stepped into the kitchen. Somewhere a radio was playing softly. The 2,100-square-foot house was mostly empty of furniture or personal effects because it was for sale. Friendly Realtors had been welcoming strangers inside for the last two months. Had he been one of the forgettable looky-loos? He would have murmured, if he spoke at all. While other potential buyers asked questions, implying interest, he would have registered as faintly critical, his absorption suggesting possible disapproval. Memorization misinterpreted as judgment.

He bypassed rooms with closed doors and headed directly for the master bedroom, in the northwest corner of the house. Standing in the doorway, he faced the bed from a distance of about ten feet. A woman lay there alone. She was sleeping, positioned on her stomach, face to pillow, the kind of "flung off the cliff of consciousness" sleep that anchors rather than drifts. Who was she in the moment before he wrenched her awake from unburdened sleep? Esther McDonald* was small, what the generation when her name was popular might have called "a slip of a thing." Back home in a cold midwestern state, a marriage at nineteen had lasted a decade with no kids or staying power. Suddenly she was thirty, which is older in Middle America than on the coasts. "California Dreamin'" wasn't a song but a siren call for a sunnier future. She and a girlfriend moved to San Francisco. The Summer of Love was over, but the Bay Area retained its reputation for improvisation, a place where you could shed your past and debut a new life.

There were jobs: a wholesale florist and an electric motor repair company. A pawnbroker twenty years her senior wooed her with jewelry and invited her to live with him in Danville. The house was five miles from the Calaveras Fault, a major branch of the San Andreas. Six months later, they split amicably. He moved out, put the house on the market, and told her she was welcome to stay until it sold. A romance was bubbling with a co-worker; the pawnbroker was still around. Matters of the heart were bidirectional and unresolved.

That's who she was as she slept around two a.m. on a cold night in December: a woman starting over in a state where the covered wagons stopped and storied reinventions began, a woman navigating an unremarkably complicated love life, a woman about to be irrevocably changed. What is the lasting damage when you believe the warm spot you were just sleeping in will be your grave? Time sands the edges of the injuries, but they never lose their

---

* Pseudonym

hold. A nameless syndrome circulates permanently through the body, sometimes long dormant, other times radiating powerful waves of pain and fear.

A hand gripped her neck. A blunt-tipped weapon dug into the side of her throat. At least a dozen investigators in Northern California could have correctly predicted the first words whispered in the dark.

"Don't move."

"Don't scream."

He was back. Or, more accurately, he had doubled back. The uncertainty of his course, the randomness of his strikes made him an unpredictable dark force, a one-man crime wave.

The first deputies alerted by dispatch arrived at 5:19 a.m. Tension ratcheted at the telltale signs. Knotted white shoelaces. Torn strips of orange towel. Cut phone lines. The house was bracingly cold. He'd turned off the thermostat, along with the radio, apparently for optimal hearing. Radio calls went out. Phones rang. People began arriving in the blue-black light of dawn. Crime-scene investigator Larry Crompton pulled up. The search for meaningful details focused him, made him alert despite the early hour. He noted the Realtor's sign in the front yard, the vacant property next door, and the railroad tracks out back—all ideal conditions that stoked the EAR's compulsions and telescoped his roving to a single target.

In a few weeks, Crompton would be promoted to sergeant and join the urgently formed EAR Task Force. He was unaware as he entered the house, the door shutting behind him, that this case would be the one he would carry for the rest of his life. It would become like a game of hangman he refused to lose, all the guesses wrong, the stick figure nearly fatally hung; Crompton kept the last move open, staving off defeat by waiting until he, or one of his successors, could reverse the momentum and fill in the blanks. Only then, the final letter correct, would the long, bruising chase in the dark end in the simplest but long-sought-after prize: a man's name.

The first of three bloodhounds, Pita, arrived. She exhibited excitement immediately, her nose wrenching the air. Who knows what goes through the minds of tracking dogs, whether they absorb the hopes of the solemn people milling around them. Pita's job was enviably clear-cut. Find the scent and follow it. A small group of handlers and cops, including Crompton, watched Pita exit the house through the back patio and head confidently to the southwest corner of the backyard. She agitated at the fence, wanting over. She was led out the yard and around the other side, to the abandoned railroad tracks. She raised her nose.

They were sifting once again through the fresh wreckage of the faceless wrecker. Foam still clung to a bottle of Schlitz Malt Liquor he'd taken from the refrigerator and set down in the backyard. Scuff marks on the fence were photographed. The group at the railroad tracks huddled in the cold, waiting for Pita to make her next move. Their hope lay in a dog's nostrils connecting with a molecule.

Then a jerk of movement. Pita caught it; she smelled him. She surged forth, galloping south down the left path alongside the tracks. She was, as police K-9 units say, "in odor." Her stride was controlled but accelerating, relentless drive her genetic gift. She was, in every sense of the word, unleashed. Crompton and Pita's handlers chased after her. The sudden commotion on the tracks, with its whiff of danger and unrest, was unusual for a Saturday morning in Danville. It was an unwelcome disruption, one that would repeat in the coming months.

Pita stopped abruptly about a half mile from where she started, at the point the railroad tracks intersected a residential street. Two other bloodhounds, Betsey and Eli, were also brought in to work the crime scene. Pita's handler, Judy Robb, noted in her follow-up report that time and even minute changes to wind velocity can alter scent pools. However, the three handlers were in agreement on several points. The dogs had sniffed along many fences and darted down numerous side yards. Their behavior suggested that the suspect had spent a lot of time prowling the area. He entered the victim's backyard by the north-side fence. He left by crossing over the southwest corner of the back fence and headed south along the tracks until at the cross street he likely entered a vehicle.

The victim had been taken to the hospital by a sergeant. He drove her back home after her exam was finished, but when he parked his county vehicle outside her house, she didn't move. Raw anguish pinned her to the seat. Daylight provided no comfort. She didn't want to go back inside. It was tricky. The investigators sympathized, but they needed her. The importance of walking the crime scene with them was gently stressed. She consented to a quick walk-through, then left. Friends came and retrieved her belongings later. She never entered the house again.

There's always the question of what to call an unknown perpetrator in police reports. The choice is often "the suspect," occasionally "the offender," or sometimes simply "the man." Whoever wrote the Danville reports elected to use a term that was stark and unambiguous in its charge, its tone of reproach as if a finger were pointing from the very page. The term affected me the moment I read it. It became my private shorthand for the EAR, the simple term I returned to when I lay awake at three a.m. cycling through a hoarder's collection of murky half clues and indistinct facial features. I admired the plainness of its unblinking claim.

The responsible.

———

HOLES PARKS ON A RESIDENTIAL STREET IN DANVILLE THAT'S ADJA-cent to the Iron Horse Regional Trail, a path for bikers, horses, and hikers that meanders for forty miles through central Contra

Costa: the old Southern Pacific Railroad right-of-way paved over and made pedestrian friendly.

"We'll get out here and walk," he says.

We head south down the trail. We've walked maybe ten feet before Holes directs my attention to a backyard.

"The bloodhounds tracked the EAR's escape to the corner of the victim's yard," he says. He steps forward. A row of agave plants shields the backside of the fence, hindering any attempt at getting closer.

"He jumps the fence here," says Holes, pointing. He stares for a long moment at the thick, sword-shaped leaves of the agave plants.

"I bet this homeowner got so freaked out about the attack, they planted this cactus," he says.

We continue walking. We're following the path that criminalist John Patty took thirty-five years ago when he scoured the area for evidence after the bloodhounds established the EAR's exit route. Patty found something during his search. He labeled what he found and sealed the items in a plastic bag; the bag went into a box that was taken to the Property Room and slid in tight against hundreds of identical boxes on a steel shelf. There it remained untouched for thirty-three years. On March 31, 2011, Holes called Property to inquire about the ski cap of an EAR suspect from the 1970s whom he was resurrecting. The director of Property had a box ready when Holes arrived. The ski cap was there. Then Holes noticed a Ziploc bag with a tag that read, "Collected from RR Right of Way." What he found inside changed the course of his investigation.

Evidence collection, like everything else in police work, requires a paper trail. John Patty's Scene Evidence Inventory form is hand-scrawled, the answers brief—"1 a) 2 sheets of spiral, 3-hole binder paper bearing pencil writing; b) 1 sheet of spiral, 3-hole binder paper bearing a pencil drawn map; c) 1 length of purple yarn 41 inches in length; d) fragment of paper with typewriting."

Were the items found together? Scattered across the ground? No photograph or sketch of the scene exists to orient Holes. Patty left a brief notation explaining where along the tracks he found the evidence. That's it. Holes is able to subject the paper to touch-DNA technology and high-resolution scanning, have multiple experts parse and analyze every aspect of the map, but he lacks one crucial authority who'd give him context: John Patty. He died of cancer in 1991. The bane of cold cases: knowledge disregarded as irrelevant but later deemed critical has died with the knower.

At first, Holes didn't know what to make of "the homework evidence." One page appeared to be the start of a poorly written school-assigned essay on General Custer. The content of the second page was more intriguing. "Mad is the word," it begins. The author rants about sixth grade and the teacher who humiliated him by forcing him to write sentences repeatedly as punishment. "I never hated anyone as much as I did him," the writer says of the unnamed teacher.

The third page is a hand-drawn map of a residential community, depicting a business area, cul-de-sacs, trails, and a lake. Holes noticed some random doodling on the back of the map.

The evidence puzzled Holes and drew him in fast. Unexpected flashes of clarity kept him pursuing the lead. He cold-called experts for input. An offhand observation by a real estate developer shifted his conception of who the EAR could be. Clues were reconsidered in a new light. Holes knew his theories diverged from his fellow investigators'. He decided not to care too much. He carved out a place for himself as the guy whose views were, as he puts it, "left field." He asked more questions. He was given several compelling explanations for the curious mix of juvenile writing and obvious design skill exhibited in the evidence. Insights accumulated. The danger of taking a wrong turn in the catacombs always looms in this case. Possibilities extend seductively to the horizon. Individual compasses have built-in design flaws of bias and the need to believe. Still, though no specific bull's-eye had emerged, a larger target began inching laterally into Holes's view.

Unexpected discovery is rare in an investigation. It thrills. Deciphering the code that might identify a criminal like the EAR is the turnstile click in the roller-coaster line for a detective. Synapses crackle. The once even-keeled multitasker is officially gripped. The obsessive always remembers the inciting moment. After Holes was finished in Property, he took the pages he found to the nearest photocopier. He was in his lab examining a copy of the hand-drawn map when his clerk spoke up.

"Paul?"

"Hmm?"

"*Paul.*"

Holes lowered the map and raised his eyebrows. The clerk gestured that he should turn the map over. Holes did. He'd noticed doodling on the back earlier but hadn't paid close attention. Now he saw what his clerk meant.

There were several illegible words, open to interpretation. Two words had been scribbled out, one vigorously so. The name Melanie could be faintly made out. But there was something else. The word was so incompatible with the rest of the nonsensical doodling that it took a second to absorb its meaning; that, and the fact that the construction of the letters was different, too— outsize, combining cursive with print, the last letter, a *T*, repeated unnecessarily, taking on a hard, triangular shape. The word's letters were darker than the others on the page, as if the writer had been pressing down angrily. The rest of the doodles had been scribbled in standard linear fashion, but not this. The word was scrawled diagonally. It took up most of the bottom half of the page. The first letter, a *P*, was bigger than the other letters and, most disconcertingly, it was backward.

The overall impression was of an unbalanced mind at work.
"PUNISHMENT."

Holes was hooked.

OUR WALK ON THE IRON HORSE REGIONAL TRAIL STOPS ABRUPTLY
in front of an electrical pole. It's the second pole north of an intersection a couple hundred yards in the distance, the spot where
the bloodhounds lost the EAR's scent and it's believed he entered
a vehicle.

"The homework evidence was found in this area," says Holes.

He has practical reasons for believing that the pages belonged
to the EAR. Tracking dogs aren't infallible, but the fact that three
independent bloodhounds indicated that he escaped south down
the tracks is strong evidence; more important to Holes, the route,
and where the scent trail ended, is consistent with the usual distance from the target that the EAR was known to park before
making an approach. John Patty was a well-respected criminalist
and heavily involved in the Contra Costa County cases; if Patty
collected the evidence, he must have thought it might be important. The other two items found with the homework evidence
are dead ends. The length of purple yarn is a mystery, and the
fragment of paper with some typing on it is illegible. But spiral
notebook paper isn't as incongruous at a sexual crime scene as one
might imagine. Serial sex offenders and killers frequently take
notes as they prowl for victims, sometimes even developing their
own code words. More than one witness who called in a suspicious person during the EAR attacks in Sacramento described a
man holding a spiral notebook. And the EAR, despite his ability to elude authorities, did drop things occasionally; whether on
purpose or not is unclear: a screwdriver, a bloody Band-Aid, a
ballpoint pen.

The ricochet between rage and self-pity in "Mad is the word"
is another clue. Violent criminals like the EAR, that is to say,

serial sex offenders who escalate to homicide, are not only rare but also so varied that generalizing about their backgrounds and behavior is unwise. But common themes do exist. The future nightmare maker begins as an adolescent daydreamer. His world is bisected; violent fantasies act as a muffler against a harsh, disappointing reality. Perceived threats to his self-esteem are disproportionately internalized. Grievances are collected. He rubs his fingers over old scars.

Violent fantasy advances to mental rehearsal. He memorizes a script and refines methods. He's the maltreated hero in the story. Staring up at him anguished-eyed is a rotating cast of terrified faces. His distorted belief system operates around a central, vampiric tenet: his feeling of inadequacy is vanquished when he exerts complete power over a victim, when his actions elicit in her an expression of helplessness; it's a look he recognizes, and hates, in himself.

The majority of violent fantasizers never act. What makes the ones who do cross over? Stress factors coalesce. An emotional match is lit. The daydreamer steps out of his trance and into a stranger's house.

The "Mad is the word" author exhibits the kind of disproportionate emotional response common to violent offenders. A sixth-grade teacher who punished him "built a state of hatred in my heart." The author chooses self-pitying, melodramatic words to describe his experience. "Suffer." "Not fair." "Dreadful." "Horrid."

We begin the walk back to the car. I consider what I know of Danville, which has a trajectory similar to that of many Northern California towns. Once upon a time, it was populated by Native Americans who camped out on Mount Diablo to the northeast, but in 1854 a white man flush with gold rush earnings swooped in and bought ten thousand acres. His name was Dan. Fruit and wheat farming hung in until the 1970s, when new residential construction boomed and people moved in, transforming the town into one of the coziest, wealthiest suburbs of the East Bay. Holes says aerial photos he consulted didn't show a huge construction spike in the neighborhood during the period when the EAR was prowling its backyards. The victim's house was built in the midsixties. Danville's quaint history was a draw. The population doubled by 1980.

The rap on Danville today is that it's homogeneous and status conscious. It was recently ranked number one in America for highest per capita spending on clothing.

"Do you think he grew up in an area like this?" I ask Holes.

"Middle class? Yeah, I think it's likely he's not coming from an impoverished background," he says.

I raise the issue of the EAR's unmatched DNA profile. I'm in wildly speculative territory, I know, but I've always thought it might indicate that he operates behind a front of respectability. I prod Holes for his opinion on the DNA.

"It surprises me," he says. "We've had DNA for over ten years on the national level, and we haven't hit on the guy."

"Does it surprise you there's no familial hit either? Doesn't that suggest someone who comes from a more straitlaced family?"—an opinion thinly veiled as a question.

"I think that could be, versus somebody that's constantly committing criminal acts," he says cautiously.

Holes and I have now spent several hours together. He's great company. Effortless. In fact, his manner is so easygoing and mild that it takes me longer than usual to recognize his conversational patterns. When he's not on board with a particular idea, he'll tell me with equanimity. But when he's uncomfortable with a line of questioning, he sidesteps more obliquely, either by not really answering or by pointing out something of interest in the landscape.

I sense a similar deflection from him on the topic of the EAR's socioeconomic background. Holes is a criminalist, I remind myself. He's a professional quantifier who works with scales and calipers. He's not pedantic, but when presented with lazy inferences, he separates hard fact from mud. He corrects me when I allude to the EAR's thick calves. The witness actually said heavy thighs. Later in the day, he'll show me, via an impressive spreadsheet, how foolhardy it is to conclude anything about the EAR's physicality from victim statements. Eye color and hair color are all over the place. Poor lighting and trauma obscure perceptions. Physical stature is the only constant, Holes points out. The EAR was around five nine. Six feet would be considered on the tall side for a suspect. But they'd still look into him, Holes adds.

"You always want to err on the side of caution."

Ever the scientist.

Prudence and scientific accuracy await me in the future. But at this point, as we prepare to leave Danville, I'm still in theory-riffing mode. I continue to rattle off other clues that the EAR might wear a mask of normalcy. Most of the murder victims were white-collar professionals who lived in upper-class neighborhoods. He must have presented as though he belonged there. He must have had some type of regular employment. He had ways and means.

"We know he had a vehicle," I say.

Holes nods, his face shadowed. He seems to be turning something over in his mind, debating internally the wisdom of sharing a thought.

"We know he had a vehicle," he says. What he says next he says very slowly: "I think he may have had more than that."

I'm momentarily unable to imagine what that could be.

Holes tells me: "I think he may have had a plane."

I stumble over the first and only word that comes to mind.

"Really!?"

He smiles an enigmatic smile. I'd misread him. He wasn't disapproving of my speculative questions. He was considering when to add his own narrative line.

"I'll elaborate at lunch," he promises.

First, we need to make one last stop in Contra Costa County: Walnut Creek.

WALNUT CREEK

The Frank Lloyd Wright–designed Sidney Bazett house on Reservoir Road in Hillsborough, outside San Francisco, is located at the end of a winding, tree-cloaked driveway and not visible from the street. Its extraordinariness is murmured about but rarely seen. One afternoon in 1949 the owner's mother-in-law, who was there alone, was surprised by a knock at the front door. The visitor was a middle-aged businessman in thick-lensed glasses. A half-dozen men in professional attire with serious expressions stood behind him. The man explained that his name was Joseph Eichler. He and his family had rented the house for three years, from 1942 until 1945, when the present owners bought it. The Bazett house, with its redwood built-ins and glass walls, where daylight filtered in from so many directions and changed the mood of each room throughout the day, was a work of art that stirred Eichler. He'd never forgotten the house, he explained. In fact, living in it had changed his life. Now a merchant builder, he'd brought along his colleagues to show them the source of his inspiration. The group was invited inside. Crossing the threshold, Eichler, who got his start on Wall Street and was a notoriously tough businessman, began to cry.

By the mid-1950s, Joseph Eichler was one of the Bay Area's most successful developers of single-family homes in the California Modern style—post-and-beam construction, flat or low-sloping A-frame roofs, open floor plans, glass walls, atria. His ambition grew with his business. He wanted the rapidly expanding postwar middle class to enjoy clean geometric lines; he wanted to bring the

Modernist aesthetic to the masses. Eichler began scouting central Contra Costa County for land to build a subdivision. He needed several hundred acres. More than that, he needed the right feeling. It should be an area on the cusp, unspoiled by urban sprawl but with budding infrastructure. In 1954 Eichler visited Walnut Creek. The town was essentially horse country. Ygnacio Valley Road, now a major thoroughfare, comprised two lanes occupied not infrequently by cows. But the area's first shopping center had recently opened. There was a new hospital. Plans for a freeway were in the works.

In a walnut orchard in the northeast part of town, across from Heather Farm Park, Eichler's search came to an end. Mount Diablo shimmered in the distance. Here was the perfect place, he thought, for a community of creative professionals, progressive types who appreciated modern art and design, people who were tired of living in cookie-cutter houses where you could find your way around blindfolded. The subdivision of 563 houses, 375 Eichler homes, the rest standard tract, was completed in 1958. A brochure shows a beautiful woman in a flowing dress gazing out a wall of glass into her tidy backyard. The roof is post and beam; the chairs, Eames. Eichler named his new community Rancho San Miguel.

The neighborhood had its detractors. Some thought the Eichler design, with its blank wall to the street and orientation toward the backyard, was antisocial. Waving from the front window at neighbors was no longer possible. Others thought the houses were ugly and resembled garages. Nevertheless, Eichlers, as people call them, have developed a devoted cult following, and Rancho San Miguel, with its parks and good schools, has remained a consistently coveted place to live. But the unusual homes, with rear glass walls, sliding doors, and high fences sealing off individual backyards, have also attracted another kind of following, not forward-thinking but darkly motivated, a fact that isn't mentioned publicly but has been puzzled over privately for years.

Holes and I pull up to the site of the first Walnut Creek EAR attack, an Eichler in Rancho San Miguel.

"I call this the Bermuda Triangle of Contra Costa County," says Holes. "We've had other serial killers attack in this same neighborhood. A missing girl. A known serial-killer attack. A housewife in 1966 that was strangled and her panties torn off. The two EAR attacks. And it's like, why?"

In the spring of 1979 a seventeen-year-old girl who lived in Rancho San Miguel in Walnut Creek began to receive a series of anonymous calls. What was especially unsettling was that the calls followed her to homes where she was babysitting. The parents would leave, the kids put to bed. A ring would knife through the quiet. "Hello?" The familiar blankness was always followed by a *click*, the only sign there was a human being with intent on the other line.

The girl sat regularly for two families who lived in Eichlers across from each other on El Divisadero. In early May, a nightgown and telephone directory went missing from her own house; even so, she didn't feel the hot breath of a threat moving in close. The thing about Eichlers is, they draw your attention to the outside. Walls of glass display occupants like rare museum objects. At night the play of light against dark means your view is limited to your reflection. The opaqueness fires the queasy imagination.

In five months, the movie *When a Stranger Calls* would be released. Based on a well-known urban legend, the story involves a teenage babysitter who's tormented by a series of increasingly sinister calls. "Have you checked the children?" an unidentified man asks. The off-white rotary phone sits menacingly in the living room like a time bomb. The drip of fear spikes at the end of the opening scene, when the detective trying to help the babysitter calls her back with an urgent message.

"We've traced the call. It's coming from inside the house."

Animal fear writ modern.

When a Stranger Calls hadn't come out yet on June 2, 1979. No anonymous calls came for the babysitter in Walnut Creek that Saturday night; there was no sense that a silent phone meant that an alternate approach was being considered and planned.

She was sitting at the kitchen table when she heard footsteps or a man's voice; she couldn't remember which came first, only that he shot up suddenly, as if spring-loaded from the dark hallway and into her terrified heart.

He said little and repeated what little he said. He communicated with jerky, unpredictable bursts of violence. He shoved her head down. He tied her wrists tightly with plastic cable ties. He bit her left nipple. Criminalists are required to take photographs of victims at the scene. No one looks happy, but everyone looks into the camera. Not the babysitter. Her gaze is averted, eyes anchored low. They seem unlikely to ever come up.

A large open field and a school were across the street at the time. The house next door was empty and posted for lease. Dogs tracked the EAR's scent around the corner, where he'd evidently gotten into a vehicle; he'd parked in front of a house where a pool was being built.

Police patrolling the neighborhood after the rape stopped a drunk driver with a knife and sheath. They stopped a man with his pants down who said he was looking for his lost cat. In his car were photographs of unsuspecting women taken with a zoom lens. They were just two of the dark compulsives scuttling through the suburbs at night, like the waterways cemented over but still churning underneath Walnut Creek.

Twenty-three days later, the EAR returned to Rancho San Miguel.

Investigators who've worked the lead on serial cases say there are times when they feel that the offender is speaking to them, as if their private thoughts have been telegraphed and he's responding. It's a wordless dialogue familiar to obsessive competitors, an exchange of small gestures whose meaning only the two people locked in battle understand. In the first leg of the race between cop and at-large criminal, the investigator is the clock-watcher with the anxious, racing mind, and the offender is the string puller with the haunting smirk.

The second Eichler was just a hundred feet from the first. The victim was a thirteen-year-old this time. Her father and sister were in the house, unaware of what was taking place. The tracking dogs yanked their handlers around a corner and stopped abruptly in a familiar place: the same spot as before, in front of the house where the pool was being built.

The details of the crime coalesced to form a disembodied shit-eating grin.

"Has he ever gone back?" the thirteen-year-old asked the investigators interviewing her after the attack.

"Never," said the first investigator.

"Never, ever, ever," said the second.

"The safest house in the area," said the first.

As if any house was ever going to feel safe again.

THE NEIGHBORHOOD DOESN'T FIT EXACTLY WITH HOLES'S CON-struction angle. The Eichlers were all built in the 1950s. Rancho San Miguel didn't have active development going on at the time, though there was some adjacent development. It's two miles from the 680 freeway.

"It's a little off the beaten track," says Holes, looking around. "Something is pulling him out to this outside neighborhood."

The drive through Contra Costa County is different for Holes than it is for me. I'm seeing the neighborhoods for the first time. Holes is driving through old murders. Every "Welcome to . . ."

sign is accompanied by the memory of forensic evidence, of blurry-eyed afternoons spent in the lab hunched over a microscope. Walnut Creek particularly resonates for Holes, reminding him of the mystery of a missing girl.

Elaine Davis was going to sew a brass button on her navy peacoat. Her mother left their home on Pioneer Avenue, in north Walnut Creek, to pick up Elaine's father from work. It was ten thirty p.m. on December 1, 1969, a Monday night. When the Davises returned home, Elaine, a seventeen-year-old straight-A student with sandy blonde hair and a heart-shaped face, was gone. Her three-year-old sister was still asleep in her crib. The house appeared undisturbed. Elaine, who was nearsighted, had left her badly needed glasses behind. Items of Elaine's began to surface. The button she intended to sew on her coat was found in a field behind her house. Her brown loafer with a gold buckle was picked up on Interstate 680 in Alamo. A housewife spotted a petite girl's navy peacoat on a remote stretch of highway in the Santa Cruz Mountains, seventy-five miles away.

Eighteen days after Elaine disappeared, a female body floated ashore at Lighthouse Point in Santa Cruz. A radiologist studied the bones and concluded that the woman was twenty-five to thirty years old. It wasn't Elaine. The Jane Doe was buried in an unmarked grave. The Davis disappearance went cold.

Thirty-one years later, a Walnut Creek police detective nearing retirement brought the case file to Holes, who reviewed it. Holes concluded that the radiologist was wrong and couldn't have made an accurate determination of age. Holes joined other officials in an effort to exhume the Jane Doe's body. Twenty-five feet deep on the side of a hill, shovels connected with a plastic body bag filled with bones.

Elaine's father was dead. Her mother lived in Sacramento. Two days after the exhumation, Walnut Creek detectives asked to speak with her. Elaine's younger sister came in from out of town for the meeting. The detectives told the mother and sister the news: we've identified Elaine.

"The family buries her," says Holes. "A week later, Mom dies."

We leave Walnut Creek, heading north. Mount Diablo, a mass of strange protrusions towering above valleys cut precisely into planned communities, recedes. Black mountain cats are said to slink among the high rocks on Mount Diablo. Mysterious lights have been glimpsed. In 1873 a live frog was found partially embedded in a slab of limestone 228 feet underground, according to local legend. In late August and early September, just after the first fall rain, hundreds of male tarantulas emerge from holes in the ground. They skitter through mint-scented mountain sage in search of burrows delicately draped in silk, where females are ready to mate. Visitors armed with flashlights flock to the mountain around sunset or just after dark, the best time to see the tarantulas. Bats wheel over gray pines and live oaks. Great horned owls hoot solemnly. Beams from flashlights weaving across trails sometimes catch a piece of earth that's moving; closer inspection reveals the scuttling of saucer-size tarantulas. The male tarantulas never return to their holes. They mate as much as they can and then die, from starvation or cold.

We cross the bridge to Solano County, where we'll turn east toward Davis.

"On a clear day, you can see Sacramento from here. And the Sierras," says Holes.

He lives halfway between Sacramento and the East Bay. On weekends he often finds himself visiting the crime scenes.

"I like to drive," he says. Whenever he's in Southern California, he visits the crime scenes there too. During trips to Disneyland with his family, when the kids grow drowsy, his wife oversees naptime at the hotel while Holes takes a drive. To the Northwood subdivision in Irvine, to 13 Encina, where Janelle Cruz lived, or to 35 Columbus, where Drew Witthuhn cleaned up his sister-in-law Manuela's blood.

"Each time I'm trying to look for Why here?" Holes says. "Why this?"

DAVIS

[EDITOR'S NOTE: This section features selections from the audio transcript from the trip to Davis.]

PAUL HOLES: This is how the EAR would have traveled down to the East Bay. Along I-80, right here.

MICHELLE: If you had to guess his point of origin, in terms of where he went to school . . . I won't keep you to it. I'm just curious.

PAUL HOLES: If I were to guess? Sac State. If he was college-educated. Locationwise, if you take a look at where his attacks are, you know, you have the whole Rancho Cordova cluster. You have the attacks along La Riviera. You have the attacks that are right there, right by Sac State. Sac State seems likely. Now, you have some community colleges up in the Sacramento area that he could have gone to. Uh, high school? Uh . . . whew. There's so many possibilities.

MICHELLE: I mean, you don't feel like, maybe he grew up in Goleta?

PAUL HOLES: I wouldn't say that, but when I look at the Sac cases, and—this is one thing I want to show you at some point—when you do a flyover of the order of his attacks in Sacramento, you see very early on, he is literally crisscrossing Sacramento. He is showing intimate familiarity with the area.

MICHELLE: He's not showing up just to go to Sac State.

PAUL HOLES: No, no. I think he has a history up in Sacramento.

Now, does he have a history in Goleta? I mean, anything's possible. We don't know. But down south, Goleta is—for me—that's ground zero down south. And there's something in Irvine. Some reason why he has two cases there.

MICHELLE: And that are not far apart at all.

PAUL HOLES: No. No. Ventura and Laguna Niguel are the two outliers. *[EDITOR'S NOTE: Holes is referring to the Dana Point case here; some people mistakenly consider Dana Point part of Laguna Niguel.]*

PAUL HOLES: Davis/Modesto, to me, is significant.

MICHELLE: Modesto was just once or twice?

PAUL HOLES: Twice.

MICHELLE: Okay.

PAUL HOLES: So, when I did my initial geographic assessment, I broke the EAR into phases. The first phase being up in Sacramento. Second phase being Modesto/Davis. Third phase being East Bay, and then the fourth phase being down in Southern California. When you get to this phase two—I lump Stockton into Sacramento because the EAR goes back to Sacramento after Stockton, but then once he hits in Modesto, he doesn't go back to Sacramento until after he comes down into the East Bay. And he's toggling back and forth between Modesto and Davis. It's a hundred ten driving miles between those two cities. And between the second Modesto attack and the second Davis attack, it's just twenty-two hours' difference. Why is he toggling back and forth? I think it's work-related. He's not doing this to throw law enforcement off. I think there's a work-related reason why he's being sent to Modesto and having to go to Davis, and going back and forth.

MICHELLE: There's only a twenty-two-hour difference?

PAUL HOLES: Twenty-two-hour difference.

MICHELLE: Wow. I didn't know it was so close in time.

PAUL HOLES: And it just so happens, in those two cases, and

only those two cases . . . In the Modesto case, you have the cab driver that picks up the strange man from the airport, who he drops off and is last seen headed toward new construction under way that's just south of where the victims are attacked. And in the Davis case, that's where the footprints lead back from the victim's house to the UC-Davis airport. Shoe prints. That's what I'm going to show you. So, is it possible that you've got the EAR flying into Modesto for that one attack, and then flying up to UC-Davis for the second attack?

MICHELLE: For work?

PAUL HOLES: For work. And, what does that say about who he is?

MICHELLE: Yeah.

PAUL HOLES: Well, your common joe ain't flying an airplane.

MICHELLE: No.

PAUL HOLES: Your common joe ain't producing a diagram that is, "How should I lay out this land?"

MICHELLE: Right.

PAUL HOLES: It takes somebody with resources. Because when you read the case file on the EAR, you don't think this is somebody of wealth, right?

MICHELLE: Right.

PAUL HOLES: I don't get that. This seems contradictory to that. But that's what the EAR was about. Everything about him was misdirection.

MICHELLE: So, you're leaning toward thinking he had more resources?

PAUL HOLES: I think he has . . . well, I think if this turns out EAR was doing this not for just a school project, but he's actually looking at developing land and working for a developer, he's at least minimally hooked in to the company at a level where he's got a lot of say in that company.

PAUL HOLES: So, this is Village Homes in Davis. Village

Homes is a very famous development. What I'm showing you is, coincidentally, an aerial photo of Village Homes as it was in between the first and second Davis attacks. So, literally, they just happened to take this picture eight days before attack number thirty-six. This is what it looked like. And look at all of this new construction that's going on just north of the attack. I'll take you out and show you the whole airport thing.

PAUL HOLES: The Stockton victim I've been talking to, she worked for a major developer in the Central Valley. The victim did a lot of work for him. She ended up leaving his company when she got pregnant. I was showing this diagram [the "homework" evidence map] to a friend of mine who works in development. He told me, "This was done by a professional. . . . He's drafting these symbols." Now, this is an opinion that's coming from a forensic expert in the construction business. So I put a lot of credence in that opinion.

MICHELLE: I think you're right. I don't believe this is a fantasy.

PAUL HOLES: I don't think so. You know, you have a landscape architect from UC-Davis going, "There's unique features in here that are only seen in Village Homes."

MICHELLE: Oh really?

PAUL HOLES: Yes. And you'll see this when we go out there. Village Homes is a very unusual development. So, you have the EAR going and attacking there. Could it be possible that the EAR is going to Village Homes and when he sees some of those features, he incorporates those in this diagram, for whatever he's working on?

MICHELLE: Right. As something he would submit, along the lines of "Hey, we should do this," or something like that?

PAUL HOLES: Yeah.

Holes arrives at the apartment complex where the first Davis attack took place.

This attack, number thirty-four, occurred at approximately three fifty a.m. on June 7, 1978—two days after the EAR's first attack in Modesto. The victim was a twenty-one-year-old UC-Davis student who lived in a multistory apartment building, which Larry Pool would later deem a "structural anomaly"—as this was the only time the EAR was known to have targeted such a dwelling.

He entered the second-story apartment through the patio sliding glass door. He was particularly violent with this victim, punching her several times in the face after she initially resisted. While raping her, he forcefully shoved her face into the floor, leaving her with a broken nose and a concussion.

Certain factors suggest that this attack may have been more impulsive than most of the others: he was wearing a nylon stocking instead of a ski mask; the only known weapons were a nail file and a screwdriver; and the assailant appeared to be wearing his T-shirt inside out. The crime was undoubtedly an EAR attack, however, based on verbiage and the signature element of the rapist placing his penis in the victim's bound hands and forcing her to masturbate him.

PAUL HOLES: Alright, so the first Davis one was the college girl that was attending UC-Davis. A textile major.

MICHELLE: This is the one where they thought they saw him peeling out of the parking lot?

PAUL HOLES: Yep. It was a black Camaro, or something like that. But I'm not sure that was him.

PAUL HOLES: So, this has changed. I actually lived here once myself.

MICHELLE: Oh, wow. Is this technically campus housing?

PAUL HOLES: These are off-campus dorms. I think they were different back in the seventies. This has even changed since I was here.

Holes stops and lets the car idle.

PAUL HOLES: This is all college kids. Russell Boulevard, you see all the college kids biking. So, if he's up in Davis for any reason, I think this would be a case where he's seeing somebody that he follows back.
MICHELLE: Oh, okay.
PAUL HOLES: He sees a girl that, for whatever reason, catches his eye, and then he figures out where she lives. I don't think he's prowling or burglarizing. This is atypical from his . . .
MICHELLE: Usual thing.
PAUL HOLES: Yeah.

They move on to the second location, which was the scene of attack number thirty-six. The second of three Davis strikes, it occurred around three a.m. on June 24, 1978—one day after EAR rape number thirty-five, in Modesto.

The victim was a thirty-two-year-old housewife whose husband was in bed with her. Both were bound. Also present was the couple's ten-year-old son, whom the attacker locked in the bathroom. He rummaged through the house before returning to the female, moving her to the living room, and raping her. Prior to leaving the house, he stole seventeen rolls of pennies.

PAUL HOLES: We're now entering Village Homes.
MICHELLE: Okay.
PAUL HOLES: All the streets are named after *Lord of the Rings*.
MICHELLE: Oh. Really?
PAUL HOLES: Yep. The developer, Michael Corbett, was heavily involved in *Lord of the Rings*.

MICHELLE: Heavily involved meaning . . .

PAUL HOLES: Well, big fan.

MICHELLE: Oh, okay. He was a nerd.

PAUL HOLES: He and his wife, Judy Corbett, are the ones that pushed this development. All these houses . . . we're on the street, these are the backs of these houses. The fronts of the houses face a green common area. And that was to help facilitate more of the community feel. So, neighbors are coming out. They have gardens—community gardens; green spaces that are shared.

MICHELLE: So, if you were a student, you wouldn't live here?

PAUL HOLES: Unlikely. I mean, you could, but at that time, these were new houses. Students couldn't afford these.

Holes drives through the community looking for the home where the attack took place.

PAUL HOLES: So, our victim . . . lived in this one. Right here on the right-hand side.

MICHELLE: Hmm.

PAUL HOLES: And all of that on this side was actively being constructed at the time. So, you see the long, narrow cul-de-sacs, to which the city said, "Absolutely not." And then the Corbetts had the fire departments bring the fire trucks out here, to show them, yes, you can turn around back here. I'll drive around so you can kind of see some of the features of this place. Solar. All the houses were passive solar. That was big, back in the day.

PAUL HOLES: Here's an example here. This is a pedestrian bridge over the open-swale drainage. And this is the way the EAR came up.

MICHELLE: How do you know that?

PAUL HOLES: Shoe prints. Corbett was telling me this area down here was like a sandbox. Every day, he raked it smooth. And after the attack, he's out here, and there's a shoe impression in his freshly raked sandbox. And he followed that shoe impression to the victim's house, around the house, through the green area. And I'm talking to him, and he goes, "Well, I was in the Boy Scouts, and one of the things I really enjoyed doing was tracking. And I used to track all the time." And so, he says, "I found these shoe prints and I felt I needed to track them." So, he's got more of an elevated ability than the average person. I wouldn't say he's some search-and-rescue expert, but . . .

MICHELLE: He kinda knew what he was doing.

PAUL HOLES: Yeah. So, then he's saying, these shoe prints came down through here and went out this way.

MICHELLE: Huh.

PAUL HOLES: It's like a common green area.

MICHELLE: Wait, so they kind of went in a loop, around?

PAUL HOLES: Yes, so, he went and he came up this way, and looped around from the victim's house, and these shoe prints were in the victim's backyard.

MICHELLE: This is an interesting development. I really don't think I've ever been inside something like this.

PAUL HOLES: It's unique. Village Homes was world-famous. François Mitterrand flew in in a helicopter to visit this area because of how novel it was. Students from all over, and developers, were coming here to take a look at it. And so that's where you can see, you know, "Village Homes in Davis. We're doing a development; let's see what they're doing and what we can incorporate into our thing." It was featured . . . on the cover of *Sunset* magazine. Betty Ford rode her bike around here. I drove my wife through here, and she goes, "I'd never live here."

MICHELLE: It is a little claustrophobic.

PAUL HOLES: It's claustrophobic, and it's a predator's paradise. You can't see anything. I mean, he can come in, he can attack, and he can leave, and nobody would ever know.

PAUL HOLES: The third victim—and I'll take you by that after this—was in the neighborhood that's right over there. So, the three Davis attacks are pretty close together.

MICHELLE: Yeah, they are.

PAUL HOLES: One of the interesting things is that this victim and the third Davis victim carpooled together. Their kids were at the same nursery school. And that's the only known connection between victims that I'm aware of. But that's never really been explored.

MICHELLE: Right.

PAUL HOLES: Nobody's gone back to these victims to talk to them. Could the EAR have seen them together in a carpool and that's why he chose them, or was it just coincidence because he attacked so close together?

MICHELLE: Right. Did each know that the other was a victim? You don't even know that?

PAUL HOLES: I don't even know that, no.

PAUL HOLES: So, EAR came out here . . . and now he's tracking along on this side. And they kind of dismissed some of this at first; the initial officer that Corbett called out, Corbett tells him, "Hey, I've tracked these shoe prints," and the officer goes, "Well, this is a common jogging path, and it's so far away, I can't see the offender ever parking his vehicle down here and then getting up here to attack." Well, the shoe prints end up going down, following the path on this olive grove, down that way.

PAUL HOLES: So, here's the other side of this olive grove.

MICHELLE: Okay. So, he might have been parked like on a shoulder right here?

PAUL HOLES: Nope. 'Cause the shoe prints continued.

MICHELLE: Oh my gosh. Isn't that a little risky that he'd be seen?

PAUL HOLES: Late at night? This is pitch-black!

MICHELLE: Okay. And he's probably wearing dark clothing.

PAUL HOLES: I mean, what does he do all the time? And he's in neighborhoods, with houses. Walking around. That's probably riskier than this.

MICHELLE: Yeah, I guess that's true.

Holes drives deeper into UC-Davis property, with various research buildings spread out to the right and agricultural fields to the left.

PAUL HOLES: So, he tracks the shoe prints . . . all the way down to here. I can't get through here. This is what's called Bee Biology. They do a lot of bee studies here.

MICHELLE: Oh, uh huh.

PAUL HOLES: When I initially read this case file, I couldn't make it out. I thought it was Boo Biology. And I'm thinking it's on campus way over there, and I'm going, "This is nothing." But when you look at where he says he lost track, the shoe prints ended up veering down to the left. What's down here? Well . . . look here. It's the airport!

MICHELLE: Oh!

PAUL HOLES: So, I'm now calling airports saying, "What kind of records do you have?"

They both laugh.

PAUL HOLES: My naive thought about flying is, you know . . . every time you flew a plane, you had to file a flight plan; you fly into an airport, they know you're there, and everything else. But they told me, "No, no. Anybody can come and go here. We have no idea they're here. If they come in after hours, they tie their plane down. They go do their thing, they come back, we'll never know they're here."

MICHELLE: Is that right?! That is strange.

PAUL HOLES: So, here we've got this case, twenty-two hours after the case in Modesto occurred. The case in Modesto has the strange man being picked up at an airport, being dropped off, near new construction, seemingly heading toward the victim's home.

MICHELLE: But why was that man so strange?

PAUL HOLES: The cab driver said he just had a single bag. And he just says, "Take me to Sylvan and Meadow." And then, "Drop me off right here." He gets out and just wanders to where the cab driver says there's nothing there but houses being built. And then the next case . . . we have an airport connection.

MICHELLE: I'm trying to think of what kind of person would have a plane like that. Like, a small plane?

PAUL HOLES: Well, a small plane opens up possibilities. You know, these developers typically had your multiseat corporate jets. If you're talking about somebody with a small plane, somebody who's not a millionaire, you know, or somebody with huge resources, having a . . .

MICHELLE: Yeah.

PAUL HOLES: So, if you're talking to these developers, and saying, well, "Would you fly? If you have developments across the state, would you fly there?" They answer, "Yeah, we would fly there. Flying an airplane is very expensive, but it was sort of an ego thing. So, we would want to be perceived as successful, because we have our own jet that we're flying in. And yeah, occasionally we would go and check on our kingdoms that are being built."

MICHELLE: Right. Hmm. Were there any other little clues from

any of the cases that tied into a plane? Like, any kind of . . .
didn't he have, like, a navigator's something?

PAUL HOLES: No, not that I can think of.

*Holes is trying to locate the home of the third Davis victim. This
attack, number thirty-seven, occurred on July 6, 1978, at 2:40 in the
morning. The victim was a thirty-three-year-old woman—recently
separated and in the bed alone—whose sons were sleeping in another
room. The EAR used them as leverage, threatening to kill them if
she didn't do what he said. After raping and sodomizing the victim,
he sobbed. A three-month hiatus would then follow, after which he
resurfaced in the East Bay area.*

PAUL HOLES: It was a corner house. I want to say it was the end.
I don't think these houses were here at the time. And there are
no houses behind. And then you had the construction going
on at the school. So, the attack occurred here. There was lots
of construction going on in this area. . . . Here it is. So . . . this
victim carpooled with the previous Davis victim.

MICHELLE: Wow. A lot of these scenes are a lot closer to each
other than I thought they were. I mean, some aren't, but . . .
some, it's interesting.

PAUL HOLES: Right. Well, neighborhoods. He got familiar
with the neighborhoods. Danville is tightly clustered. Concord.
Walnut Creek.

MICHELLE: Certainly, I mean, Rancho Cordova . . . weren't
some right next to each other?

PAUL HOLES: Yeah. Not quite right next to each other, but
right around the block. You know, the house between.

MICHELLE: Right. I mean, and if you're walking away without
your pants on, you either live there or your car is right there.
Or you're kind of crazy. Or all of the above.

PAUL HOLES: Well, one of these guys I spent a lot of time on, a serial killer by the name of Phillip Hughes . . . in his interviews with the psychiatrist, he admits to, when he was in high school, leaving his house in the middle of the night—parents had no idea—he'd be nude, and he'd break into other houses in the neighborhood to steal the clothing from the women.

MICHELLE: And this was before he'd actually been violent with anyone?

PAUL HOLES: Yeah, as far as we know. He had killed some animals. You know . . . the whole serial-killer triad thing [the theory that torturing animals, setting fires, and bedwetting past early childhood predict sexual violence in adulthood].

MICHELLE: Right.

PAUL HOLES: But this was at the high school age. I think there's a certain . . . thrill to being out without the clothes on.

MICHELLE: Right.

PAUL HOLES: Now, there could be a practical thing too, you know? Let's say it's his first attack, and he's going, "Well, how am I going to deal with the pants? I'm just not going to wear them. I don't want them in the way."

MICHELLE: Right. Yeah, that's why it's interesting to me that in a lot of the murders, he killed them with whatever was handy there.

PAUL HOLES: Yeah. He had a gun, but in terms of the bludgeoning, he used what was there.

MICHELLE: Is there anything about people who bludgeon that's different from people who do other stuff?

PAUL HOLES: Well, bludgeoning and stabbing in essence are the same thing. You know, it's very personal. You're taking out a lot of violence, a lot of anger, on that person. Now, strangulation . . . beating with your fists or strangling, that's all . . .

MICHELLE: So anything you do with your hands is kind of out of the same thing?

PAUL HOLES: Yeah, it's all the same. Versus killing with a gun—it's less personal. And it's easy. Anybody can kill anybody with a gun. You can kill from a distance. But when you're in physical confrontation with the person, that's a personal thing. You know, you read about these guys who are looking in the victim's eyes as they're strangling them . . .

MICHELLE: Right.

PAUL HOLES: You know, and they feel Godlike because, in essence, they are controlling whether this victim lives or dies.

FRED RAY

I'M NOT ENJOYING MY SECOND CUP OF TERRIBLE COFFEE IN A CAFÉ
in Kingsburg, California, twenty miles southeast of Fresno, when
I'm given an explanation to a mystery that's puzzled me for years.
The man who provides the answer, Fred Ray, is tall and laconic
and possesses a slightly nasal drawl befitting a descendent of generations of Central Valley farmers. When Ray isn't using his long
fingers to emphasize a point, he folds his hands and rests them
gently on his chest like a scholar. His mostly brown hair is envi-
ously abundant for a retired detective who's being asked about a
thirty-five-year-old double murder he once investigated. I formed
a certain ungenerous impression when Ray first loped in with his
battered briefcase and Dust Bowl twang. He wanted to meet on
the early side to avoid the high school crowd, he told me, but I spot
no one under seventy in the tiny café, which consists of a handful
of tables covered in thick, clear plastic, shelves of Swedish knick-
knacks (Kingsburg is known as Little Sweden), and a narrow glass
counter displaying scattered pastries. Two of the café's few patrons
are Ray's wife and then his pastor, who asks me where I'm from
even though I haven't been identified as an out-of-town visitor. I
tell him I'm from Los Angeles.

"Welcome to the state of California," the pastor says.

But my impression of Ray changes abruptly early in our conversation, when he's describing his time as a detective with the
Santa Barbara County Sheriff's Office, in particular his experience

interrogating a certain kind of troubled kid. Outwardly the kids, young white males mostly, presented little threat. The laid-back pace of an old-money coastal town trickled down to them, even if they didn't live in upscale Hope Ranch, with its horse paths and private beach, but the trailer park on Hollister. These were Garys and Keiths, shaggy-haired late-seventies burnouts who started but never finished Dos Pueblos or San Marcos High. They dragged beat-up armchairs into the avocado groves and hid out smoking homegrown weed. They surfed Haskell's Beach all day and gathered around bonfires at night, drunk and feeling safely out of reach; they knew the cops would never hike down the sage-scrub-covered bluffs to break up a beach party. Their troubles were petty stuff. Minor aggravations. Except that Ray discovered a surprising number of them engaged in a chilling pastime, one they kept secret even from each other: they got a thrill out of breaking into strangers' homes in the middle of the night.

They were prowlers. Peepers. Burglary was an afterthought. What they took pride in, Ray learned from talking to them, was their ability to get inside a house, crawl along a floor, and stand unnoticed in the dark, watching people sleep. Ray was amazed at the details they would share with him once he got them started.

"I always had a way of getting guys to talk to me," Ray says.

"How would you do it?"

He opens his hands. His features soften almost imperceptibly.

"Well, you know, everyone does that," he says, his tone both conspiratorial and direct. "Everybody has wanted to see what's going on in someone else's house."

That sounds reasonable. I nod.

"Right," I say.

But then Ray snaps back to his former self, his real self, and I realize that, without my noticing, he'd assumed a slight slouch and slackened his expression to appear more casual. This wasn't the ham-fisted method used to coax information out of a suspect as seen on *Law and Order*. The abrupt transition was startling. I bought the act completely. One of Ray's most winning mannerisms is a huge, unpredictable smile that's the opposite of eager and therefore more gratifying when you prompt it. He got me, and he knows it. He grins.

"They all want to tell their story, but they want to tell it to somebody that's not going to freak out on them. When you sit there showing no emotion, kind of agreeing with them, almost like you're enjoying what they're telling you, they'll talk."

The parade of troubled young men whom Ray questioned decades ago interests me for a specific reason.

"You interviewed these guys, these prowlers," I say. "Do you think you might have talked to him?"

"No," he says quickly.

Then carefully, "I could have."

But he's shaking his head.

Him. The third person at every interview I conduct, the faceless killer whose tennis-shoe impressions Ray once tracked through the neighborhood, retracing the man's path as he crept from window to window, searching for victims. Ray was deeply involved in the case of a serial killer who picked up hitchhikers, shot them in the side of the head, and then had sex with their corpses; over the course of his career, he has stood over headless bodies and examined ritualistic carvings on the decomposing skin of a young woman. Yet the only killer he mentions who made, as he says, "the hair on the back of my neck stand up," was the one who brought me here. Him.

That Ray doesn't believe he talked to the unidentified man I've dubbed the Golden State Killer doesn't surprise me. Every detective I've interviewed who's worked the case insists the same thing. They've held precut ligatures he left behind and stared at his spermatozoa under a microscope. They've played and replayed audio recordings of hypnotized witnesses and survivors, listening for any throwaway clues to his identity. Decades after retirement, one detective found himself squatting in the woods outside a possible suspect's house in Oregon, waiting for the trash to come out so he could swipe a DNA sample. The Golden State Killer haunts their dreams. He's ruined their marriages. He's burrowed so deeply inside their heads that they want to, or have to, believe that if they locked eyes with him, they'd know.

"It's kind of like a bloodhound thing," a detective said to me. "I believe if I were at a mall and he passed by me, I'd know."

I explain to Ray that the reason I'm interested in his memories of young prowlers is that I recently visited Goleta, the city eight miles west of Santa Barbara on California's Central Coast where the killer attacked three times between 1979 and 1981. All three attacks took place in an unassuming neighborhood in northeast Goleta, an area occupying less than two square miles. Shoe tracks and twine ligatures presumably dropped by accident from his pockets show that he moved along San Jose Creek, a narrow gorge that begins in the mountains to the north and meanders through the neighborhood of tract homes until emptying into the Pacific Ocean. His victims all lived close to the creek.

I walked along the creek bed, I tell Ray, and was struck by how captivating the overgrown path, shrouded in huge, draping trees and strewn with moss-covered rocks, would be for a certain kind of suburban adolescent boy, a semiwild, underparented kid yearning for refuge. Rope swings dangled from sycamore trees. Adults who'd grown up in the neighborhood told me that in the midseventies some boys built a BMX track down there. There were secret tunnels and cement-lined drainage ditches where kids skateboarded. There were no lights, and the path was confusing and hard to follow. It felt like the kind of place you'd know only if you'd spent a lot of time down there as a kid.

"Especially when you consider the first attack on Queen Ann

Lane," I say. The Queen Ann Lane house isn't even visible from the street, as it's located behind another house. You'd notice it only from the path along the creek.

The mention of the October 1, 1979, attack on Queen Ann Lane hardens Ray's otherwise matter-of-fact face.

"You know, they could have caught him that night," Ray says.

That was the night he realized he had to kill. The night the victims survived and their neighbor, an off-duty FBI agent, pursued the suspect as he fled on a stolen ten-speed bike. I've walked the route of the pursuit and stopped at the place where the agent lost him. The agent was in radio contact with deputies who were on their way. I've never quite understood how he wasn't apprehended.

"I knew what was going to happen," Ray says. He shakes his head. "I knew exactly what the deputies were going to do."

What they did was let him slip away.

THE ONE

THE FIRST MOMENT OF JIM WALTHER'S* OVER THIRTY-YEAR ENTAN-glement with the EAR case began in Danville, in the early morn-ing hours of February 2, 1979, when he was roused awake by Contra Costa Sheriff's Deputy Carl Fabbri's flashlight. Walther said he'd pulled his gray-primer-coated 1968 Pontiac LeMans off Interstate 680 to sleep after leaving his job as a brakeman for the Western Pacific Railroad. Fabbri didn't buy the story. Walther's car was parked on Camino Tassajara, a good mile and a half from the freeway. Why drive that far for a nap? He searched Walther's eyes for signs of sleep. Fabbri's hackles were up. He was patrolling the neighborhood because he'd unsuccessfully chased a prowler here the night before. Five months earlier, Sacramento's most infa-mous phantom, the East Area Rapist, had writhed his way seventy miles southwest to their area. Four attacks. A thirty-two-year-old divorcée living in a corner house near the Iron Horse Regional Trail had been the most recent victim, in December. "Do you like to raise dicks?" he whispered to her. "Then why do you raise mine every time I see you?" The attack was just over a mile from where Walther was now parked.

Deputy Fabbri ordered Walther to stay put and ran a check on him. The kid had an open warrant for outstanding vehicle-code violations. His record showed a low-grade marijuana bust

---

* Pseudonym

two years earlier—in Sacramento. He was twenty-one, five ten, 150. The broad outline was looking good, if not the particulars. Fabbri and his partner placed Walther under arrest. His protests were routine white noise until Fabbri's partner took out a Polaroid camera to snap a mug shot, and a switch flipped. Walther went apeshit. Fabbri had to physically subdue him. It was weird. The kid had a minor record. Why was he so freaked out about having his picture taken? They had to hold his head up to get the shot.

En route to jail, Walther conducted a strange, mostly one-way conversation with his arresting officers.

"Nobody ever catches the real criminals," Walther told them. "They always get away."

DAMNING COINCIDENCES PILED ON FROM THE START. WHEN asked for his address, Walther put down Sutter Avenue, Carmichael. East Sacramento. A deputy recalled seeing a car like Walther's distinct one in nearby San Ramon around the time of the EAR attacks there. Shortly after his arrest, Walther ditched the car and got a new one. He shut down when EAR Task Force investigators questioned him, and he lawyered up, courtesy of his mother—an overbearing woman who referred to her adult son as "my Jimmy" and who'd once nearly come to blows with his probation officer. The lawyer told investigators his client wouldn't chew on gauze for a saliva sample because "it might be incriminating." The task force continued to lean on Walther. He continued to resist. He volunteered in passing that his blood type was A and he wore a size 9 shoe, same as the EAR's. Finally, in August, they called him out of his girlfriend's apartment and told him they knew she was growing marijuana in there. They gave him a stark choice: either chew on gauze now, or we're arresting her. He chewed on gauze.

The saliva results eliminated Walther. He was a secretor. The

EAR was a nonsecretor. The task force dropped him as a suspect and moved on to fresher dirtbags.

————————

MORE THAN THIRTY YEARS LATER, PAUL HOLES QUESTIONED THAT elimination. As a veteran of the crime lab, he knew that the secretor-status testing method back then was less than ideal. In the 1980s, quality-control experts had found serious glitches in the method. In the intervening years, scientists had also discovered that a small segment of the population are aberrant secretors, individuals who may express ABO type in some of their fluids but not others. Holes felt that suspect eliminations based on secretor status were unreliable.

Holes also had the benefit of retrospection, three decades' worth. They knew much more about the EAR now. Holes could open Google Earth on his computer and fly over the attack locations and scenes of suspicious circumstances in chronological order, a dizzying flight from yellow pushpin to miniature blue car to little people representing footprints or witnesses. He could adjust for speed and height. He could sit at his desk and follow the killer's trail with his eyes. The zigzag path looked random, but for someone, the One, it was not.

Holes regrets not making a switch to the investigations unit twenty years ago, when he was first tempted. Certainty won. He had two small kids. He was climbing the ranks in forensic science. You can see why he's chief material. He's blond and fit, with a handsome, genial face. He never winces or eye-rolls. His parents are from Minnesota, and he retains a hint of the long *o*. I once referred to Rupert Murdoch and he shrugged, not recognizing the name. "We run in different circles," he said. Looking at him, you'd never guess that his parents once gave him the book *Sexual Homicide: Patterns and Motives* as a "thinking of you" gift.

DNA testing once required hours of tedious manual work. In a sexual assault case, for example, you would take a swab from a plastic tube, isolate the sperm, and locate the DNA markers via a dot-blot technique that involved a series of white strips, trays, and specialized washes. Increasingly, as technology advanced, robotic arms and instruments did the work. In turn, Holes had more time to dedicate to cold cases. Holes believed Walther might be the One.

When he first came across the "homework" evidence in the Sheriff's Property Room that spring afternoon in 2011, he had been looking for a ski mask—Walther's ski mask. He knew that back when Walther was suspect number one, task force investigators had interviewed his friend, a guy who'd been arrested with him for selling marijuana in Sacramento in '77. The friend gave them a few of Walther's belongings, including a black ski mask. Walther's DNA profile wasn't currently in the system; Holes wondered if he could develop a profile from hairs or skin cells extracted from the mask.

Unfortunately, Walther was in the wind. The man had disappeared off the face of the earth. He'd failed to appear for a court date related to a misdemeanor domestic violence charge in 2003, and there was a warrant out for his arrest. His driver's license was suspended in June 2004. After that, nothing. No credit. No job trail. No welfare. Holes tried to reconstruct Walther's messy life as best he could. He requested and received Walther's school records and noted with interest that his sixth-grade teacher was male, somewhat unusual for the time. Holes got the teacher on the phone. The elderly man said he didn't recall Walther. But sentence writing would fit with the kind of schoolroom punishment he meted out then, he said.

The teacher mentioned that about ten years ago an unidentified male called him and sang "Freedom Isn't Free," a song he'd made unruly kids sing in class. "Remember that," the caller said, and hung up. The call had upset the teacher enough that he changed his number and kept it unlisted. He told Holes he was sorry he couldn't be more helpful.

Holes looked up the words to the song "Freedom Isn't Free," by Paul Colwell.

"There was a general by the name of George," starts the fourth verse, "With a small band of men at Valley Forge."

————

RON GREER* HAD TO BE THE ONE. HE WAS A THREE-PACK-A-DAY smoker living in a rundown apartment, and here they were, casually offering him what they knew through surveillance was his preferred brand of cigarettes, and he wouldn't take a single smoke. He was tightly wound and wary. Sacramento Sheriff's Detective Ken Clark and his partner did everything they could to relax the guy. They weren't going to leave without eyeballing a direct DNA deposit. But Greer declined to take even a sip from a water bottle. He knows what's up, Ken figured. Yep. Nervous and forensically wise. He's the One.

Greer came to them via a thirty-year-old supplemental report. Many of the investigators share the belief that the EAR's name is lost in the paperwork somewhere, jotted down on a vehicle stop or suspicious-circumstance report. His cover story was either airtight, or he was eliminated by a lousy but accepted alibi. Ken and his partner began methodically reviewing the old reports. Greer's name popped up early.

He was stopped driving southbound on Sunrise Boulevard in a two-door yellow Datsun at 4:27 a.m. on April 15, 1977, just minutes after an EAR rape had been called in blocks away. He told police he was on his way to his job working as a janitor at a

————
* Pseudonym

rice mill. They noted that he was extremely quiet and coopera-
tive. They opened his trunk; their interest grew considerably. He
consented to a residence search. His mother had recently died, he
told them, and he was living with his sister now. Or, more specifically, on his sister's property, in a trashed storage trailer buried in
some bushes on a steep hillside in Fair Oaks. The trailer couldn't
have been more than eight feet long and wasn't tall enough to
stand up in. He seemed to have a solid work alibi for an earlier
EAR rape. Still, the investigators who dealt with Greer never forgot him. They couldn't shake the memory of what they found
inside his car.

That's why Ken and his partner had tracked him down thirty
years later. Greer had significant medical issues now. Still, no water, thank you. No cigarettes. Finally, their patience and ruses running out, they persuaded him to lick an envelope. They swabbed
all his car door handles when he wasn't looking just to be sure.

Greer was pulled over on that spring night in 1977 near an
EAR rape because he fit the general physical description of the
attacker; he was a white male, twenty-five, five nine, 150. The first
thing the patrol officers picked out with their flashlights was a
plastic bottle of hand lotion on the front seat of his car. There was
a white mask, similar to the kind used for painting or surgery, on
the passenger side dashboard. When they popped his trunk they
found rope in an opened cellophane wrapper. There was also a
pair of tennis shoes.

And two large, zippered bags. Inside the bags, they found a
handgun and a hunting knife.

Ken and his partner sent the DNA collected from Greer to the
crime lab. They waited. The results came back.

Unbelievable.

Greer wasn't the One.

As I've said, falling for a suspect is a lot like the first surge of
blind love in a relationship. Focus narrows to a single face. The

world and its practical sounds are a wan soundtrack to the powerful silent biopic you're editing in your mind at all times. No amount of information on the object of your obsession is enough. You crave more. Always more. You note his taste in shoes and even drive by his house, courtesy of Google Maps. You engage in wild confirmation bias. You project. A middle-aged white man smiling and cutting a cake decorated with candles in a picture posted on Facebook isn't celebrating his birthday, but holding a knife.

I first sensed the parallels when a weary-looking Larry Pool admitted to me that he used to "feel more" about suspects in the beginning, when as an Orange County cold-case detective, he first got the Original Night Stalker case in 1997. He was "fresher then," he said, his face drawn, sounding like a middle-aged serial dater toughened by the vagaries of love.

Pool recalled an early moment of excitement in the summer of 2001, when he got a call asking him to report to the assistant sheriff's office. Such calls always meant good news. When he walked in, a group turned to smile at him—his captain, his lieutenant, members of the administrative staff, and most tellingly, Mary Hong, the Orange County criminalist who developed the Original Night Stalker's DNA profile. Hong worked in a different building.

Pool pumped his fist in the air before he even closed the door. "Yes!" he said. He'd worked the case nonstop, maybe even obsessively, for three years by then.

There's been a fingerprint match, the assistant sheriff told Pool. A print left on a lamp at one of the East Area Rapist's Danville scenes was believed to be the killer's. The victim had heard him turn on the light; the lamp had been recently unpacked and wouldn't have had anyone else's prints on it. A retired investigator from Contra Costa had fished out an old copy of the print and recently sent it down to Orange County.

"Excellent," Pool said.

The suspect died of natural causes five years ago, the assistant sheriff continued, and he slid the man's file across the table toward Pool. Pool, who knew more about the killer than anyone in the room, opened the folder. Everyone stared at him expectantly. Pool experienced his first pang of disappointment.

"Oh, man. I don't like his age," Pool said. The suspect was born in 1934. Pool flipped through the report. He didn't like the guy's criminal history, either. Weapons charges. Trafficking. Bank robberies. The guy had been in witness protection. Pool wasn't feeling it.

He could sense the mood in the room shift.

"I don't care for him as a suspect," Pool admitted. "But who knows, maybe that's why we haven't found the guy. He's not what we expect."

"Find out where this man's buried," the assistant sheriff said.

"Got it, boss," said Pool.

Pool discovered that the dead suspect had been a friend of the victim's boyfriend. The two men had had a falling-out several weeks before the attack. The victim and her boyfriend had their stereo stolen around the same time, and Pool theorized that the suspect was the robber, probably exacting some revenge on his friend for their fight. He must have touched the lamp when he was in the house stealing the stereo. He wasn't the killer, just a lousy friend with a burglary habit.

But Pool's bosses wanted certainty.

"We gotta dig him up and check his DNA," the assistant sheriff said.

Pool got on a plane and flew to Baltimore to exhume the body. This was the first time the Orange County Sheriff's Department had dug up a suspect—victims, yes, but never a suspect before. Baltimore Homicide assisted in the exhumation. When they opened the vault, the *shoop* sound reminded Pool of a huge Pepsi can opening. The corpse was in remarkably good condition, just covered in mold. But the smell.

"Imagine the worst decomp times ten," Pool said.

No wonder the Baltimore Homicide detectives had lit up cigars as they crested the hill where the man was buried.

Pool packed the suspect's teeth and hair in his carry-on bag. The femur and parts of flesh they put on dry ice in a box, checked in at the airport. Back in Orange County, when Pool went to grab the box as it came around the baggage carousel, he discovered that it was leaking.

DNA proved Pool's suspicion. The dead fingerprint guy wasn't the One.

DOUG FIEDLER* HAD TO BE THE ONE.

An e-mail materialized in my inbox one night at 12:01 a.m. from "John Doe."

John Doe never explained his preference for anonymity. He was concerned with another matter: he'd heard me on a podcast talking about the case, and wanted to share what he considered to be a good tip. "Worldcat.org is a valuable research tool for finding what libraries carry a specific book or media. When you search for Det. Crompton's *Sudden Terror* it gives the following locations Salem, Oregon, Post Falls, Idaho, Hayden Lake, Idaho, Sidney, Nebraska, Los Gatos, California. Maybe EAR-ONS used his library to acquire the book to avoid buying it online?"

It was an interesting idea. *Sudden Terror* was self-published; it was unlikely that any library would carry it without a borrower specifically requesting that the library acquire it. I was pretty sure I knew who was responsible for Oregon and California (retired

---

* Pseudonym

detectives), so I concentrated on Idaho and Nebraska. I knew the libraries weren't going to share the names of the borrowers with me, as it's important to them to protect patrons' privacy. I stared at my computer. A blank search bar waited for me to find a way to use it. I decided to enter the relevant zip codes along with the name of a high-profile group I felt the EAR might have joined in the intervening years: registered sex offenders.

For about an hour, I scrolled through the rough mugs of the perverted and depraved. The exercise was feeling like a waste of time. Then I saw him. I experienced a flash, the first since I'd started investigating the case: *You.*

I eyeballed his stats. The man, Doug Fiedler, was born in 1955. He was the right height and weight. He was originally from California, and in the late eighties was convicted there of several sexual offenses, including rape by force or fear and lewd and lascivious acts with a child under the age of fourteen.

From a genealogy website, I learned that his mother was from a large family from Sacramento County. My pulse quickened with every new piece of information I gathered. In the early 1980s, and possibly earlier, she lived in north Stockton, close to the EAR rapes there. Doug's ex-wife had addresses all over Orange County, including one in Dana Point, just 1.7 miles from the house where Keith and Patty Harrington were murdered.

He had an animal tattoo on his arm that could easily be mistaken for a bull (during hypnosis a young girl who saw the EAR in her house recalled a tattoo she thought looked like the Schlitz Malt Liquor bull on his forearm).

I ran his name through a Google News archive. I nearly jumped out of my chair when I saw the results. An August 1969 *Los Angeles Times* story detailed how a nineteen-year-old boy was hit on the head with a frying pan and stabbed to death by his younger half brother, who had gone to his mother's aid during a family fight. The younger brother? Doug Fiedler.

Bludgeoning. Knife. The EAR did a lot strange things during the commission of his crimes, but in my opinion one of the weirdest was his occasional whimpering and crying. Those occasional plaintive calls amid the sobs: "Mommy! Mommy!"

Doug now lived with his elderly mother in a small town in Idaho. Google Street View revealed it to be a modest white house obscured by overgrown weeds.

I didn't say it explicitly, but when I e-mailed Pool about Doug Fiedler, I felt there was a very good chance I was handing him the killer.

"Nice catch," Pool wrote back. "Good profile and physical. I just confirmed via phone and other data that he's been eliminated by DNA (CODIS)."

For hours I'd felt as if I was hurtling down the street with nothing in my way, like catching a series of green lights. Now the transmission had just fallen out. The wisdom of the time traveler, I realized, can be deceiving. We return to the past armed with more information and cutting-edge innovations. But there are hazards in having so much wizardry at hand. The feast of data means there are more circumstances to bend and connect. You're tempted to build your villain with the abundance of pieces. It's understandable. We're pattern-seekers, all of us. We glimpse the rough outline of what we seek and we get snagged on it, sometimes remaining stuck when we could get free and move on.

"Keep throwing me suspects like him!" Pool wrote.

He was letting me down gently. He'd been there. After he told me how excited he'd get about certain suspects when he first started on the case, I asked how he responded now, fifteen years later. He mimed getting a report and looking it over, taciturn and severe.

"Okay," he said curtly, and pretended to throw it in the pile.

But I'd seen him reenact another moment, the one when he walked through his boss's door, when he spotted the group assembled there for him, on the cusp of a moment you can spend a career in law enforcement imagining but never experience. I knew how quickly he sometimes got back to me through e-mail when something interesting popped up.

I'd seen him imitate that fist pump and "Yes!" I knew that he quietly longed for that moment again.

LOS ANGELES, 2014

"WHAT PEOPLE FORGET ABOUT ROCKY IS THAT FIRST SCENE, WHEN he goes out to train. His legs are killing him. He's past his prime. It's freezing. He's staggering. He can barely get up those steps."

Patton was trying to buoy my spirits by telling me about *Rocky*. I'd been talking to him about dead ends. How many could the average person face before they gave up?

"But Rocky just kept getting up every morning and doing it. Over and over. It's like with these cold-case guys. You invest all this time and energy. You call around. You dig through boxes. You coax out stories. You swab. Then, the answer is no. You can't let that kill you. You have to wake up the next morning, get your coffee, clear your desk, and do it all over again."

Patton was talking about himself too, I realized, the way he kept getting back onstage as a young comedian, for no money, to hostile crowds. He had that burning determination in him, and he's partial to stories about people who do too. Sometimes when he's standing at the sink doing the dishes, I notice his lips moving but there's no sound.

"What are you doing there?" I asked him once.

"Working out a joke," he said.

Starting over. Making it better. Doing it again.

"Rocky didn't beat Apollo Creed, remember," Patton said. "But he shocked him, and the world, because he refused to give up."

We were having dinner to celebrate our eighth wedding anniversary. Patton raised his glass of wine. I could tell he hoped to shake me from my listless defeat in the face of dead ends.

"You have a rogues' gallery of villains in your future," he said.

"Stop it!" I said. "Don't say that."

His intentions were good, I knew. But I couldn't, or refused, to imagine the future.

"I don't want a rogues' gallery of villains," I said. "He's the only one."

The moment I said it, I realized how sick that sounded. What I meant was that after the EAR, I couldn't imagine ever wanting to feverishly search, to breathlessly catch a series of green lights only to keep crashing, ever again.

From under the table, Patton brought out a large present wrapped beautifully in vintage wrapping paper. He's an amazing gift giver. He loves to find young artists and artisans and collaborate with them on unique gifts. One year he had made what we jokingly refer to as an inaction figure of me—I'm sitting in bed in my pajamas holding a Starbucks vanilla latte, my laptop open to my true-crime website. Another time he had a young metal worker build me a wooden box. The house we lived in for seven years is depicted in a bronze plate on the front. Inside are a series of hidden miniature drawers, each containing mementos from our life together—ticket stubs, Post-it notes.

Last year he commissioned artist Scott Campbell to paint three small watercolors of me facing off against notorious crime figures. In one I'm holding a cup of coffee and staring down the Zodiac Killer. In another, I clutch a notebook as if I'm about to interrogate D. B. Cooper, the infamous plane hijacker. And in the third, I'm holding my laptop, a curious smile on my face, standing face-to-face with the One, masked and unknowable, my bane, the EAR.

I opened this year's present. Patton had had my *Los Angeles* magazine article professionally bound and placed in a custom-made black slipcase. The case had a compartment where I could store the most important notes from my story. A DVD of an interview I did on the local news was in a bottom drawer.

I realize later that for two years in a row my wedding anniversary gift has been, in some way or another, about the EAR.

But that's not even the most telling sign of how much he's come to dominate my life. That would be the fact that I've forgotten to get Patton as much as a card.

SACRAMENTO, 2014

HOLES DUG RELENTLESSLY INTO WALTHER'S BACKGROUND. THE LO-cation of Walther's family's home on Sutter Avenue in Carmichael was a central buffer zone around which the EAR preyed. In the midseventies, Walther helped his mom in her job managing low-income apartment complexes in Rancho Cordova; one of the complexes was next door to an EAR attack. Holes learned that in May 1975 Walther was in a bad car accident in Sacramento that resulted in scars on his face. Victim number seven had tried reverse psychology and told the EAR he was good at sex. He responded that people always made fun of him for being small, a presumably truthful statement, because he was indeed underendowed. The EAR also mentioned to her that "something happened to my face."

Four attacks were a half mile from Del Campo High School, where Walther went to school. The father of one of the victims taught at the continuation school that Walther transferred to after dropping out of Del Campo. Walther worked in 1976 at a Black Angus restaurant that two victims mentioned to detectives was a frequent dining location for them.

Walther began working for the Western Pacific Railroad in 1978; the job took him to Stockton, Modesto, and through Davis (on his way to Milpitas), just as the EAR began branching out in those areas. In August 1978, he received two speeding tickets in Walnut Creek. The EAR's East Bay attacks in that area started two months later. A court date related to one of Walther's Walnut Creek traffic tickets occurred two weeks before the attack there.

In 1997 Walther was pulled over for running a stop sign. Two steak knives were found in a duct-tape sheath in his waistband. Court documents from his domestic violence arrest reveal that he threatened his ex-wife, saying, "I'm going to cut you up into little pieces."

"Be quiet or I'll cut you up," the EAR said. He frequently threatened to cut off ears, toes, and fingers.

Walther was either dead or making a Herculean effort not to be found. Holes repeatedly called coroner's offices to ask if they had any similar-looking John Does. Finally, he tracked down Walther's only child, an estranged daughter. A detective from the Contra Costa Investigations Unit told the daughter they were looking for her dad because he was owed money from a jail stint he did in 2004. The daughter said she hadn't spoken to Walther since 2007. He called her once from a pay phone, she said. He was homeless in Sacramento at the time.

Holes asked Sacramento law enforcement agencies if they could dig up any paperwork at all on Walther; transients frequently have small interactions with police. If Walther was homeless in the Sacramento area, his name was probably jotted down on some report. Maybe the notation never made it into the system, but it was buried there somewhere. Finally, Holes got the call.

"We don't have Walther," the officer said, "but his brother is listed as a witness in a crime. He lives in a car behind a Union 76 in Antelope."

Holes took out a copy of the brother's property deed, which he had in his file on Walther. There was no mortgage associated with the house, as it was passed to the brother through his father. Holes was confused.

"Why would Walther's brother be homeless?" Holes asked out loud. There was a pause on the phone.

"Are you absolutely sure it was Walther's brother you were talking to?" Holes asked.

Soon after, the Sacramento Sheriff's Office called Holes, the call he'd been waiting for. They'd approached Walther's brother with serious expressions and a mobile fingerprint device, and he'd crumpled and thrown up his hands. He confessed. The thumb-print confirmed it—the homeless man was Jim Walther. They swabbed him and rushed the DNA sample to the lab.

Holes was taking me on a driving tour of the relevant East Bay locations when he stopped the car and pointed out the exact spot in Danville where Walther was found sleeping in his parked Pon-tiac LeMans on February 2, 1979. Holes still has questions that nag him. Why would someone go underground for eight years just to avoid a thirty-day sentence?

But the most important question, the one he spent eighteen months investigating, has been answered.

"He wasn't the EAR," Holes said. He shook his head. "But I tell you, he was the EAR's shadow."

We stared at the spot.

"You're sure they did it right?" I asked about the DNA test.

Holes paused for a fraction of a moment.

"Sacramento is very, very good at what they do," he said.

We drove on.

SACRAMENTO, 1978

DETECTIVE KEN CLARK AND I WERE STANDING OUTSIDE THE SCENE of a double homicide that occurred in east Sacramento in February 1978 when he interrupted his train of thought to ask, "Do you support Obama?" We smiled at each other for a moment and then both started laughing. He shrugged off our political difference and kept pouring forth. Clark was a nonstop chatterer. I didn't get a word in edgewise, and that worked to my advantage. We stood outside the yard where Clark believes the East Area Rapist shot a young couple to death. The Maggiore murders were never conclusively linked to the EAR, but Clark recently found police reports showing EAR-like prowling and break-ins in the area that night, moving closer and closer until Katie and Brian Maggiore were mysteriously gunned down while out walking their dog. Witnesses got a good glimpse of the suspect. When a composite was released, the EAR suddenly moved west to Contra Costa County. Though Paul Holes already told me he doesn't buy the "scared away" theory, Clark thinks he was spooked. He shows me the composite. "I think this is the closest image we have of him."

Clark shows me the old police reports he's now digging through for clues. They include traffic stops and Peeping Tom incidents. So much wasn't considered relevant then. Clark can't explain why. It kills him. "They let a good suspect go because his sister-in-law said she once went skinny-dipping with him and she thought he had a decent-size penis." (The EAR did not). "Another, I'm not kidding, had 'too big a lower lip.' "

Sacramento teems with angles to explore. What brought him here? Is it a coincidence that all branches of the military transferred their navigation training to Mather Air Force Base on July 1, 1976, just as the rapes began? What about California State University–Sacramento? Their academic calendar dovetails perfectly with the crimes (he never attacked during a school holiday). Using new technology, a geographic profiler pinpoints streets where he believes the EAR may have lived. I revisit the neighborhoods. I talk to old-timers. I feed what I find to the laptop DIY detectives engaged in the hunt.

[EDITOR'S NOTE: Michelle McNamara died on April 21, 2016.]

PART THREE

[EDITOR'S NOTE: When Michelle died, she was midway through the writing of I'll Be Gone in the Dark. *To prepare the book for release, Michelle's lead researcher, Paul Haynes, aka the Kid, and acclaimed investigative journalist Billy Jensen, who was a friend of Michelle's, worked together to tie up loose ends and organize the materials Michelle left behind. The following chapter was written collaboratively by Haynes and Jensen.]*

A WEEK AFTER MICHELLE'S DEATH, WE GAINED ACCESS TO HER HARD drives and began exploring her files on the Golden State Killer. All 3,500 of them. That was on top of the dozens of notebooks, the legal pads, the scraps of paper, and thousands of digitized pages of police reports. And the thirty-seven boxes of files she had received from the Orange County prosecutor, which Michelle lovingly dubbed the Mother Lode.

Thousands of pieces of a jigsaw puzzle, and only one person knew what it was supposed to look like. That one person wasn't Michelle. It was the killer himself.

Michelle's white whale was not the Black Dahlia Killer, or the Zodiac Killer, or even Jack the Ripper—infamous agents of unsolved crimes whose "bodies of work"—and thus the files of investigative source material—were relatively small.

No. Michelle was after a monster who had raped upward of fifty women and had murdered at least ten people. There were more than fifty-five crime scenes, with thousands of pieces of evidence.

We opened Michelle's main hard drive and began going through the chapters she had completed. They reminded us why we were drawn to her writing in the first place.

Her prose jumps off the page and sits down next to you, weaving tales of Michelle on the streets of Rancho Cordova, Irvine, and Goleta on the trail of a killer. The amount of detail is massive. But her writing, at once dogged and empathetic, works the specifics into a fluent narrative. Just when the average reader might get fatigued by too many facts, she turns a phrase or shows a telling detail that brings it all around again. In the manuscript and on *True Crime Diary*, Michelle always found the perfect balance between the typical extremes of the genre. She didn't flinch from evoking key elements of the horror and yet avoided lurid overindulgence in grisly details, as well as sidestepping self-righteous justice crusading or victim hagiography. What her words evoked was the intrigue, the curiosity, the compulsion to solve a puzzle and resolve the soul-chilling blank spots.

But there were parts of the story that Michelle had not completed. We laid out what she *had* finished. She had a nuance that one doesn't normally encounter in true crime (except maybe in Capote—and when he was looking for a hook, he sometimes would just make it up). Michelle was writing a nonfiction book with a style that couldn't be replicated. We thought about it and even took a brief stab. But it was fruitless. She had told this story in so many forms—in the chapters she had completed, in the story for *Los Angeles* magazine, and in her numerous blog posts—that there was enough material to fill in many of the gaps.

That being said, there were topics she would have definitely expanded on had she been able to complete the book. Many of those files or scribbled notes presented a lead she wanted to follow—or a red herring she might have disregarded. Where a friend's bucket list might be littered with items like "Trip to Paris" and "Try skydiving," Michelle's included "Go to Modesto," "Complete the reverse directory of Goleta residents," and "Figure out way to submit DNA to 23andMe or Ancestry.com."

BACK IN 2011, AFTER SHE POSTED HER FIRST STORY ON *TRUE CRIME Diary* about EAR-ONS (she hadn't yet given him the Golden State Killer moniker), Michelle first became aware of Paul when he posted a link to her piece on the A&E *Cold Case Files* forum, which at that time was the only place where a dialogue about the case was taking place.

Michelle wrote him immediately.

"Hi!" she began. "You're one of my favorite posters." She proceeded to describe a rare surname she'd stumbled upon, whose few bearers shared some interesting geography. Maybe they were worth looking into.

"I struggle with insomnia," she explained, "and when I can't sleep, I sleuth around for good EAR suspects. I don't know what your system is, if any, but I've been doing two things—running down names in the Goleta cemetery, and running names gleaned from alumni lists from multiple schools in Irvine, particularly the Northwood neighborhood. Not counting sheep, exactly, but hypnotic in its own way."

The results of Michelle's insomnia were laid bare on her hard drive:

- Old maps and aerial photographs of Goleta, used to compare against the "homework" evidence map
- Images of the soles of shoes and bindings from the crime scenes
- An analysis of the turf-plugger tool, possibly used in the Domingo murder

- A folder bursting at the seams about the Visalia Ransacker, and theories she was putting forth to connect him to EAR-ONS

There was a list of some specific items taken from the victims of the East Area Rapist:

- Silver Dollar "MISSILE"
- Silver Dollar "M.S.R." 8.8.72
- Ring with "For my angel" 1.11.70
- One set of cuff links, yellow gold, initial "NR" in script
- Man's gold ring, 80 pt diamond, square shape, 3 gold nuggets
- Ring "*[redacted]* Always *[redacted]*" 2.11.71
- Gold initial ring WSJ
- Antique silver spoon ring by Prelude by International
- Class ring Lycoming College 1965

As well as a note mentioning that the rapist had a particular penchant for clock radios, having stolen five of them.

Nestled among the array was a spreadsheet containing the names and addresses of the 1976 Dos Pueblos High School cross country team, a rabbit hole she went down with the thought that the EAR might have been a young runner with muscular legs.

One document was titled "Possibly Interesting People." It was a list pasted together over time, with notes and nuggets added as Michelle ran down the names and birth dates of potential suspects. Some of the fragments retained the tag "Sent from my iPhone"—betraying its contents' origin as a quick note to self while Michelle was killing time at a movie premiere.

In another notepad, she wrote: "Don't underestimate the fantasy: not raping in front of men—afraid of male; functional; privacy, writhing male not part of his fantasy. Mommy and crying. No remorse. Probably part of fantasy."

There were even notes on her own psychology:

- He was a compulsive prowler and searcher. We, who hunt him, suffer from the same affliction. He peered through windows. I tap "return." Return. Return. Click Mouse click, mouse click.
- Rats search for their own food.
- The hunt is the adrenaline rush, not the catch. He's the fake shark in *Jaws*, barely seen so doubly feared.

Michelle would reach out to witnesses from the old reports if she felt there was some detail left unelaborated or a nagging question the investigators neglected to ask. One of those witnesses was Andrew Marquette.*

The night of June 10, 1979, was an especially hot one, and Marquette had left his bedroom window open to catch a breeze while he tried to sleep. Around midnight, he heard the crunch of footsteps on the rock path beneath his window. He peered out and saw a stranger creeping slowly alongside his house, his eyes fixed on the window of his neighbors. Marquette looked into the same window and could see the couple that lived there putting their child to bed.

Marquette continued observing the subject as he slunk toward a pine tree and receded into the grassy darkness. He fetched a .22 pistol he kept near his bed and racked the slide. It was a sound the prowler must have recognized, as he immediately sprang into motion and scrambled over the fence into the front yard. Marquette went to his neighbors' house and knocked on the front door. No one answered.

---

* Pseudonym

He returned the pistol to his house and began heading back next door to try his neighbors' again. Midway there, a passing car's headlights swept across the homes on the north side of the block and briefly illuminated the prowler, who was now on a bike, leaning against a house. As Marquette started to approach, the subject began pedaling furiously across the lawn, fleeing from Marquette and disappearing into the night. Marquette called the police. They cruised up and down the neighborhood, searching for the prowler to no avail.

Several hours later, the forty-seventh EAR attack occurred half a block away. Investigators reconnected with Marquette during the canvass, and he told the same story.

The prowler was a white male in his twenties with collar-length hair, wearing Levi's and a dark-colored T-shirt—consistent with what the latest EAR victim described. The bicycle on which the prowler had fled was found abandoned later that morning, several blocks away, next to an Olympia beer can from the victim's fridge. Investigators quickly realized that this was the same bike stolen several hours before the attack from an open garage a mile away. Near that garage, detectives found a pair of white, knotted shoelaces.

Michelle felt that Marquette was someone worth reinterviewing. She contacted him in late 2015.

She sent him a map she had sketched, along with her understanding of the schematic of that night's events, and asked him to confirm and amend where appropriate. Paul compiled a seventeen-picture photo lineup, and Michelle asked Marquette which of the individuals most closely resembled the man he saw that night.

On the phone, she asked Marquette to spit out the first word that came to mind to describe the prowler he observed. Marquette replied without missing a beat: "Schoolboy."

In a 2011 file called "EAR CLUES," Michelle attempted to consolidate many of the known facts about the man into a profile:

- Physically he's most often described as 5′ 9″ to 5′ 11″, with a swimmer's build. Lean, but with a muscular chest and noticeably big calves. Very small penis, both narrow and short. 9–9½ shoe size. Dirty blond hair. Bigger than normal nose. Type A blood type, nonsecretor.

- He used the phone to contact his victims, sometimes before an attack, sometimes after. Sometimes just hang-up phone calls. Sometimes with theatrical, scary-movie deep breathing and threats.

- He wore ski masks. He brought guns. He had what looked like a pen style navigator flashlight, and he liked to startle his victims awake by beaming it at them, blinding them. He tore towels into strips, or used shoelaces, to bind victims.

- He had a script, and he stuck to it. Some variation of, "Do what I say, or I'll kill you." He alleged he only wanted money and food. Sometimes he said it was for his apartment. Other times he mentioned his van. He would make the woman tie up the man, then separate them. Sometimes he'd stack dishes on the man's back and tell him if he heard a crash he'd kill the female victim.

- He frequently brought baby lotion to the scene to use as a lubricant.

- He liked to steal neighborhood bicycles and escape on them.

- Some personal items associated with him: a bag with a long zipper, like a doctor's bag, or duffel bag; blue tennis shoes; motocross gloves; corduroy pants.

- He took driver's licenses and jewelry, particularly rings.

- Some of the things he said, which may or may not be true but are nevertheless interesting: Killing someone in Bakersfield; moving back to LA; "I hate you, Bonnie"; being thrown out of the Air Force.

- Something may have been going on with him in late

October 1977. In two different attacks around then he was described as sobbing.

- Some of the vehicles possibly associated with EAR-ONS: green Chevy van, 1960s yellow sidestep pickup truck, VW bug.

An e-mail forwarded to Michelle by Patton reveals that she had even enlisted her father-in-law, a career US Marine, to do some research on military bases in the area back then, as there was a theory that the rapist might have been an airman.

Begin forwarded message:

From: Larry Oswalt

Date: April 18, 2011, 2:01:06 PM PDT

To: Patton

Subject: Air Force Bases around Sacramento

    Mom said Michelle had some questions about Air Force Bases around Sacramento. Here is the list.

    Near Sacramento:

        McLellan closed 2001

        Mather Closed 1993

        Beale still active—40 miles north of Sacramento

    Travis is located in Fairfield, CA sort of north of San Francisco and a good ways from Sacramento.

    Let me know if you need any additional info.

    Dad

Many have attempted to profile EAR-ONS over the years, but Michelle wanted to go one step further and dive deep into the locations of the rapes to see whether geographic profiling could lead to his identity. Among the pieces she left behind were her musings about EAR-ONS's geography:

- My feeling is that the two most important locations are Rancho Cordova and Irvine.
- The first and third rapes were only yards apart in Rancho Cordova. He walked away in an unhurried fashion from the third attack without his pants on, suggesting he lived close by.
- He murdered Manuela Witthuhn on February 6, 1981, in Irvine. Five years later he murdered Janelle Cruz. Manuela and Janelle lived in the same subdivision, just two miles apart.
- Interestingly, Manuela's answering machine tape was stolen in the attack. Was the suspect's voice on the tape? If so, was he worried it was recognizable as someone in the neighborhood?

A document Michelle created in August 2014, entitled "Geo-Chapter," has her rethinking the map after more than three solid years of nonstop research. When you open it, there is just one line: "Carmichael seems like central clearing, like a buffer zone."

FINDING THE KILLER WITH GEO-PROFILING

While his most fundamental characteristics—his name and his face—are unknown, it can be said with reasonable certainty that the East Area Rapist was, among approximately seven hundred thousand other humans, a resident of Sacramento County in the mid-to-late 1970s.

The EAR's connection to the many other places in which he struck—Stockton, Modesto, Davis, the East Bay—is less clear.

The East Area Rapist was a highly prolific offender in Sacramento, exhibiting the familiarity and ubiquity of someone who was undoubtedly local. With places like Stockton, Modesto, and

Davis, where he struck two or three times apiece, one questions what connection he had to these cities, if any. Perhaps he had family there or had business there. Maybe he was just passing through. Maybe he flung a dart at a map.

But you'd be hard-pressed to find an investigator who doesn't believe the EAR lived or at least worked in Sacramento.

If we accept that the EAR was living in Sacramento from 1976 through 1978 or 1979, which is nearly certain, and then lived in Southern California during the first half of the 1980s, which is *highly* probable, then the haystack gets considerably smaller. Devise a list of people who lived in both areas during those time periods, and the suspect pool shrinks from nearly a million to maybe ten thousand.

It would be ideal if the process were as simple as, say, applying filters to a product search on Amazon. With a few clicks, one could filter by gender (male), birth year (1940–1960), race (white), height (5′ 7″ to 5′ 11″), places lived (Carmichael AND Irvine; or Rancho Cordova AND in the 92620 zip code; or Citrus Heights, Goleta, AND Dana Point), and maybe occupation for good measure (real estate agent, construction worker, painter, landscaper, landscape architect, nurse, pharmacist, hospital orderly, cop, security guard, OR serviceman—all of which are among the many occupations that various investigators and armchair sleuths have posited the EAR may have had). Just set all these search parameters and voilà! You'd be left with a manageable yet all-inclusive list of potential suspects.

But it's not that easy. The names have to come from somewhere, and there's no central database of, well, people. It must be either composited or built. And creating such a list is indeed one of the projects Michelle felt most optimistic about.

He may have come from Visalia. Or perhaps Goleta was his hometown. He may have lived in the 92620 zip code of Irvine. He may have gone to Cordova High School. His name may appear in both the 1977 Sacramento phone book and the 1983 Orange County phone book. We didn't need access to restricted information or an official suspect list to uncover some potential suspects who might otherwise have flown under the radar. All the necessary information and tools that could be used to process it were already available in the form of online public records aggregators, vital records, property records, yearbooks, and yellowed phone directories from the 1970s and '80s (many of which have fortunately been digitized).

In the year prior to Michelle's death, Paul had begun creating master resident lists for Sacramento and Orange Counties for the relevant time periods, which combined names from sources such as Ancestry.com's marriage and divorce records, the appropriate county's registry of deeds (which entailed using a Web scraper), alumni lists, and old crisscross directories and telephone books.[†]

Michelle then connected with a computer programmer in Canada who offered to volunteer his help in whatever way he could. Per Paul's specifications, the programmer built a cross-referencing utility that processes multiple lists and finds matching lines of text. With that application, Paul could begin feeding it two or more lists and then analyze its match results—now numbering over forty thousand.

Once the list of matches had been generated, Paul would go through it and weed out the false positives (far more likely with

---

† The text from the directories and phone books was collected by using a software process known as optical character recognition, or OCR, to convert the image of the scanned material into text. Because it's a digital eye reading analog material of variable print and scan quality, the output is lousy with syntax and transcription errors, ranging from failure to distinguish, say, the letter *D* from the letter *O*, to chaotic arrays of punctuation marks, symbols, and other errant nonalphanumeric characters. These issues necessitated hundreds of hours of cleanup in order to turn these scans of decades-old volumes into readable and consistently formatted lists of names.

common names like John Smith) by using public records aggregators. Paul would then collect as much information as possible
on each match until he was satisfied that neither he nor any of
his male relatives was viable. The names of those he was unable
to rule out would be added to a master list of potential suspects.

IN CASES OF SERIAL BURGLARY, RAPE, OR MURDER, THE SUSPECT
lists often swell to several thousand names and beyond. Difficulty
in managing a list of this size enforces the need to devise a prioritiza-
tion system, whereby suspect ranks are determined by factors such
as prior criminal offenses and police contacts, availability for all
crimes in the series, physical characteristics, and—if a geographic
profile has been done—the suspect's work and home addresses.

Geographic profiling is a specialized criminal investigative
technique—perhaps more useful and scientific than behavioral
profiling, which is arguably closer to an art than a science—
whereby the key locations in a linked crime series are analyzed for
the purpose of determining the likely anchor points (home, work,
etc.) of a serial offender. This allows one to focus on isolated bub-
bles within a much broader suspect pool.

Although the general technique has informally been around
for a while—you see investigators employing it to find a kidnap-
per in Akira Kurosawa's *High and Low* (1963)—the methodol-
ogy of geographic profiling didn't even have a name until the late
1980s, about ten years after the phrase "serial killer" first entered
the popular lexicon. Given that it wasn't yet an established investigative procedure, awareness of geo-profiling could not have been
a factor motivating the EAR—a lover of misdirection—to misdirect geographically by commuting great distances to faraway
neighborhoods in Southern California. Moreover, his Southern
California crimes were not generally recognized as EAR crimes
(and he specifically seemed to want to avoid this recognition,
which is likely one reason he began killing his victims—to elim-

inate witnesses) until DNA evidence established them as such. The logical conclusion, per the principle of Occam's razor, is that the EAR was living in Southern California during the period in which he was offending there.

That said, while we would not advocate completely eliminating someone merely because a Southern California residence cannot be established, it would take some damn compelling reason to muster any interest in such a suspect.

However, Southern California—due to the infrequency of the EAR's known offenses there, and the broad distance covered—is not ideal for a geographic profile. Because Sacramento was the area in which our offender was most prolific over the ten-year span of his known crimes, it is the ripest of the case-relevant locations for building a geographic profile.

With twenty-nine distinct locations linked to confirmed EAR attacks and close to a hundred likely connected burglaries, prowler reports, and other incidents, there is more than sufficient data for developing a geographic profile that would spotlight the neighborhoods in which the EAR *most likely* lived. In geo-profile-speak, these areas are known as buffer zones. Buffer zones are like an eye of a hurricane, carved out by the typical serial offender's reluctance to strike too close to home.

So, at least in theory, identifying the EAR should simply be a matter of finding people who were living in Southern California in the early 1980s who had previously lived in Sacramento County in the mid-to-late 1970s—most likely living in one of those buffer zones.

BY LOOKING AT THE AREAS FAMILIAR TO THE OFFENDER IN THE early phases of the series, as opposed to the ones to which he branched out later on, one can analyze the chronology of attacks in Sacramento and break them up into multiple phases. We've chosen five:

- Attacks 1–4 (pre–media blackout)
- Attacks 5–8 (pre–media blackout)
- Attacks 9–15 (post–media blackout following the first news stories about a serial rapist operating in the East Area of Sacramento)
- Attacks 16–22 (beginning with the EAR's major m.o. shift from lone women to couples, and preceding his three-month hiatus in the summer of 1977)
- Attacks 24–44 (following the EAR's summer '77 hiatus as well as his first known attack outside of Sacramento County)

Creating a Google Map with a layer for each phase allows you to isolate and toggle between phases, comparing the spread within each and determining if a prospective anchor point or an apparent buffer zone remains consistent through the offender's incrementally expanding radius of activity. In addition, tighter clusters of attacks tend to signify neighborhoods the offender may not know very well.

Of particular interest is the swath of Sacramento County where Carmichael, Citrus Heights, and Fair Oaks meet, a part of town where the EAR's attacks were the most spread out—and which also exhibited the most clear-cut buffer zone. (See figure 1.)

Paul adopted the assumption that the EAR lived somewhere in the vicinity of what's labeled the North Ridge Country Club on the map, and he observed that, each time the EAR attacked in this area, it was on the opposite side of that ostensible buffer zone from where he attacked previously—a possible interplay between instinct (change of pace) and calculation (avoidance of areas with increased surveillance).

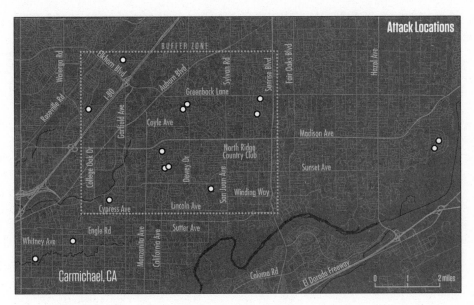

FIGURE 1

Paul decided to attempt a geographic profile using an entirely improvised and nonscientific approach. He ported screenshots of his Google Map into Photoshop and began drawing lines between the attacks in this area, pairing successive ones. Plotting both the midway point of each line as well as where each line intersected with another, and then connecting each set of plot points resulted in shapes that Paul then shaded. The most densely shaded area would theoretically represent the EAR's approximate home base. (See figure 2.)

Alternately, lines were drawn through the midway points that were perpendicular to the lines connecting the paired attacks, in order to find the densest concentration of intersections. The result was similar. (See figure 3.)

Paul then took a different yet equally ad hoc approach by forming a triangle that connected the three most outlying attacks in the East Area, and then, in order to find its true center, creating a smaller, inverted triangle by connecting the midpoints of the larger shape's three sides. He repeated the process until he was left

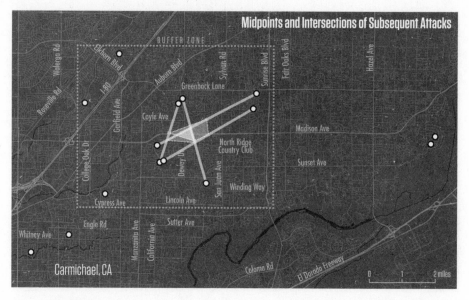

FIGURE 2

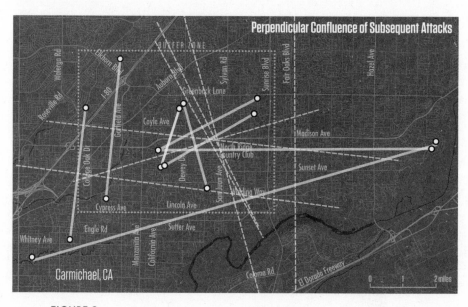

FIGURE 3

with a triangle small enough that it was analogous to a sheet of
paper he couldn't fold in half again. (See figure 4.)

Each effort, both those described above and those omitted out

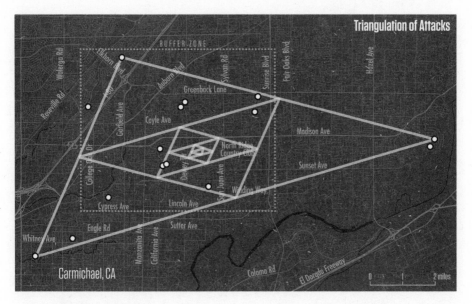

Triangulation of Attacks

Carmichael, CA

FIGURE 4

of mercy toward the reader, yielded a similar result, which suggested that the EAR's anchor point was somewhere close to the intersection of Dewey Drive and Madison Avenue, at the border between Carmichael and Fair Oaks. This conclusion was supported to some extent by a 1995 FBI study (Warren et al.), which found that the fifth attack in a series was closest to the offender's home in a plurality of instances (24 percent of cases, versus 18 percent of cases where the first attack was closest). The fifth EAR attack was second closest to the proposed anchor point, whereas attack number seventeen was only nominally closer (by approximately three hundred feet).

A couple of years later, Michelle got ahold of a geographic profile performed on the EAR Sacramento attacks by none other than Kim Rossmo, the father of modern geographic profiling. In fact, Rossmo himself coined the term.

Rossmo's anchor point was near the intersection of Coyle Avenue and Millburn Street—less than half a mile northwest of the anchor point Paul had postulated without ever having seen Rossmo's analysis. (See figure 5.)

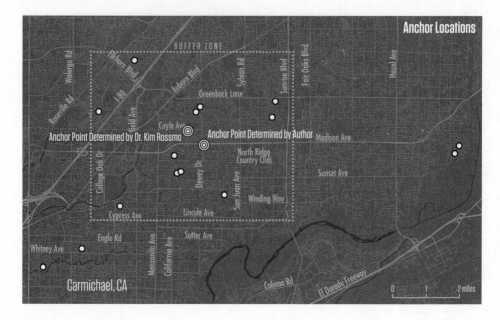

FIGURE 5

FINDING THE KILLER WITH FAMILIAL DNA

Scrolling through the rest of the 3,500 documents in Michelle's hard drive, one comes upon a file titled "RecentDNAresults," which features the EAR's Y-STR markers (short tandem repeats on the Y chromosome that establish male-line ancestry), including the elusive rare PGM marker.

Having the Golden State Killer's DNA was always the one ace up this investigation's sleeve.

But a killer's DNA is only as good as the databases we can compare it to. There was no match in CODIS. And there was no match in the California penal system's Y-STR database. If the killer's father, brothers, or uncles had been convicted of a felony in the past sixteen years, an alert would have gone to Paul Holes or Erika Hutchcraft (the current lead investigator in Orange County). They would have looked into the man's family, zeroed in on a member who was in the area of the crimes, and launched an investigation.

But they had nothing.

There are public databases that the DNA profile could be used to match, filled not with convicted criminals but with genealogical buffs. You can enter the STR markers on the Y chromosome of the killer into these public databases and try to find a match, or at least a surname that could help you with the search.

Paul Holes had done this in 2013, and just like Michelle smiling and proclaiming "I've solved it!" Holes thought he had finally caught the man via this technique.

Michelle tells the story in this half-finished section, titled "Sacramento, 2013."

Paul Holes can still hear the sound of his filing cabinet drawer slamming shut. He'd emptied out everything pertaining to the EAR, boxed it up, and FedEx'ed it to Larry Pool in Orange County.

"Larry's got it," Holes thought. Only a matter of time.

A decade later, Holes was sitting in his office, bored out of his mind. He was chief of the crime lab now. On his second marriage. Two more small children with the second wife. He'd worked at the crime lab long enough to see entire specialties discredited. Hair analysis? Made him cringe to even think about it. He and his co-workers sometimes sat around and laughed at the tools they used to have to work with, unwieldy and defective instruments, like the first generation of mobile phones.

He was starting to make good on the promise he always said he would, that he put off for a decade in order to accrue steady promotions and provide for his family. Investigator Paul Holes. He always liked the sound of it. He was meeting the right people. Getting the right credentials. A move to the DA's office to work cold-case investigation full time was already in the works.

But there was one problem, one he knew full well he was going to take with him to the DA's office. The EAR. Each year he hadn't surfaced, nabbed by DNA or turned in by a tipster, Holes's interest grew. His wife might call it an obsession. Spreadsheets were made. Leisurely car rides turned into crime-scene tours. Not once, but weekly.

Sometimes when he thought of the destruction wrought by one faceless man, not just the victims but also the victims' families, the detectives' shame, the wasted money and time and effort and family time and ruined marriages and sex foregone for lifetimes . . . Holes rarely swore. Wasn't him. But when he thought about all this, he just felt, fuck you. Fuck. You.

The first generation of detectives who worked the case were having health problems. The second generation of detectives, who worked it when they could grab time here and there, were retiring soon. Time was running out. The EAR was looking back at them, smirking from a door half-closed.

Holes scooted his chair over to his computer. In the last year, ancestral DNA had become popular with people curious about their genealogy and, though this was much less publicized, as a tool for finding unidentified criminals. Many in law enforcement were wary. There were quality-assurance issues. Privacy issues. Holes knew DNA. Knew it well. In his opinion, ancestral DNA was a tool, not a certainty. He had a Y-DNA profile generated from the EAR's DNA, which means he isolated the EAR's paternal lineage. The Y-DNA profile could be input into certain genealogical websites, the kind that people use to find first cousins and the like. You input a set of markers from your Y-DNA profile, anywhere from 12 to 111, and a list of matches is returned, surnames of families with whom you might share a common ancestor. Almost always the matches are at a genetic distance of 1 from you, which doesn't mean much, relative-seeking-wise. You're looking for the elusive 0—a close match.

Holes did this every couple of weeks. He kept his expectations at zero. A way to feed the obsession. So it was that on an afternoon in mid-March 2013 he input the familiar sequence and hit return. After a moment the list appeared, many of them familiar surnames from his previous searches. But he didn't recognize the name at the very top of the list.

The EAR has one extremely rare marker. Only 2 percent of the world's population has this marker. When Holes clicked on the link of the top name he saw that the profile contained this rare marker. It also matched eleven other EAR markers, all the same—0 genetic distance. Holes had never received a 0 gdistance before.

He didn't know what to do first. He picked up the phone to call Ken Clark, the Sacramento County Sheriff's detective he talked to the most, but then hung up before dialing. Sacramento was an hour drive from Holes's office in Martinez. He grabbed his car keys.

He'd go to the place where, thirty-six years ago, it all began.

Michelle never got to finish the punchline—the kind of punchline that could have driven anyone who had been working on this case for so long over the edge. It turns out that a retired Secret Service agent and amateur sleuth named Russ Oase had anonymously uploaded EAR's markers into the same database.

So the match Paul Holes thought he had was actually the result of two guys uploading the same killer's DNA profile and getting a mirror-image match.

DNA was the thread Michelle felt was the best way to get out of the maze of the Golden State Killer. California was one of only nine states in America that allowed testing of familial DNA within the state's database. If the GSK's brother was arrested for a felony tomorrow, we would see a hit. But that database contains only people who have been convicted of a crime.

Michelle thought she might have found the killer when she had uploaded his DNA profile to a Y-STR database available online from Ancestry.com.

On quick glance, at the top of the page, it looks promising. The name at the top (we are obscuring all the names) has many hits, as seen by the check marks. The name is very uncommon (only a handful in the United States and England). Next to the name, MRCA stands for Most Recent Common Ancestor, and the number is the number of generations you have to look back in your family tree to have a 50 percent probability that you will find

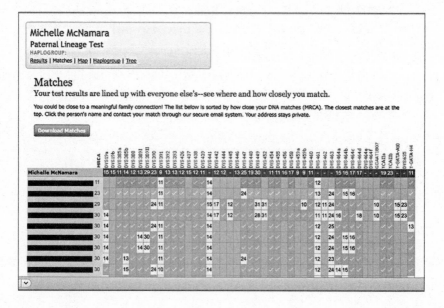

a common ancestor. The MRCA between the man and Michelle (standing in for the killer's DNA) is estimated to have lived eleven generations ago (with a 50 percent probability).

After sharing her find with Paul Holes and other experts, Michelle would discover that it wasn't quite as significant as she initially thought. You would have to go back through this guy's family 330 years, and even then you'd have only a fifty-fifty chance of finding him.

Finding the exact person with these results was a no-go with this test.

One of those experts Michelle consulted was Colleen Fitzpatrick, a forensic genealogist who aids people in finding their birth parents—and who has been instrumental in helping solve some major crimes, including Phoenix's infamous Canal Killer. Fitzpatrick wrote the book on forensic genealogy—literally[†]—and spent many hours, some of them the early a.m. variety, on the phone with Michelle, discussing the various ways of approaching the genealogical route to identifying the GSK.

After Michelle died, Colleen explained to Billy that even though we don't have a usable lineage to follow from the above comparison, we do have a clue:

"Even if you come up with Y-matches that are distant, but they all have the same name, you can say that is probably Mr. X's last name and he belongs to the same extended family as those matches (along the direct line), maybe going back many generations. But in this case, there are a variety of names, so you can't pin one down. The 'flavor' of the names can sometimes give you some ethnicity for your Mr. X. Say, if his list is made of all Irish names, you can say he's probably Irish. That is what I did on the canal murders. Not only did I come up with the name Miller for their Canal Murderer, I also told the Phoenix PD that he was a

---

† *Forensic Genealogy*, by Colleen Fitzpatrick, was published in 2005.

Miller of Irish extraction. A few weeks later, they arrested Bryan Patrick Miller. That's where I got the idea that the EAR had a German name but was from the UK. In the tests I ran for Michelle, that's the 'flavor' of names I was coming up with."

So we were looking for a guy with a German name whose family at some point lived in the UK. Of course, he could have been adopted; then all bets are off.

IT ALL COMES DOWN TO THE SIZE OF THE DATABASE YOU ARE TRYing to compare your sample to. By 2016, there were numerous companies offering to run your DNA profile and add it to a rapidly expanding data set. These companies use autosomal DNA testing. For around a hundred dollars and a little bit of your saliva, the companies deliver your DNA profile. On top of learning whether you might possibly get Alzheimer's in the future, or the odds of your eye color, the test is used by adoptees or people who were raised by single moms. The results that come back to them can deliver previously unknown first cousins, and from there, they can find their birth fathers and other information about their own identities. If you don't get a hit at first, there is still hope. The companies send you e-mails when new family members have uploaded their DNA. "You Have New DNA Relatives" read one Billy recently received from 23andMe, having submitted his own DNA a few years back. "51 people who share DNA with you have joined DNA Relatives over the past 90 days." The tests do not connect just male lineage. They connect everyone.

Most important, the databases are huge—23andMe has 1.5 million profiles and Ancestry has 2.5 million.

Just think of how many murders, rapes, and other violent crimes could be solved if law enforcement could enter the DNA from crime scenes into these databases and be pointed in the right direction via a cousin of the perpetrator found in the system. Unfortunately, neither company will work with law enforcement, citing privacy issues and their terms of service.

The idea that the answer to this mystery is probably hiding in the databases of 23andMe and Ancestry.com kept Michelle up at night.

If we could just submit the killer's actual genetic material—as opposed to only select markers—to one of these databases, the odds are great that we would find a second or third cousin and that person would lead investigators to the killer's identity.

So the answer may very well be sitting behind this locked door. A lock made up of privacy issues and illegal-search-and-seizure issues.

Michelle wanted to be able to enter the killer's DNA into these rapidly expanding commercial databases. She would have eschewed their terms of service to do so. But to enter your DNA into those databases, the company sends you a tube that you spit in and send back to them. Michelle did not have the killer's spit or even a swab. She had the profile on paper. But according to a scientist friend of Billy's, there was a way around that. Nevertheless, when critics talk privacy, the terms of use of the businesses, and the Fourth Amendment, they evoke the classic statement by Ian Malcolm as played by Jeff Goldblum in *Jurassic Park*: "Your scientists were so preoccupied with whether or not they could, they didn't stop to think if they should."

———

WHEN MICHELLE BEGAN WORKING ON THE FEATURE FOR *LOS AN-geles* magazine that served as the basis for this book, official case files began trickling into her possession. She read the materials carefully and began building an index of people, places, and things named in the reports. The purpose was threefold: to promote easy

location of investigative elements within the reports, to disambig-
uate individuals and find those who may be of interest on the basis
of later geographic movement, and to find overlapping names or
possible common bonds among victims.

Michelle had cultivated relationships with investigators both
active and retired that evolved into open exchanges of information. She was like an honorary investigator, and her energy and
insight reinvigorated the case's tired blood. She passed our findings, along with the Master List, to some of the active investigators.

The collection of official case materials continued to grow.
The culmination was a stunning acquisition of physical case materials in January 2016, when Michelle and Paul were led to a
narrow closet at the Orange County Sheriff's Department that
housed sixty-five Bankers Boxes full of EAR-ONS case files. Remarkably, they were permitted to look through them—under
supervision—and borrow what they wanted.

This was the Mother Lode.

They set aside thirty-five of the boxes along with two large
plastic bins to take back to L.A.

Michelle had thought ahead. Instead of sharing a day trip
in one vehicle, they motorcaded into Santa Ana in dual SUVs.
They stacked the Bankers Boxes onto dollies and wheeled them
down to the loading dock behind OCSD headquarters, where
they stuffed them into the two vehicles while the undersheriff,
unaware of what they were doing, emerged from the building
and luckily didn't seem to notice what was going down. They
moved as quickly as physically possible, lest people at OCSD
changed their mind.

They returned to L.A., and the boxes were moved to the second floor of Michelle's house. What had been her daughter's playroom would now become the Box Room.

They soon began digging through the materials. All the holy
grails, the holdouts Michelle had not yet seen, were there, as

were mountains of supplemental reports. Supplemental reports—
compiled from the orphans and outliers, the one-offs that drifted
to the back of the EAR filing cabinet in the absence of real estate in a specific case folder—were among the materials that they
coveted the most. Michelle and Paul shared the belief that if the
offender's name was anywhere in these files, it was likely one of
those clues in the margins: the forgotten suspect, the overlooked
witness report, the out-of-place vehicle that was never followed
up on, or the prowler who at the time gave what seemed like a
reasonable explanation for his presence in the area.

Michelle purchased two high-volume digital scanners, and
they began scanning the materials. Much of this material had
not been seen by active investigators like Paul Holes, Ken Clark,
and Erika Hutchcraft. Scanning would not only allow the files
to become easily accessible and make the text searchable, but it
would allow Michelle to reciprocate the generous spirit of these
investigators by providing them an invaluable service.

This was the single most exciting break since the investigation
began. This was a major pivot, a game changer. Michelle believed
that the probability of the offender's name being somewhere in
those boxes was about 80 percent.

AFTER THE *LOS ANGELES* MAGAZINE ARTICLE WAS PUBLISHED,
Michelle wrote a blog post about the letters she was getting from
armchair detectives who had read the story and became obsessed—
even for just a few hours—with cracking the case.

In the last week, I've received dozens of responses from
readers about my article "In the Footsteps of a Killer."
Many emails contained insights about the evidence and

fresh ideas for how best to catch the Golden State Killer, the elusive serial violent offender that from 1976 to 1986 preyed on victims up and down California.

The map drew the most ideas, with many readers contributing theories based on their professional or academic backgrounds. One reader, a general contractor with experience with "golf planned communities," felt the map looked like many of the communities he'd worked on. The hand-drawn paths, he said, resembled golf cart paths.

Another had a chilling insight into the detailed property lines. They're indicating fence lines, the tipster wrote, because the mapmaker is showing barriers he would encounter while moving around in the dark.

One reader felt there was a clue in the "Mad is the word that reminds me of 6th grade" journal entry. The "6" in "6th" grade looked more like a "G," she pointed out, adding that the writer clearly went back and inserted the word "the" before the "6," as if changing what he was originally going to write, which in her opinion was probably the name of the town he grew up in. A town, she surmised, which begins with "G."

The "Mad is the word" evidence details the writer's anger toward his male sixth-grade teacher. More than one reader pointed out that male sixth-grade teachers were relatively unusual in the 1960s, when the writer presumably was in elementary school.

Another reader noted that Visalia, where the Golden State Killer may have started out as a younger offender, was home to many pilots from nearby Lemoore Naval Air Station. The killer may have been the son of a pilot, the tipster theorized, as several other locations in the crime series are close to military air bases.

Some of these clues might help form the picture of the killer. And some might have absolutely nothing to do with him, like a jigsaw puzzle you buy at a garage sale that's been mixed up with pieces from twenty other jigsaw puzzles.

Michelle was determined, to the end, to investigate each and every piece to see if it fit.

One of the last documents modified on her hard drive—dated April 18, 2016, three days before her death—was titled "StillToDo."

- Find out from Debbi D about flashlight; would they have brought flashlight from other house. To her knowledge did Greg visit Toltec?

- [One of the detectives] needed psychiatric leave after O/M [Offerman/Manning], and Ray said worst crime scene he ever saw (this was in email to Irwin.) Why worse than Domingo/Sanchez?

- For Erika: Since my training isn't in reading crime scenes, what do you think happened at Cruz?

- For Ken Clark: Was there a public/press link to Maggiore at the time of the homicide? Is it true FBI ran familial and expected 200 to 400 hits for names and got zero?

- Find out from Ken exactly what he meant about the husband or the guy in the clown suit walking down the street.

The questions go on for pages and pages. On Michelle's blog, *True Crime Diary*, we will begin to try to get the answers to the questions she had left open. The discussions of the case are ongoing, and we invite readers to join in and follow the numerous message boards that light up day and night with new clues and different theories about the killer. Michelle always said she didn't care who solved this case, just as long as it got solved.

There's no question as to Michelle's impact on the case. In

the words of Ken Clark, she "brought attention to one of the least known, yet most prolific serial offenders ever to operate in the United States. If I hadn't read the reports for myself during my years of investigation on this case, the story would be almost unbelievable. Her professional research, attention to detail, and sincere desire to identify the suspect allowed her to strike a balance between the privacy of those who suffered while exposing the suspect in a way that someone may recognize."

"It is not easy to gain the trust of so many detectives across so many jurisdictions," Erika Hutchcraft told us, "but she managed to do so and you knew it was by her reputation, her perseverance, and the fact that she cared about the case."

Paul Holes concurred, going so far as to say that he considered Michelle to be his detective partner on the case. "We were constantly in communication. I would get excited about something and would send it to her and she would also get excited. She would dig and find a name and send it to me to look into. This case is the ultimate emotional roller coaster—the highs are amazing when you think you have found the guy, and then you crash when you eliminate the promising suspect through DNA. Michelle and I shared in those ups and downs. I had my good suspects and she had hers; we would send e-mails back and forth in a growing crescendo of excitement only to experience the finality of an elimination.

"Michelle was able to accomplish gaining not only my trust but the trust of the entire task force and proved herself as a natural investigator, adding value with her own insights and tenacity. The ability to learn the case, have insights that many do not have the aptitude for, the persistence, and the fun and engaging personality all wrapped up in one person was amazing. I know she was the only person who could have accomplished what she did in this case starting out as an outsider and becoming one of us over time. I think this private/public partnership was truly unique in a criminal investigation. Michelle was perfect for it.

"I last saw Michelle in Las Vegas where we spent a lot of time together talking about the case. Little did I know this would be the last time I would see her face-to-face. Her last email to me was Wednesday, 4/20. As always, she let me know she was sending me some files she and her researcher had found and thought I should know about. She ended that email with 'Talk to you soon, Michelle.'

"I downloaded those files she sent after I found out about her passing Friday night. She was still helping me."

In an e-mail to her editor in December 2013, Michelle addressed what every true-crime journalist has to come to grips with when writing about an unsolved crime: how does the story end?

> I'm still optimistic about developments in the case, but not blind to the challenge of writing about a currently unsolved mystery. I did have one idea on that front. After my magazine article was published, I received tons of emails from readers, almost all starting along the lines of, "You may have thought of this, but if not, what about (insert some investigative idea)." It really confirmed for me that inside everyone lurks a Sherlock Holmes that believes that given the right amount of clues they could solve a mystery. If the challenge here, or perceived weakness, is that the unsolved aspect will leave readers unfulfilled, why not turn that on its head and use it as a strength? I have literally hundreds of pages of analyses from both back in the day, and more recently—geo-profiles, analysis of footwear, days of the week he attacked, etc. One idea I had was to include some of those in the book, to offer the reader the chance to play detective.

We will not stop until we get his name. We'll be playing the detective as well.

— PAUL HAYNES AND BILLY JENSEN

May 2017

AFTERWORD

MICHELLE WAS BORED BY ANYTHING WITH MAGIC OR SPACESHIPS. "I'm out," she'd say with a laugh. Ray guns, wands, glowing swords, superhuman abilities, ghosts, time travel, talking animals, superscience, enchanted relics, or ancient curses: "All of that feels like cheating."

"Is he building *another* suit of armor?" she asked during a screening of the first *Iron Man* movie. Twenty minutes into the movie, Tony Stark tweaks and improves his boxy gray Mark I armor into the candy apple red and regal gold supersuit. Michelle chuckled and cut out to go shopping.

Spaghetti Westerns were too long and too violent. Zombies were scientifically implausible. And diabolical serial killers with complex schemes were, as far as she was concerned, unicorns.

Michelle and I were married for ten years, and together for thirteen. There was not a single pop-culture point of connection between the two of us. Oh, wait—*The Wire*. We both liked *The Wire*. There you go.

When we met, I was a burbling, fizzing cauldron of obscure ephemera and disjointed facts. Movies, novels, comics, music.

And serial killers.

I knew body counts, and modi operandi, and quotes from interviews. Stockpiling serial-killer lore is a rite of passage for guys in their twenties who want to seem dark and edgy. I was precisely the kind of dork who, in my twenties, would do *anything* to seem dark and edgy. And there I was, all through the flannel nineties, rattling off minutiae about Henry Lee Lucas and Carl Panzram and Edmund Kemper.

Michelle knew those facts and trivia as well. But for her, it was background noise, as unimportant and ultimately uninteresting as poured cement.

What interested her, what sparked her mind and torqued every neuron and receptor, were *people*. Specifically, detectives and investigators. Men and women who, armed with a handful of random clues (or, more often than not, *too many clues* that needed to be sifted through and discarded as red herrings), could build traps to catch monsters.

(Ugh—that was the movie tagline description of what Michelle did. Sorry. It's hard for me not to spiral upward into hyperbole when I talk about her.)

I was married to a crime fighter for a decade—an emphatically for-real, methodical, "little grey cells," Great Brain–type crime fighter. I saw her righteous fury when she'd read survivor testimony or interview family members who were still reeling from the wrenching away of a loved one. There were mornings when I'd bring her coffee and she'd be at her laptop, weeping, frustrated and worn flat by another lead she'd chased that left her smashed nose-first against a brick wall. But then she'd have a slug of caffeine, wipe her eyes, and hammer away at the keyboard again. A new window opened, a new link pursued, another run at this murderous, vile creep.

The book you just read was as close as she got. She always said, "I don't care if *I'm* the one who captures him. I just want bracelets on his wrists and a cell door slamming behind him." And she meant it. She was born with a true cop's heart and mind—she craved justice, not glory.

Michelle was an incredible writer: she was honest—sometimes to a fault—with her readers, with herself, and *about* herself. You see that in the memoir sections of *I'll Be Gone in the Dark*. And you see how she was honest about her own obsessions, her own mania, her at times dangerous commitment to the pursuit—often at the expense of sleep and health.

The mind for investigation and logic. The heart for empathy and insight. She combined those two qualities in ways I'd never encountered before. Without even trying, she made me rethink my own path in life, my own way of relating to people, and the things that I valued. She made everything about me and everyone around her better. And she did it by being quietly, effortlessly original.

Let me give you a specific, anecdotal example and then a broader, more universal one.

ANECDOTAL: IN 2011 I WORKED WITH PHIL ROSENTHAL TO DE-velop a sitcom based on my life. *Louie* had been on the air for a year, and I was besotted by the new ground it was breaking in terms of how to structure a sitcom and how to present the personal in a comedic way. I basically wanted my own *Louie*. And so Phil and I sat down and walked through the details of my day-to-day life.

"What does your wife do?" Phil asked during an afternoon writing session.

I told him. I told him that she'd started a blog called *True Crime Diary*. I said it began as a way for her to write about the numerous cold cases and developing cases she followed online. I explained that she'd incorporate possible suspects' Myspace entries. Social media is a gold mine for investigators, she realized. The old, pulling-teeth method of getting suspects to talk was nothing compared to the mind-dump these sociopathic narcissists offer daily on their own Tumblr, Facebook, and Twitter accounts. She used Google Maps and a dozen other new platforms to construct solutions to seemingly dead-end cases. She was especially adept at linking data from an obscure, decade-old case to a seemingly unconnected current crime: "You see how he's improving his m.o.? Failed kidnapping attempt on a street without easy freeway access has evolved into a clean snatch right near a cloverleaf where he can merge and reverse. He built up his courage and his skills. It's the same car in each case, and he's going unnoticed 'cause it's a different state, and a lot of times different police forces won't share info." (That particular monologue, I remembered, was delivered one night in bed, laptop propped up against her knees; this was Michelle's idea of pillow talk.)

Her blog entries led to interest from cable news shows, then to *Dateline NBC*, which hired her to reinterview suspects in a Mormon black-widow murder case. The persons of interest had stonewalled when approached by a major network, but they were more than happy to blab to a blogger. They just didn't realize that the blogger they were talking to had invented a mutant, more expansive form of homicide investigation. They told her everything.

Phil mused over all of this for a minute or so after I finished talking. Then he said, "Well, that's a *way* more interesting show than what we're working on. How 'bout your TV wife is a party planner? Sound good?"

Now for the more universal example of Michelle's uniqueness. We live in a swipe-right, blip-span culture of clickbait, 140-character arguments, and thirty-second viral videos. It's easy to get someone's attention, but it's almost impossible to *keep* it.

Michelle was dealing with a subject that demands sustained, often unrewarded attention to yield any sort of satisfaction or closure. It requires the attention of not just a single reader but of dozens of cops, data miners, and citizen journalists to spark even a minor breakthrough.

Michelle earned and sustained that attention through flawless, compelling writing and storytelling. You understand everyone's point of view in her writing, and none of her subjects are characters she invented. They're people she got to know, cared about, and took the time to really *see*: the police, the survivors, the bereaved, and, as hard as it is for me to fathom, even a wounded, destructive insect like the Golden State Killer.

I'm still hoping he hears that cell door slam behind him. And I hope she hears it somehow too.

———

THIS PAST CHRISTMAS, ALICE, OUR DAUGHTER, OPENED A PRESENT that Santa had left her. She was happy, unwrapping her little digital camera and messing around with the settings. Fun gift. Happy holiday, sweetie.

Later that morning, she asked, out of the blue, "Daddy, why do you and Santa Claus have the same handwriting?"

Michelle Eileen McNamara is gone. But she left behind a little detective.

And a mystery.

—PATTON OSWALT

Herndon, VA
July 2, 2017

EPILOGUE: LETTER TO AN OLD MAN

YOU WERE YOUR APPROACH: THE THUMP AGAINST THE FENCE. A temperature dip from a jimmied-open patio door. The odor of aftershave permeating a bedroom at three a.m. A blade at the base of the neck. "Don't move, or I'll kill you." Their hardwired threat-detection systems flickered meekly through the sledgehammer of sleep. No one had time to sit up. Awakening meant understanding they were under siege. Phone lines had been cut. Bullets emptied from guns. Ligatures prepared and laid out. You forced action from the periphery, a blur of mask and strange, gulping breaths. Your familiarity freaked them. Your hands flew to hard-to-find light switches. You knew names. Number of kids. Hangouts. Your pre-planning gave you a crucial advantage, because when your victims awoke to the blinding flashlight and clenched-teeth threats, you were always a stranger to them, but they never were to you.

Hearts drummed. Mouths dried. Your physicality remained unfathomable. You were a hard-soled shoe felt fleetingly. A penis slathered in baby lotion thrust into a pair of bound hands. "Do it good." No one saw your face. No one felt your full body weight. Blindfolded, the victims relied on smell and hearing. Floral talcum powder. Hint of cinnamon. Chimes on a curtain rod. Zipper opening on a duffel bag. Coins falling to the floor. A whimper, a sob. "Oh, Mom." A glimpse of royal blue brushed-leather tennis shoes.

The barking of dogs fading away in a westerly direction.

You were what you left behind: a four-inch vertical cut in the window screen at the ranch house on Montclair, in San Ramon. A green-handled hatchet on the hedges. A piece of cord hanging in a birch tree. Foam on an empty Schlitz Malt Liquor bottle in the backyard. Smears of unidentifiable blue paint. Frame 4 of Contra Costa County Sheriff Department's photo roll 3, of the spot where they believe you came over the fence. A girl's purpled right hand, which was numb for hours. The outline of a crowbar in dust.

Eight crushed skulls.

You were a voyeur. A patient recorder of habits and routines. The first night a husband working dispatch switched to the graveyard shift, you pounced. There were four-to-seven-day-old herringbone shoe impressions beneath the bathroom window at the scene on the 3800 block of Thornwood, Sacramento. Officers noted that standing there you could stare into the victim's bedroom. "Fuck me like your old man," you hissed, like you knew how that was done. You put high heels on one girl, something she did in bed with her boyfriend. You stole bikini Polaroids as keepsakes. You stalked around with your needling flashlight and clipped, repetitive phrases, both director and star of the movie unspooling in your head.

Almost every victim describes the same scene: a time they could sense you return after a period of distracted ransacking in another part of the house. No words. No movement. But they knew you were standing there, could imagine the lifeless gaze coming from the two holes in your ski mask. One victim felt you staring at the scar on her back. After a long while of hearing nothing she thought, *He's gone.* She exhaled, just as the knife tip came down and began tracing the end of the scar.

Fantasy adrenalized you. Your imagination compensated for failed reality. Your inadequacies reeked. One victim experimented with reverse psychology and whispered, "You're good." You abruptly got off her, amazed. Your tough-guy bravado smelled like a bluff. There was a shakiness to your clenched-teeth whisper, an occasional stutter detected. Another victim described to police how you'd briefly grabbed her left breast. "Like it was a doorknob."

"Oh, isn't this good?" you asked one girl as you raped her, and held a knife to her throat until she agreed.

Your fantasies ran deep, but they never tripped you up. Every investigation into an at-large violent offender is a footrace; you always maintained the lead. You were savvy. You knew to park just outside the standard police perimeter, between two houses or on a vacant lot, to avoid suspicion. You punched small holes in the glass panes, used a tool to nudge wooden latches, and opened windows while your victims remained asleep. You turned off the AC so you could hear if someone was coming. You left side gates open and rearranged patio furniture so you had a straight shot out. Pedaling a ten-speed, you escaped an FBI agent in a car. You scuttled across roofs. In Danville on July 6, 1979, a tracker's dog reacted so strongly to an ivy shrub on Sycamore Hill Court that the tracker believed the scent pool was just moments old.

A neighbor witnessed you escape the scene of one attack. You exited the house the way you entered: without pants.

Helicopters. Roadblocks. Citizen patrols taking down plate numbers. Hypnotists. Psychics. Hundreds of white males chewing on gauze. Nothing.

You were a scent and shoe impressions. Bloodhounds and detectives tracked both. They led away. They led nowhere.

They led into the dark.

For a long time, you have the advantage. Your gait is propulsive. In your wake are the police investigations. The worst episode in a person's life is recorded in sloppy cursive by an often rushed and sleepy officer. Misspellings abound. Pubic hair texture is described by a doodle in the margin. Investigators follow leads using slowly dialed rotary phones. When no one is home, the phone just continues to ring. If they want to look up an old record, they dig through stacks of paper by hand. The clattering Teletype machine punches messy holes in paper tape. Viable suspects are eliminated based on their mothers' alibis. Eventually the case report is put in a file, a box, and then a room. The door is shut. Yellowing of paper and fading of memory commence.

The race is yours to win. You're home free; you can feel it. The victims recede from view. Their rhythm is off, their confidence drained. They're laden with phobias and made tentative by memory. Divorce and drugs beset them. Statutes of limitations expire. Evidence kits are tossed for lack of room. What happened to them is buried, bright and unmoving, a coin at the bottom of a pool. They do their best to carry on.

So do you.

But the game has lost its edge. The script is repetitive and requires higher stakes. You began at windowsills, then crossed inside. The fear response stirred you. But three years in, grimaces and pleading will no longer suffice. You yield to your darker impulses. Your murder victims are stunners all. Some have complicated love lives. To you, I'm certain, they are "whores."

It was a different set of rules. You knew you had at least fifteen minutes to flee a neighborhood when your victims were left bound and alive in their homes. But when you walk out of Lyman and Charlene Smith's in Ventura on March 13, 1980, you feel no need to rush. Their bodies won't be found for three days.

Fireplace log. Crowbar. Wrench. You kill your victims with objects picked up at their homes—unusual maybe, but then it's always been your habit to be fleet of foot and unencumbered by very little but rage.

And then, after May 4, 1986, you disappear. Some think you died. Or went to prison. Not me.

I think you bailed when the world began to change. It's true, age must have slowed you. The testosterone, once a gush, was now a trickle. But the truth is memories fade. Paper decays. But technology improves.

You cut out when you looked over your shoulder and saw your opponents gaining on you.

THE RACE WAS YOURS TO WIN. YOU WERE THE OBSERVER IN POWER, never observed. An initial setback came on September 10, 1984, in a lab at Leicester University, when geneticist Alec Jeffreys developed the first DNA profile. Another came in 1989, when Tim Berners-Lee wrote a proposal for the World Wide Web. People who weren't even aware of you or your crimes began devising algorithms that could help find you. In 1998 Larry Page and Sergey Brin incorporated their company, Google. Boxes with your police reports were hauled out, scanned, digitized, and shared. The world hummed with connectivity and speed. Smartphones. Optical character recognition technology. Customizable interactive maps. Familial DNA.

I've seen photos of the waffle-stomper boot impressions you left in the dirt beneath a teenage girl's bedroom on July 17, 1976, in Carmichael, a crude relic from a time when voyeurs had no choice but to physically plant themselves in front of windows. You excelled at the stealth sidle. But your heyday prowess has no value anymore. Your skill set has been phased out. The tables have been turned. Virtual windows are opening all around you. You, the master watcher, are an aging, lumbering target in their crosshairs.

A ski mask won't help you now.

One victim's phone rang twenty-four years after her rape. "You want to play?" a man whispered. It was you. She was certain. You played nostalgic, like an arthritic former football star running game tape on a VCR. "Remember when we played?"

I imagine you dialing her number, alone in a small, dark room, sitting on the edge of your twin bed, the only weapon left in your arsenal firing up a memory, the ability to trigger terror with your voice.

One day soon, you'll hear a car pull up to your curb, an engine cut out. You'll hear footsteps coming up your front walk. Like they did for Edward Wayne Edwards, twenty-nine years after he killed Timothy Hack and Kelly Drew in Sullivan, Wisconsin. Like they did for Kenneth Lee Hicks, thirty years after he killed Lori Billingsley in Aloha, Oregon.

The doorbell rings.

No side gates are left open. You're long past leaping over a fence. Take one of your hyper, gulping breaths. Clench your teeth. Inch timidly toward the insistent bell.

This is how it ends for you.

"You'll be silent forever, and I'll be gone in the dark," you threatened a victim once.

Open the door. Show us your face.

Walk into the light.

—MICHELLE McNAMARA

ABOUT THE AUTHOR

MICHELLE McNAMARA (1970–2016) was the author of the website *True Crime Diary*. She earned an MFA in fiction writing from the University of Minnesota and had sold television pilots to ABC and Fox and a screenplay to Paramount. She also worked as a consultant for *Dateline NBC*. She lived in Los Angeles and is survived by her husband, Patton Oswalt, and their daughter, Alice.